Improving the Targeting of Social Programs in Ghana

Edited by Quentin Wodon

THE WORLD BANK
Washington, DC

Library of Congress Cataloging-in-Publication Data

Improving the targeting of social programs in Ghana / edited by Quentin Wodon.
   p. cm.
 ISBN 978-0-8213-9593-6
1. Social work administration--Ghana. 2. Ghana--Economic policy--21st century. I. Wodon, Quentin.
HV41.I4277 2012
361.2'509667--dc23

                                                                          2012023625

Contents

Tables

Figures

Acknowledgments

This volume was prepared by a core team led by Quentin Wodon and consisting of Harold Coulombe, Eunice Yaa Brimfah Dapaah, George Joseph, Juan Carlos Parra Osorio, and Clarence Tsimpo under the guidance of Ishac Diwan (Country Director) and Rakesh Nangia (Director for Operations and Strategy in the Human Development Network). The peer reviewers were Theresa Jones, Sam Carlson, Johan Mistiaen, and Lucian Bucur Pop. Valuable comments and suggestions were also received among others from Mawutor Ablo, Kathy Bain, Peter Darvas, Sebastien Dessus, Chris Jackson, Qaiser Khan, Julianna Lindsay, and Kalanidhi Subbarao. The collaboration of UNICEF and the Ministry of Employment and Social Welfare in launching the work and gathering the data necessary for analyzing the targeting performance of social programs is especially appreciated.

Acronyms and Abbreviations

CAS	Country Assistance Strategy
CCT	Conditional Cash Transfers
CHAG	Christian Health Association of Ghana
CLIC	Community LEAP Implementation Committees
CWIQ	Core Welfare Indicators Questionnaire
DHS	Demographic and Health Survey
FBO	Faith-based Organization
GDP	Gross Domestic Product
GFSP	Ghana School Feeding Program
GH¢	Ghana Cedi
GLSS	Ghana Living Standard Survey
HIV	Human Immunodeficiency Virus
IFPRI	International Food Policy Research Institute
JHS	Junior High School
LEAP	Livelihood Empowerment Against Poverty
MDG	Millennium Development Goal
MESW	Ministry of Employment and Social Welfare
MOFA	Ministry of Food and Agriculture
MOE	Ministry of Education
MOH	Ministry of Health
NGO	Nongovernmental Organization
NHIS	National Health Insurance Scheme
NYEP	National Youth Employment Program
ODI	Overseas Development Institute
OECD	Organization for Economic Co-operation and Development
OVC	Orphans and Vulnerable Children
PROGRESA	Programa de Educación, Salud y Alimentación
PPP	Purchasing Power Parity
PSU	Primary Sampling Unit
PURC	Public Utilities Regulatory Commission
SHS	Senior High School
SSNIT	Social Security and National Insurance Trust
STEP	Skills Training and Employment Placement Program
VAT	Value Added Tax
VDT	Volume Differentiated Tariff
WFP	World Food Programme

CHAPTER 1

Improving Targeting in Ghana: A Brief Overview

Quentin Wodon

This study provides a diagnostic of the benefit incidence and targeting performance of a large number of social programs in Ghana. Both broad-based programs (such as spending for education and health, and subsidies for food, oil-related products, and electricity) as well as targeted programs (such as Livelihood Empowerment Against Poverty (LEAP), the indigent exemption under the National Health Insurance Scheme (NHIS), school lunches and uniforms, or fertilizer subsidies) are considered. In addition, the study provides tools and recommendations for better targeting of those programs in the future. The tools include new maps and data sets for geographic targeting according to poverty and food security, as well as ways to implement proxy means-testing. The purpose of this introductory chapter is to briefly synthesize the key findings and messages from the study.

Over the last two decades, Ghana has made tremendous progress towards the targets set forth in the Millennium Development Goals. The share of the population in poverty has been reduced from 51.7 percent in 1991–92 to 28.5 percent in 2005–06, and large gains have also been achieved for other social indicators. Such rapid progress has implications for policy. Several factors suggest that there is an opportunity today for Ghana to continue to make progress by implementing better social programs both in terms of the targeting mechanisms to be used and the type of benefits and incentives to be provided.

Consider first the issue of targeting. Poverty has been reduced dramatically, but there also remain pockets of deep poverty, especially in the northern savannah area. This increase in the concentration of poverty provides a way to target interventions geographically. Yet while geographic targeting can help very substantially, it may not be sufficient since many poor and near-poor households live in other parts of the country and remain vulnerable to external shocks. Thus a combination of targeting mechanisms could be used to target various programs to the subset of the population that needs those programs the most.

Consider next the issue of the types of programs to be implemented. Traditional programs for poverty reduction such as public works have an important role to play, provided they are well targeted geographically and implemented properly in terms of the choice of the local infrastructure to be built, the wages to be paid to beneficiaries, and the seasonality of the jobs to be created. Other programs aiming to reduce the cost of schooling for very poor households, such as the planned distribution of free school uniforms are also useful, and the same could be said of school lunches, although in the case of Ghana an effort should be made to better target them geographically. Yet some of the more innovative poverty reduction programs (such as conditional cash transfers) implemented in middle income countries in the last decade, and especially in Latin American countries, have gone beyond these traditional programs. It may be time for Ghana to consider implementing on a pilot basis some of these innovative programs.

While conditions and opportunities are there to further improve the design and targeting of social programs in Ghana, there is also an urgent need to do so from a budget point of view. Ghana's fiscal deficit has been increasing rapidly in recent years. Reducing budget deficits should not be done at the expense of the poor, but for this a better targeting of social programs is key.

Given the above context, this study aims to contribute to the discussion of how to improve the design and targeting of social programs in Ghana. Due to the limited scope of what can be achieved within a single study, the emphasis is placed much more on program targeting than program design. This is an important limitation insofar as we do not aim to measure or simulate medium- to long-term program impacts; we are simply assessing who benefits or could benefit today from immediate benefits from various programs.

Table 1.1 provides the key results in terms of the targeting performance to the poor of various programs. LEAP is probably today the best targeted program in Ghana. Other well targeted programs include the indigent exemption under the NHIS, as well as three simulated programs: the free school uniforms at the primary school level (which would need to be targeted to the poorest districts), pilot conditional cash transfers for the poor at the primary or junior high level (which would require geographic targeting and/or proxy means-testing), and labor intensive public works (if these are implemented in the poorest areas). The next set of programs in table 1.1 tends to benefit large segments of the population, and thereby also the poor. This includes broad-based basic education and health spending, as well as the Ghana school feeding program, although this program should be much better targeted to the poor than it currently is. Programs with some benefits for the poor include funding for senior high and vocational education, as well as (to a lower extent) the NHIS and the NYEP. Poorly targeted programs include general consumption subsidies for rice, electricity (through the tariff structure), tertiary education, and oil-related products (although the estimations do not take into account multiplier effects).

Decisions on which programs to fund in priority should not be based only on an assessment of the targeting performance of these programs. The impact of any given program in the medium-term is also essential, and some programs do not target the poor in priority. Still, targeting performance does matter, and the following tentative recommendations can be made on the basis of the findings from this study.

LEAP appears to be one of the best targeted programs in Ghana. An expansion of the program would thus generate substantial benefits for the poor and would also help in reducing the share of program costs currently devoted to administration and delivery. LEAP's targeting mechanisms should however be reviewed to assess if it could be improved in terms of both its proxy means-testing and community-based components. In addition, a LEAP-inspired household questionnaire could be used to assess eligibility for other programs (possibly on a pilot basis) and for assessing ex post the targeting performance of some programs such as public works. There is thus scope for building on LEAP's experience to progressively design targeting mechanisms that could be used for

Table 1.1: Summary results on the share of the benefits from various programs accruing to the poor

	Share of outlays benefiting the poor (%)	Simulated versus actual
Well or potentially well targeted programs		
LEAP (Livelihood Empowerment Against Poverty)	57.5	Actual (good data)
NHIS indigent exemption	<50.0	Actual (partial data)
Free School uniforms for primary schools in poor areas	49.9	Simulated
Labor intensive public works in poor areas	<43.2	Simulated
Proxy means-tested conditional cash transfers for JHS	42.2	Simulated
Programs/subsidies benefitting the population fairly evenly		
General funding for primary education	32.2	Actual (good data)
General funding for health service delivery by Christian Health Association of Ghana (CHAG)	30.8	Actual (good data)
Potential connection subsidies for electricity	29.4	Simulated
Free maternal (ante- and post-natal) and child care	29.1	Actual (good data)
General funding for kindergarten education	27.2	Actual (good data)
General funding for junior high school (JHS) education	24.0	Actual (good data)
General funding for health care	22.4	Actual (good data)
Ghana School Feeding Program	<21.3	Actual (partial data)
Kerosene subsidies	20.7	Actual (good data)
Programs and subsidies with limited benefits for the poor		
General funding for vocational (TVET) education	19.0	Actual (good data)
Fertilizer subsidy scheme	15.8	Actual (partial data)
General funding for senior high school (SHS) education	15.1	Actual (good data)
Public Utilities Regulatory Commission (PURC) pilot access to safe water through tankers in cities	13.1	Simulated
National Youth Employment Program (NYEP)	12.7	Simulated
NHIS general subsidies	12.4	Actual (partial data)
Poorly targeted programs and subsidies		
Tax cut on imported rice during food price crisis	8.3	Actual (good data)
Electricity subsidies embedded in tariff structure (in 2005–06)	8.0	Actual (good data)
General funding for tertiary education	6.9	Actual (good data)
Subsidies for petrol and diesel products (except kerosene)	>2.3	Actual (good data)

Source: Author using various sources of data including the Ghana Living Standard Survey (GLSS)5 and 2003 Core Welfare Indicators Questionnaire (CWIQ).

multiple programs, or at least for those programs that are not geographically targeted (for programs serving the north, geographic targeting is often enough).

The indigent exemption under the NHIS is also probably well targeted to the poor, although we have only limited data to make this assessment. Given low levels of enrollment under this exemption today as compared to the share of the population in extreme poverty, districts should be encouraged to make more extensive use of the indigent exemption. A first step could be to enable (most) LEAP households to benefit from the exemption. New applicants for the exemption could be screened with a LEAP-inspired questionnaire, and the procedure for verification of district enrollment under the indigent exemption once the share of indigents exceeds a certain threshold could also be based on a LEAP-inspired questionnaire that would be administered to a random sample of beneficiaries chosen within the district under review.

The distribution of free school uniforms should not be made on the basis of the map of educationally deprived districts, because this map relates too much to supply-side issues in the delivery of education. Instead, free school uniforms should be distributed according to the Ghana poverty map, the food security map, or a map of gaps in primary school completion at the district level. Free school uniforms should not be targeted individually—geographic targeting through public schools in poor districts is sufficient.

The government could consider testing on a pilot basis a conditional cash transfer program possibly for primary or JHS students from poor families, with a proper baseline and follow up survey so that we can measure impact. This should be done in priority in the northern districts using geographic targeting, but part of the pilot could take place in less poor districts using proxy means-testing. Possibly the program could be tested through LEAP, which has some conditionalities that are not really enforced.

Large subsidies that are not well targeted to the poor for food (rice), energy, and electricity, and possibly piped water should be reduced. This does not mean that all subsidies should be eliminated. Kerosene is for example a good that can be subsidized to protect the poor from fluctuations in world oil prices. Some subsidies for electricity or piped water can also be considered, but they need to be limited, and in general connection subsidies would tend to be better targeted than consumption subsidies.

The allocation procedure for school lunches at the district and school level should be revised given weak targeting performance (according to some other indicators, targeting performance might be weaker than what is suggested in table 1.1). This should be done firstly to have a transparent allocation procedure, and secondly to propose a more systematic use of the geographic targeting information now available, following the poverty/food security maps rather than the educational deprived district maps.

The educational deprived district formula should continue to be used for the targeting of supply-side investments with transfers provided to districts and thereafter to schools. However the formula to identify the deprived districts should be revised from a rank-based to a level-based indicator. There should also be a process of reassessment, say every two years, to reorient on a dynamic basis the funds to districts in need given that some of the variables used in the formula change substantially over time.

Labor intensive public works and so-called productive safety nets should be targeted to the poorest areas of the country. This is because in a context where a large number of workers work for no or limited pay, self-targeting through low wages may not be enough to ensure good targeting performance. Proxy means-testing would not be needed for determining eligibility of public works participants if the program is geographically targeted, but a LEAP-inspired questionnaire could be used ex post on a sample of participants to monitor targeting performance and implement corrective measures as needed.

Social protection and service delivery strategies need to take into account the important role of privately funded or privately run (and publicly funded) partners. The same tools of targeting assessment can be used to measure how well nongovernmental organizations (NGOs) and faith-based organizations (FBOs) reach the poor through their programs in Ghana.

On fertilizer subsidies/vouchers, geographic targeting as well as a cap on the size of vouchers to be received by any one household would help to improve targeting performance. Many of these measures have already been taken by the government, but data collection and monitoring is needed to measure to what extent the fertilizer voucher program is reaching the poor.

This study does not provide recommendations regarding the allocation of funding for general services in education and health, as many other considerations must be taken into account. The assessment of benefit incidence provided here is simply an input for more detailed forthcoming analysis to be conducted for an Education Country Status Report, a Health Country Status Report, and a Poverty Assessment.

The data from the 2003 Core Welfare Indicators Questionnaire (CWIQ) survey was essential to various parts of the analysis conducted in this study, including the poverty map and the work on geographic targeting. The CWIQ was important because its large sample size provides statistical reliability at the district level. Ghana Statistical Service should be encouraged to field a new large sample CWIQ survey apart from the upcoming implementation of the Ghana Living Standards Survey (GLSS6) to monitor district-level progress and assess directly participation in a range of programs at the district level. Both the new CWIQ and the GLSS6 should include new questionnaire modules aiming to measure program targeting (i.e., participation and benefits) as well as program impacts.

PART I
Synthesis of the Study

CHAPTER 2

How Well Targeted Are Ghana's Social Programs?

Quentin Wodon

This chapter provides an information base to improve the targeting of social programs in Ghana. Data from household surveys and administrative records made available by Ministries were used to assess the targeting performance of many different programs. LEAP and the indigent exemption for health coverage under NHIS are well targeted to the poor. Simulations suggest that free school uniforms for public primary school students and conditional cash transfers at the junior high school level could also be well targeted, but this will depend on the targeting mechanism used. Large transfer programs funding public basic education and health care as well as kerosene subsidies benefit relatively evenly large segments of the population, including the poor. School lunches also benefit large segments of the population but improvements in targeting performance should be sought to better target schools located in poor areas. Programs that do benefit the poor but less so than the overall population include funding for vocational and senior high education, fertilizer vouchers, and NHIS general subsidies. Programs that benefit mostly the nonpoor include electricity consumption subsidies, tax cuts on imported rice (implemented during the food price crisis), funding for tertiary education, and petrol and diesel subsidies (many of these have been recently terminated). Apart from assessing the targeting performance of a range of social programs, the study provides tools and recommendations for better targeting in the future. This includes new maps and data sets for geographic targeting according to poverty and food security, and an assessment as to whether it makes a difference to target geographically according to levels of deprivations or changes in deprivation due to external shocks. The study also discusses proxy means-testing mechanisms and compares the performance of geographic and proxy means-testing, as well as the combination of both. This overview provides a summary of the main findings from the study, while the rest of the study consists of a series of chapters with more detailed analysis in selected areas.

Introduction

Over the last two decades, Ghana has made tremendous progress towards the targets set forth in the Millennium Development Goals (MDGs). As shown in table 2.1 from World Bank (2009), and thanks in large part to rapid economic growth, the share of the population in poverty in Ghana was reduced from 51.7 percent in 1991–92 to 28.5 percent in 2005–06. The prevalence of child malnutrition was also almost reduced by half, from

24.1 percent in 1988 to 13.9 percent in 2008. The share of the children not completing primary education decreased from 38.8 percent in 1991 to 15.0 percent in 2008, thanks in part to the elimination of fees and the implementation of capitation grants to provide compensatory resources to schools. Today, the country is very close to achieving boy-girl parity in primary and secondary education, while about 20 years ago, there were roughly three girls in school for every four boys. The child (under five) mortality rate has also decreased, although at a smaller pace, from 119.7 in 1991 per one thousand to 80 in 2008. The share of birth deliveries not attended by skilled health personnel has dropped from 59.8 percent in 1988 to 43 percent in 2008. The share of the population without access to an improved water source dropped from 44 percent in 1990 to 26 percent in 2006. The only indicator in table 2.1 not showing rapid progress is the share of the population with access to improved sanitation, which decreased only from 94 percent in 1990 to 90 percent in 2006. Still, the overall progress to date represents a tremendous achievement.

Table 2.1: Ghana's progress toward the Millennium Development Goals

	Initial		Most Recent	
MDG1a. Poverty headcount ratio, national poverty line (% of population)	51.7	1992	28.5	2006
MDG1b. Malnutrition prevalence, weight for age (% of children under 5)	24.1	1988	13.9	2008
MDG2. Primary noncompletion rate, total (% of relevant age group)	38.8	1991	15.0	2008
MDG3. Ratio of girls to boys in primary and secondary education (%)	78.5	1991	95.2	2007
MDG4. Mortality rate, under-5 (per 1,000)	119.7	1990	80	2008
MDG5. Births not-attended by skilled health staff (% of total)	59.8	1988	43	2008
MDG7a. Improved water source (% of population without access)	44	1990	26	2006
MDG7b. Improved sanitation facilities (% of population without access)	94	1990	90	2006

Source: World Bank (2009).

Such rapid progress has implications for policy. Several factors suggest that there is an opportunity today for Ghana's government to continue to make progress by implementing better social programs both in terms of the targeting mechanisms to be used and in terms of the type of programs to be implemented.

Consider first the issue of targeting. Poverty has been reduced dramatically, so that a smaller share of the population is in need of government transfers. In addition there remain pockets of deep poverty. The northern savannah area, by far the poorest of the ecological zones, has been left behind in the growth process. This has resulted in an increase in the share of the poor living in the rural savannah from 32.6 percent in 1991–92 to 49.3 percent in 2005–06. The concentration of poverty in the rural savannah is even more evident when considering the depth of poverty (poverty gap) which provides information regarding how much resources would be needed to eradicate poverty through perfectly targeted transfers. In 2005–06, the rural savannah area represented 62.1 percent of total poverty in the country as measured through the poverty gap, and the proportion was even higher (70.7 percent) with the squared poverty gap, which in addition takes into account the inequality among the poor and places more emphasis on the poorest. This increase in the concentration of poverty provides a simple way to target at least some interventions geographically. Yet while geographic targeting can help in better reaching the poor, it will not be sufficient. Indeed, many poor and near-poor households in other parts of the country remain vulnerable to external shocks, as evidenced by the recent global economic crisis. Well-designed safety nets and social programs could be highly beneficial to help this vulnerable population to cope with shocks and more generally to access public services. But for this, additional targeting mechanisms are needed, such as community-based targeting and proxy means-testing (i.e., identifying households that are likely to be poor through their observable characteristics). As demonstrated by the LEAP pilot, Ghana has developed the technical capacity to implement such more refined targeted mechanisms which have been used in middle-income countries for many years.

Consider next the issue of the types of programs to be implemented. Traditional programs for poverty reduction such as public works have an important role to play, provided they are well targeted geographically and implemented properly in terms of the choice of the local infrastructure to be built, the wages to be paid to beneficiaries, and the seasonality of the jobs to be created. Other programs aiming to reduce the cost of schooling for very poor households, such as the planned distribution of free school uniforms are also useful, and the same could be said of school lunches, although in the case of Ghana an effort should be made to better target them geographically. Yet some of the more innovative poverty reduction programs implemented in middle income countries in the last decade, and especially in Latin American countries, have gone beyond these traditional programs. They have for example generated not only investments in the local infrastructure of poor areas, but also in the human capital of the population living in these areas, with probably longer lasting effects on poverty. It may be time today for Ghana to consider implementing some of these innovative programs.

Ghana has already led the way in West Africa with innovations such as the LEAP program, the National Health Insurance Scheme, and the elimination of school fees together with the implementation of capitation grants. One other area where innovative models could be adapted to Ghana is that of conditional cash transfers that in other countries often take the form of stipends given to poor children attending junior high school. More research is needed in Ghana before recommending to implement such programs at any scale, and it would thus be wise to start with small pilots. But under the condition that supply constraints can be or have been resolved (or at least reduced) in areas where such stipends would be implemented, it has been shown in many low and middle income countries that these transfers tend to increase primary school completion and junior secondary school enrollment among the poor, and that they are likely to have a long term impact on poverty reduction by increasing the expected future earnings of the children when they reach adulthood and start to work. In a context of continued internal rural to urban migration, conditional cash transfers also help build mobile human capital and are therefore a useful step to improve the skills of a large part of the population and thereby better meet the challenges posed by the progressive transformation of the economy of a country like Ghana into a more service-oriented economy. Results from simulations suggest that conditional cash transfers could also be well targeted, for example by combining geographic targeting with proxy means-testing in the less poor districts.

While conditions and opportunities are there to further improve the design and targeting of social programs in Ghana, there is also an urgent need to do so from a budget point of view. The cost of universal or poorly targeted safety nets is often high for governments and external funding from donors for such universal or poorly targeted programs is decreasing when countries reach middle income status. In Ghana itself, in part due to the economic crisis, the fiscal deficit has been increasing rapidly in recent years, reaching 14.5 percent of Gross Domestic Product (GDP) in 2008. As noted by the World Bank (2009), at the time this report was written, the 2009 budget was foreseeing a reduction of this deficit to 9.4 percent in 2009, with further consolidation to 6.0 percent in 2010 and 4.5 percent in 2011 to stabilize the debt-to-GDP ratio. Large fiscal deficits run the risk of crowding out private investment and raise interest rates, and put downward pressure on the currency and lead to inflation with negative impacts on the poor who are least able to cope with increases in the cost of living. Reducing budget deficits requires deliberate action, and is a call to reduce funding for some large but poorly targeted subsidies and increase funding instead for programs directly benefiting the poor.

Objective, Limits, and Structure of the Study

Given the above context, this study aims to contribute to the discussion of how to improve the design and targeting of social programs in Ghana. Due to the limited scope of what can be achieved within a single study, the emphasis is placed much more on program targeting than program design. This is an important limitation insofar as we do not aim to measure or simulate medium- to long-term program impact; we are simply assessing who benefits or could benefit from various programs. One could argue that it would be better from a policy point of view to implement a less well targeted program whose impact in terms of behavioral changes leads to substantial poverty reduction in the future (for example through a more educated or better trained workforce), than a well targeted program that provides some immediate transfers to the poor today but without any long term impacts. This is correct, but this aspect of the discussion will not be covered in this study, both because the issue is complex and because data to assess program impacts in Ghana are lacking. It is often not enough to rely on the experience of other countries in implementing social programs to guesstimate the likely impact of a specific program in a specific country since this impact often depends on the particular set of conditions (among others in terms of capacity, governance, and political economy) that exist at any given point in time in a given country.

Still, the issue of targeting is complex enough, and the budget amounts involved in some of the programs and subsidies implemented today are large enough to justify a study on assessing ways to target different programs and on measuring the actual targeting performance of existing programs when the available data provides enough information for such assessment. It should also be said that even if one does not address the medium- and long-term impacts of specific programs, one must still deal with a number of trade-offs embedded in any decision to rely on one targeting mechanism versus another, or to target at all. Targeting does involve administrative costs, it must be sustainable from a political point of view, and it may have negative incentive effects. Some of these considerations must be dealt with explicitly, but this is not done in this study which is devoted rather to more basic measurement issues.

In terms of structure, the study consists of two parts. The first part, which consists of the present overview, summarizes the key findings of the study. The second part consists of a series of 14 short chapters that describe more precisely some of the assumptions that have led to the results presented in this overview. After a first chapter that introduces the concepts used in discussions on targeting policy, the other chapters are devoted among others to poverty and food insecurity maps for Ghana, a geographic assessment of the impact of higher foods prices on poverty, a comparison of geographic targeting and proxy means-testing in the case of simulated distributions of free school uniforms and conditional cash transfers in junior secondary schools, an assessment of the benefit incidence of tax cuts for imported food, as well as subsidies for agricultural inputs and electricity, a benefit incidence analysis for education public spending, an evaluation of the targeting performance of school lunches, the NHIS, the LEAP program, the National Youth Employment Program (NYEP), and finally simulated public works. The quality of the data used is not the same for each of these programs, whether actual or simulated, and this is why, even though a serious effort was made to estimate benefit incidence as precisely as possible within the limits of the available data, some of the estimates provided in this study should be considered as preliminary.

Before providing a summary of the main empirical results, one more caveat is important to point out. While this study focuses in part on targeted safety nets, other programs are important to achieve good human capital outcomes and ensure social cohesion. In addition, inequality remains high in Ghana and social cohesion may have been weakened by the process of economic transformation of the country. In such a context, targeted programs need not be conceived and implemented necessarily instead of universal programs. Rather the challenge is to ensure access to what one might refer to as social entitlements through targeting. There is thus no necessary contradiction or dichotomy between universal and targeted approaches to social program. Some programs need to aim for universality (like the NHIS), while other programs need to be targeted (like the indigent exemption to be covered at no cost by the NHIS), and it is the fact that various parts of the social system complement each other that makes the whole system better than simply the sum of its parts. Dealing with the issue of complementarity is an important task, but again one that the limited scope of this study does not consider to any large extent.

Programs and Subsidies Well (or Potentially Well) Targeted to the Poor

In this section and the next three sections, we provide a review of the main empirical findings from the study in terms of the targeting performance of existing (and in a few cases potential) programs. Some broad-based public expenditures are likely to benefit large segments of the population, and therefore are likely not to be especially well targeted to the poor, although in some cases they may benefit the poor as much as other population groups. This is not necessarily a problem if broad reach is the objective of the program, as is the case with public spending for education and health. What is problematic is if the poor systematically benefit less than the nonpoor from such broad-based categories of spending. In addition to broad based public funding for the social sectors, many Ministries, Departments and Agencies are implementing social programs and it is often assumed that these programs are indeed well targeted to the poor in one way or the other. These programs use a wide array of targeting mechanisms (including self targeting, demographic targeting, geographic targeting, community-based targeting, and proxy means-testing) to reach their beneficiaries. Unfortunately, not all of these programs are well targeted.

We consider first in this section a subset of programs that appear to be already well targeted, or that could potentially be well targeted if the implementing agencies were to follow the guidance provided in this study. Table 2.2 provides a list of such programs. The table follows a useful format proposed by Akuffo-Amoabeng (2009) in a note for the Ministry of Employment and Social Welfare (MESW). The key addition provided in this study is the estimates of targeting performance that emerge from our detailed work. We have also included additional programs or categories of spending versus those initially considered by MESW, and some programs considered in the MESW note have been dropped here due to their very limited size, the lack of sufficient data to assess target-ing performance, or both. Finally, based on the information available to us, we have characterized in some cases the targeting mechanisms of the programs or categories of spending as well as their features slightly differently.

Table 2.2: Programs and subsidies with a large share of benefits accruing to the poor

Program	Share of outlays benefiting the poor (%)	Principal targeting mechanism	Benefits for households	Conditions attached
Programs that are well targeted to the poor				
LEAP	57.5	Community based and proxy means-testing	GHC 8.00–12.00, per household per month	School enrollment, health visits
NHIS Indigents	>50.0	District-level identification	Free coverage under NHIS	None
Programs that are potentially well targeted (assessment based on simulations)				
MOE school uniforms	49.9	Geographic poverty-based targeting	School uniform for 1.6 million children	Enrollment in public primary school
Public works in 3 poorest areas	43.2	Geographic and self-targeting (low wage)	Public works Wage	Employment in public works
MOE conditional cash transfers	42.2	Geographic and proxy means-testing	Cash transfer to JHS students	Enrollment in public JHS school

Source: Author, based on the material provided in this study.

The best targeted program appears to be LEAP (Livelihood Empowerment Against Poverty), a program implemented by MESW to provide cash transfers to households in extreme poverty. LEAP aims to reach the poorest of the poor, defined by the program as the bottom 20 percent of the poor. This is a very difficult task to accomplish and due to data limitations, it is also difficult to assess precisely whether the program does indeed manage to reach the poorest of the poor as opposed to simply reaching the poor. Still the data suggest that three fourths of the transfers provided by LEAP reach the bottom two quintiles of the population and the share reaching the poor is estimated at 57.5 percent. Thus, the targeting performance of the program is better than that of other programs for which data are available.

The good targeting performance of LEAP does not mean that there are no areas that could be considered for improving targeting performance. The program relies on a combination of community-based targeting, proxy means-testing, and some target-ing to poorer districts. The good targeting performance of the program does not come primarily from the district-level targeting (in fact the program is to be expanded to a larger number of districts). There are two areas that should be considered for further improving LEAP's targeting performance. First, a more detailed analysis is needed to assess the respective roles of community-based and proxy means-testing mechanisms. Community-based targeting can improve targeting performance, but it can also, if not well implemented, lead to treating similar households differently at the local level (this is referred to in the literature as a risk of horizontal inequity, and it comes from so-called errors of exclusion whereby some households that should benefit from the program do not). Second, the actual proxy means-testing mechanism used is not well documented. An analysis should be conducted to assess whether the variables used for proxy means-testing are the best possible variables (given the need to have comparability with the GLSS data to measure targeting performance), whether the statistical or econometric model used for predicting poverty is the best model that can be fitted with the available data, and finally whether the thresholds used for determining eligibility are appropriate. Still the fact that MESW today is one of very few agencies that maintain detailed information on the beneficiaries of its programs is very important. This is done by LEAP through a single registry, the use of which MESW could possibly expand on a pilot basis to provide a mechanism to improve the targeting of other social programs (we will come back to this later.)

Another issue with LEAP is that the budget allocated to the program remains limited, so that it serves only a small number of households. Increasing LEAP's budget should enable the program to reach a larger share of the poor, and reduce the share of the program's budget that is allocated to administration and implementation costs as opposed to the actual transfers to households. But there is a need to define better some of the features of the program, in terms of the demographic characteristics of whom it aims to reach, as well as the exit mechanisms to be used for facilitating graduation out of the program. Some of the thinking that is to be done on conditional cash transfers should also be of help for improving LEAP. Finally, another question in terms of future expansion is to decide whether the program should be focused on selected geographic areas, for example in the north of the country, or should be national. If the budget of the program remains limited, it may be best to start any expansion in the poorest areas of the country, since this would make administration of the program easier than having many participating communities geographically scattered. On the other hand, the proxy means-testing part of the targeting mechanism piloted by LEAP or an adaptation thereof could be used on a national basis to determine eligibility for some other programs, such as the exemption for the indigent under the NHIS, to which we turn next.

A second program that appears to be very well targeted is the indigent exemption for the registration and coverage of very poor households under NHIS. We actually do not have data at the individual level on the characteristics of the beneficiaries from this program. Based on district level data, if we assume that beneficiaries within a district have a profile similar to the district as a whole, we obtain a share of benefits accruing to the poor equal to 38.5 percent, which is already good in comparison to other programs and suggests that poorer districts have many more indigents registered than less poor districts. The actual targeting performance of the exemption is however likely to be much better, since there is relatively strict targeting within district. This is why we have indicated in table 2.2 that the share of benefits accruing to the poor could be above 50 percent (it would be useful to implement a questionnaire similar to LEAP's among a sample of beneficiaries to measure actual performance).

The next two programs listed in table 2.2 could have a good targeting performance if the guidance on how to target them proposed in this study or similar targeting mechanisms are adopted by the implementing agencies. The first program consists in providing free school uniforms in public primary schools. If the program is geographically targeted along the lines suggested in this study, 49.9 percent of the benefits should accrue to the poor. The second program, which is not yet under consideration by the government, would consist in providing conditional cash transfers to promote a better transition from the completion of primary school to the enrollment and completion of junior high school (JHS). The program could be implemented to help households so that their children complete primary school, or it could target children who have completed primary school and should register for JHS. A more detailed analysis of the latest administrative data on school enrollment and completion at the district level should be conducted to assess where the needs are highest and where such a program could best benefit the poor. But a key result from the simulations carried with the GLSS data is that if such a program were targeted using a combination of geographic and proxy means-testing, probably about 42.2 percent of the benefits would accrue to the poor at the JHS level, and the share of benefits for the poor for conditional cash transfers at the primary level would be probably a bit higher.

The last program in table 2.2 is a labor intensive public works program that would be implemented in the three poorest areas of the country (Northern, Upper East and Upper West). The estimate of targeting performance is also based on simulations using low wage levels (i.e., well below the minimum wage) provided to program participants. Leakage from the program from the point of view of poverty reduction takes into account the share of the wage benefits that do not reach the poor due to mistargeting, as well as the substitution effects whereby part of the wages paid are not additional income for households because individuals participating in the program might have done some other work without the program's existence. We also assumed that only 70 percent of the program costs are used for wages due to the need to pay for materials (we do not factor in administrative costs since this is not done for other programs; without that 70 percent markdown, the share of benefits going to the poor as additional income would be higher, at 61.8 percent). If the program were not targeted to poor areas, targeting performance would be much lower, with an estimated 26.8 percent of the benefits likely to accrue to the poor.

Programs and Subsidies Relatively Evenly Distributed in the Population as a Whole

Table 2.3 provides data on programs and subsidies that benefit the population as a whole without large differences between the poor and the nonpoor. A first set of programs in this category are the subsidies for the public education system provided by the Ministry of Education. The estimates suggest that 32.2 percent of the benefits from primary public education spending accrue to the poor, and the proportion is 27.2 percent at the kindergarten level and 24.0 percent at the junior high school (JHS) level. General funding for health care also falls in this category, with an estimated 24.0 percent accruing to the poor (although due to lack of sufficiently detailed of information on spending for various types of services, the share of the benefits obtained by the poor is likely to be over-estimated). Given that health services provided by the Christian Health Association of Ghana (CHAG) are provided to individuals with characteristics similar to the population as a whole (albeit with slightly better targeting to the poor than public facilities according to the most reliable data available), CHAG also falls in this category of programs. So do services provided for free for antenatal and postnatal care, as well as for maternal and child care more generally.

Table 2.3: Programs with benefits relatively evenly distributed in the population

Program	Share of outlays benefiting the poor (%)	Principal targeting mechanism	Benefits for households	Conditions attached
Programs with benefits accruing proportionately more to the poor				
MOE Primary Education	32.2	Children in public primary schools	Subsidized education	School enrollment and attendance
CHAG service delivery	30.8	Individuals ill or injured	Subsidized health care	Use of CHAG health centers
Programs with benefits relatively evenly distributed in the population				
Electricity and water connections	29.4	Households not connected	Access to water/ electricity	Payment of consumption
MOH antenatal and child care	29.1	Antenatal and post natal care, maternal and child health	Impregnated bed nets	Pregnant women and children aged below 5 years
MOE Kindergarten Education	27.2	Children in public kindergarten schools	Subsidized education	School enrollment and attendance
MOE Junior High. Education	24.0	Children in public JHS schools	Subsidized education	School enrollment and attendance
Programs with benefits accruing proportionately more to the nonpoor				
MOH funding for health care	22.4	Individuals ill or injured	Subsidized health care	Visit to publicly funded center
GSFP school lunches	21.3	Public Primary schools	One hot meal per child-school day	Attendance in pub. primary school
Kerosene Subsidies	20.7	Self-targeting through use of good	Lower cost of kerosene	Purchase of kerosene

Source: Author, based on the material provided in this study.

Three other programs are listed in table 2.3. The first program is the Ghana School Feeding Programme (GSFP), which provides hot meals to students in participating public primary schools. As noted by Akuffo-Amoabeng (2009), GSFP uses a range of variables to target beneficiary schools, including road access, availability of electricity, access to potable water, telecommunication non-coverage, health facility unavailability within a 15 km radius, low enrollment rates, conflict- or flood-prone areas, and poor school infrastructure. Yet we estimate that only 21.3 percent of the benefits accrue to the poor. While some other programs are faring even worse, this is not a good performance for a program that aims to reach the poor. If the program were more strategically targeted to poor areas along the lines suggested for the free school uniforms, the share of benefits that would accrue to the poor could more than double (as shown in table 2.2, about half of the benefits from a geographically targeted free school uniform programs could benefit the poor, and the share would be higher if the simulations were for a smaller program).

The second program consists of kerosene subsidies. Among all oil-related products, kerosene is the only product that is consumed in a substantial way by the poor, so that 20.7 percent of kerosene subsidies would reach the poor. This is not great, but better than other broad-based subsidies for oil-related products since for these other products, only a very small part of the subsidies directly benefit the poor (this is discussed below, with the corresponding estimates provided in table 2.5).

The third program consists of free connections to the electricity network for households that live in an area where there is access to the network, but are not connected to the network. In the case of water, targeting performance could be higher or lower depending on how the connections would be provided. For both water and electricity, simulated connection subsidies would be better targeted than consumption subsidies, which are discussed below. It is important to highlight the fact that simply expanding the network when the utilities already have a deficit is not necessarily a good option. What is needed is a reform package that makes consumption subsidies through the features of the tariff structure better targeted to the poor and less costly, so that cost recovery can be achieved, and the networks can be then extended through more connections for the poor, the benefits of which are larger for poverty reduction than the benefits of the existing consumption subsidies. Again, a more detailed analysis would be needed to propose specific and realistic policy recommendations in this area, but the finding that connection subsidies would be better targeted to the poor than existing consumption subsidies is likely to remain.

Programs and Subsidies Benefiting the Poor but Only to a Limited Extent

Table 2.4 provides data on programs that do benefit the poor to some extent, but much less so than the population as a whole. The first program consists of the subsidies provided by the Ministry of Education for technical and vocational education and training, with 19.0 percent of outlays benefiting the poor. Next is the Ministry of Agriculture's fertilizer voucher program, with an estimate benefit incidence for the poor of 15.8 percent. This estimate is based on the share of fertilizer purchases accounted by the poor in the GLSS5, but it could be that the program reached the poor more than indicated in the data due in part to some level of geographic targeting (northern districts received a larger share of the vouchers). The advantage of fertilizers is that beyond the cash transfer provided through vouchers, they also have a positive impact on future earnings for farmers by increasing quantities produced. Thus if mechanisms can be designed to ensure good targeting, lower costs for fertilizers could have a large impact on poverty.

We estimate that 15.1 percent of the public spending for senior high school education reaches the poor, and our estimate of the share of NHIS benefits accruing to the poor is 12.5 percent, based on the data from the GLSS5 (a more recent assessment based on 2007 data did not generate a higher benefit incidence for the poor as identified from wealth data; the benefit incidence was apparently slightly lower). The fact that these estimates are low does not of course mean that the programs should be reduced in scope, but rather that more efforts should be made to enable the poor to benefits from these programs.

Table 2.4: Programs with some limited benefits accruing to the poor

Program	Share of Outlays Benefiting the Poor (%)	Principal Targeting Mechanism	Benefits for Households	Conditions Attached
MOE Vocational Education	19.0	Children in public SHS schools	Subsidized education	School enrollment and attendance
MOA Fertilizer Subsidies	15.8	Vouchers for fertilizers	Lower cost of fertilizer	Use of fertilizers for food crops
MOE Senior High Education	15.1	Children in public SHS schools	Subsidized education	School enrollment and attendance
PURC access to potable water	13.1	Indirect access to potable water	Supply of water in tankers in Accra	Areas w/o access to piped water
NYEP	12.7	Unemployed youths (18–35 year old)	Training and monthly allowances	Participation in training program
NHIS General Subsidies	12.4	Social security and district schemes	Coverage of most health care costs	Registration and premiums
MOWAC Micro Credit	N/A	Community based women groups	Micro-credit loans GH¢ 100 to 500	Access to loan via rural banks

Source: Author, based on the material provided in this study.

Another program listed in table 2.4 is an initiative under the Worlds Bank's Ghana Urban Water Project to supply potable water through tankers on a pilot basis in three urban communities in Accra that do not have access to piped water. The program is a pilot and it could be extended nationally if successful. Depending on which urban communities are targeted, and given the fact that urban households who do not have access to piped water tend to be poorer than households with access, targeting performance could be good. However, because urban poverty rates are low in Ghana, the share of poor households who might benefit from such intervention would probably also be low. The estimate of 13.1 percent of benefits accruing to the poor provided in table 2.4 is the estimate from the GLSS5 of the share of the population without connection to piped water in urban areas that is in poverty (we consider all urban areas as opposed to Accra only because if successful, the program could be extended to many urban areas beyond the Accra pilot). If the intervention were to be targeted to the poorest areas in cities, something which is difficult to measure in the GLSS5, targeting performance could be better. Another reason why we mention this project here despite its small size is that to reach the poor it is often better to provide connection as opposed to consumption subsidies for basic utilities (consumption subsidies are provided through inverted or increasing block tariff structures, but many of the benefits involved tend to be captured by better off households).

The estimate of the share of outlays from the NYEP accruing to the poor is 12.7 percent. This estimate is based on simulations using household survey data rather than on actual data on the characteristics of beneficiaries. Administrative data are also available on the number of beneficiaries by district. Based on those district level data, if we assume that beneficiaries within a district have a profile similar to the district as a whole, we obtain a share of benefits accruing to the poor equal to about 30 percent. However, many of the beneficiaries of the NYEP have completed junior high school, and on that basis the benefits accruing to the poor should be much smaller. The fact that the NYEP is not well targeted to the poor does not mean that the NYEP performs poorly given that the program is not explicitly aiming to reduce poverty (or at least this is not its primary objective). However, other aspects of the program appear to suffer from weaknesses and would warrant more scrutiny so as to better assess its actual impact and cost. It would also make sense in a country like Ghana to ensure that a larger share of the benefits of such a program reach the poor.

The last program included in table 2.4 is the Ministry of Women and Children's (MOWAC) program aiming to facilitate access to micro credit for women. It is unclear to what extent this program reaches the poor. Based on district level data, if we assume that beneficiaries within a district have a profile similar to the district as a whole, we obtain a share of benefits accruing to the poor equal to 25.4 percent. However, the characteristics of the program are such that the share of benefits accruing to the poor is probably smaller. Groups of women with typically 20 to 50 members apply for credit to local microfinance and small loans centers and need to show evidence of savings as collateral for loans. Business and financial management training is provided to the groups to run small businesses and beneficiaries are encouraged to open bank accounts. Individual credits provided to group members range from GH¢100 to GH¢500. This type of program, while potentially beneficial for participants, typically does not reach the very poor and qualitative evidence suggests a lack of specific mechanisms and monitoring systems to ensure such targeting.

Programs and Subsidies Benefiting Mostly the Nonpoor

Table 2.5 lists a last group of programs that are mostly benefitting the nonpoor. The first program is the electricity lifeline embedded in the inverted (or increasing) block tariff structure for residential electricity consumption and mandated by the Public Utilities Regulatory Commission (PURC). We estimate that only 8 percent of the subsidies involved by reducing the unit price of electricity for those who consume lower amounts of electricity reach the poor. This assessment is based on the tariff structure that prevailed in 2005–06 and on the data from the GLSS5. Changes in tariff structure since 2005–06 may have increased the share of benefits accruing to the poor, but targeting performance is likely to remain limited because many residential electricity customers who benefit from the lifeline are nonpoor. Household survey data suggest that providing connection instead of consumption subsidies could substantially improve targeting, but providing such connection subsidies supposes also that cost recovery is adequate in order not to increase sector deficits further. A more detailed analysis could be performed with the PURC to help increase the share of consumption subsidies that would accrue to the poor under alternative tariff structure designs. Also, if connection subsidies were to be implemented, possibly on a pilot basis as a start, a proxy means-testing mechanism similar to that used by LEAP could be used for good targeting.

The second program is the tax cut that was implemented temporarily on imported rice at the peak of the food price crisis. Since most of the imported and domestic rice consumed in the country is consumed by the nonpoor, only 8.3 percent of the tax cut is likely to have benefited the poor. In addition, by reducing the after-tax price of imported food, the tax cut may also have reduced the price of locally produced rice, which would then have reduced the incomes of rice producers, some of whom are poor.

Table 2.5: Programs with benefits accruing mostly to nonpoor households

Program	Share of Outlays Benefiting the Poor (%)	Principal Targeting Mechanism	Benefits for households	Conditions Attached
PURC Electricity Subsidies	8.0	Inverted block tariff and lifeline	Cheaper electricity for low consumers	Residential electricity consumers
MOF Tax Cut on Imported Rice	8.3	Self-targeting through use of good	Lower cost of rice (imported/domestic)	Purchase of rice (imported/domestic)
MOE Tertiary Education	6.9	Youth in higher degree institutions	Subsidized education	School enrollment and attendance
MOF Petrol and Diesel Subsidies	>2.3	Self-targeting through use of good	Lower cost of fuel (imported/domestic)	Purchase of fuel (imported/domestic)

Source: Author, based on the material provided in this study.

Not surprisingly, the share of public spending for tertiary education that accrues to the poor is very low, at 6.9 percent. The share of subsidies for oil-related products (apart from kerosene) that were in effect until recently that accrues to the poor is even lower, at 2.9 percent, on the basis of the observed consumption patterns by households. Because oil products are used as intermediary inputs for a wide range of activities, including transportation for example, the share of the subsidies that indirectly reach the poor is likely to be higher, but it also probably will remain relatively small.

Choosing Indicators for Geographic Targeting

Apart from an evaluation of the targeting performance of existing programs and subsidies, this study provides data and tools for the implementation of better targeting mechanisms. Before mentioning these tools, it is worth emphasizing that it would not make sense to target narrowly all of the subsidies considered in the previous sections only to the poor. For example, funding for public primary education should remain broadbased, although the data presented above could possibly be used to argue that shifts in spending from, say, tertiary education to basic education would be pro-poor, at least in terms of benefit incidence (whether such a shift should be recommended requires a much more thorough analysis). But for a number of other, smaller programs, such as school lunches, public works, or electricity consumption subsidies, it would make sense to better target the programs to the poor and this could be done in various ways. We consider first geographic targeting (in the next section, we discuss proxy means-testing).

It has become customary to suggest that poverty maps, which provide detailed information on poverty at low levels of geographic disaggregation, can be used to target a wide range of programs. However, it is not clear than an education or health program should be targeted according to a map of poverty, as opposed to a map of education or health deprivation, however that would be defined. This is why this study provides different maps at the district level (using the 2005–06 GLSS5 and 2003 CWIQ surveys as well as other sources of data) for poverty (a previous poverty map was based on the 2000 census and the GLSS4) as well as food insecurity. The study also suggests that the correlation between many social indicators at the district level is not always high. In fact while there is a clear pattern of higher concentration of poverty over time in the rural savannah area, it is less clear whether the distribution of other indicators related to the MDGs display a similar geographic pattern. As an illustration, Figures 2.1a to 2.1l below provide scatter plots with the district level share of the population in poverty on the horizontal axis, and various MDG indicators on the vertical axis to display visually the correlation (or lack thereof) between these indicators and poverty.

Regarding child malnutrition, we would expect upward sloping regression lines through the scatter plots with areas with higher levels of poverty also displaying higher measures of child malnutrition. However, the relationship between poverty and malnutrition measures for children under five years of age is weak, whether measures of stunting, wasting, and the share of children being underweight are used (figures 2.1a–2.1c). The relationship is also weak with measures of severe malnutrition (share of children more than three standard deviations away from the mean; see figures 2.1d–2.1f), suggesting that policies to deal with malnutrition may have to be targeted geographically in a different way from policies dealing with monetary poverty. As discussed in more details in the study, other indicators of food insecurity, including caloric intake, are on the other hand much more closely related to poverty. Still, overall it is clear that geographic targeting of programs aiming to improve nutrition and/or food security would have to be carefully thought through.

Regarding education, net enrollment in primary school is strongly correlated with poverty (figure 2.1g), with enrollment rates significantly lower in areas with higher poverty. There is also some evidence that girls are more likely not to be enrolled in poorer areas (figures 2.1i–2.1j), especially in terms of secondary and tertiary education. By contrast, the literacy rate in the population aged 15–24 is not strongly correlated with the level of poverty (figure 2.1h). These data thus suggest that geographic targeting based on poverty could potentially be used for some interventions related to schooling (such as conditional cash transfers and school lunches that aim to reduce the cost of schooling for the poor). Yet for other education interventions such as investments at the school level, it would probably be much better to use administrative data to develop a definition of deprived districts. This has been done in Ghana, although one can show that depending on how deprived districts are defined, some of the districts eligible for transfers are likely to change.

Regarding employment, one of the MDG indicators is related to the share of women in wage employment in the non-agricultural sector. The relationship between this indicator and poverty is weak. More generally, the link between unemployment and underemployment, and poverty is less straightforward than one might think, in part because often the very poor simply cannot afford to be unemployed for long and may therefore have to take any job they may find even if it has low productivity. This may be important when planning interventions aimed at either providing jobs, or training, although one could argue that one of the primary objectives of public works is poverty reduction rather than job creation per se.

Finally in health, the relationship between maternal mortality and poverty is weak (figure 2.1k) and has an unexpected sign. Here it must be recognized that it is not easy to measure maternal mortality well with a survey like the CWIQ due to the very small sample size on which the observations are computed. Thus it may be best not to rely on sub-national data from the CWIQ in this area. The relationship between the share of births attended by skilled health personnel and poverty is by contrast very strong and of the right sign (figure 2.1l).

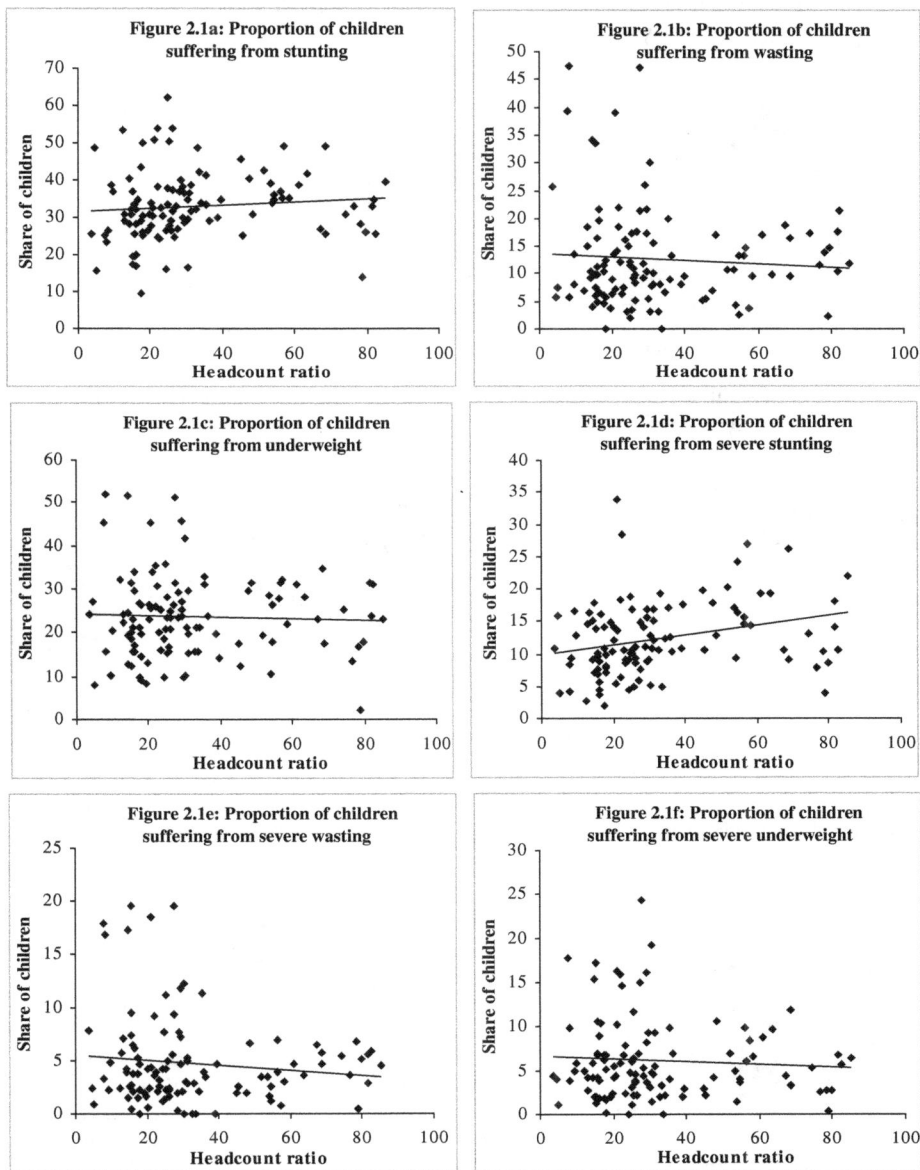

Figure 2.1: Scatter plots of various Millennium Development Goal Indicators

(Figure continues on next page)

Figure 2.1: Scatter plots of various Millennium Development Goal Indicators

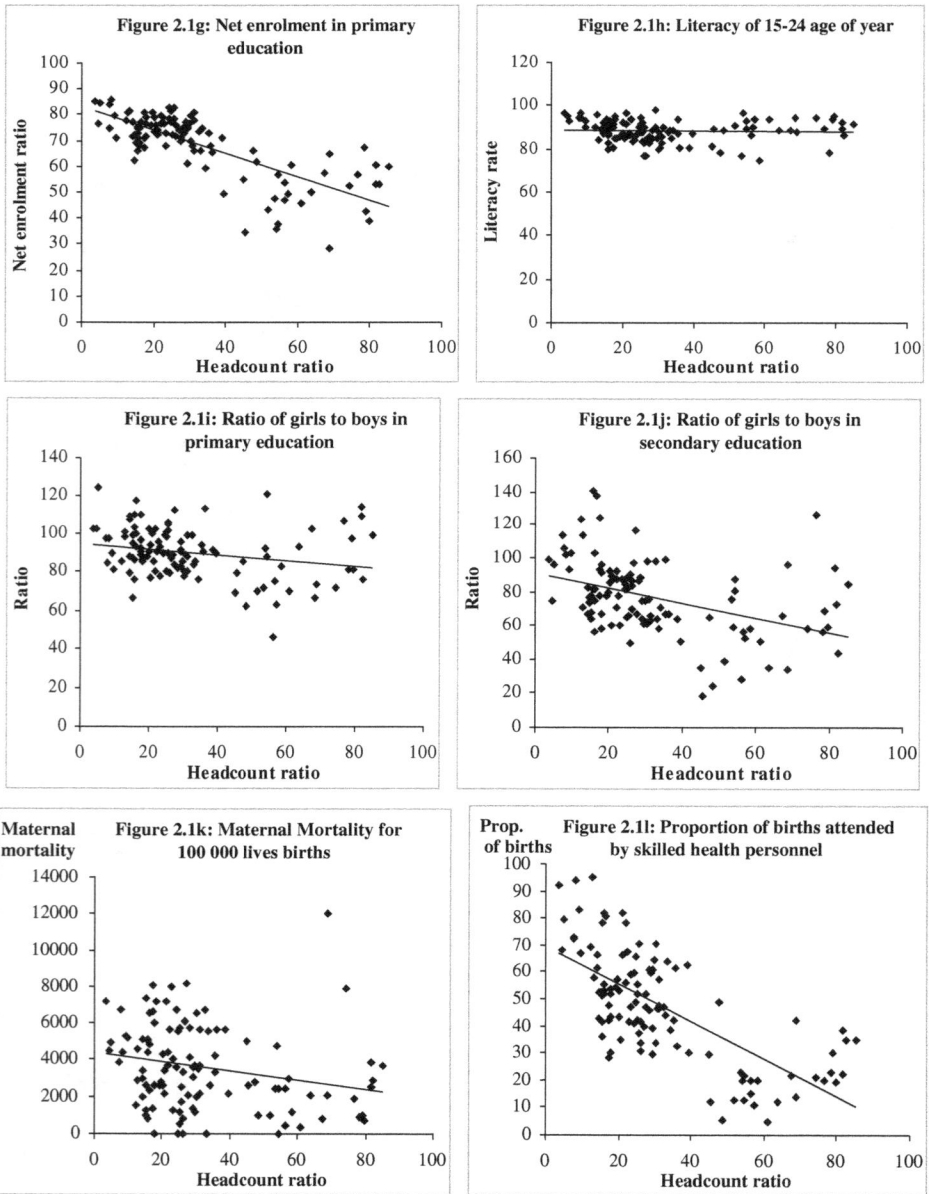

Figure 2.1g: Net enrolment in primary education

Figure 2.1h: Literacy of 15-24 age of year

Figure 2.1i: Ratio of girls to boys in primary education

Figure 2.1j: Ratio of girls to boys in secondary education

Figure 2.1k: Maternal Mortality for 100 000 lives births

Figure 2.1l: Proportion of births attended by skilled health personnel

Source: Author's estimation using CWIQ 2003 survey.

This study does not advocate strongly for the use of one versus another targeting mechanism for this or that program, but it does provide detailed data that can be used by program administrators for geographic targeting. Still we do believe that for a range of programs, geographic targeting based on poverty mapping would be appropriate, and for this reason detailed analyses are provided in subsequent chapters on the basis of simulation techniques to assess the share of benefits from various programs that would accrue to the poor under poverty-based geographic targeting (this is done for example for free school uniforms, conditional cash transfers, the NYEP, and public works).

Comparing Geographic Targeting in Levels and in Changes Due to Shocks

In the context of economic shocks, another key issue faced by policy makers when implementing or expanding a safety net or social program is whether to target areas that are affected the most by a shock, or areas that are initially the poorest or that are the poorest after taking into account the impact of a shock, such as the recent food price crisis. The same holds for food security—if higher food prices are affecting the ability of households to pay for basic food, should policy makers target areas that are the most food insecure or areas that witness the largest increase in food insecurity. In principle, from a social welfare point of view, one could argue that one should most of the time target in priority the areas with the highest level of poverty or food insecurity. But governments are also under pressure to respond to the impact of crises on households so as to offset part of that impact. To the extent that the increase in poverty or food insecurity is going to be highest in already poor or food insecure areas, the dilemma faced by policy makers is reduced.

One example of such an analysis in a chapter provided in this study focuses on the potential impact on poverty of the recent increase in food prices. The results suggest that the impact on poverty of higher food prices is likely to have been lower in Ghana than in other West and Central African countries, but that the impact was nevertheless substantial. Using poverty mapping techniques, we analyze where geographically higher food prices are likely to have had the largest negative impact. The results suggest that contrary to popular belief the poorest areas of the country are likely to have been the most affected by the increase in food prices, which would then warrant targeting these areas through safety nets independently of whether one considers that the priority is to reach poor areas or to help offset the impact of the shock. A similar analysis could be conducted for the impact of higher fuel prices, lower remittances, and lower export prices. Preliminary results suggest that in the case of higher fuel prices, there is also a somewhat positive relationship between the initial level of poverty and the impact on poverty. In the case of remittances, there is no clear relationship. In the case of export prices, using cocoa as an example, the increase in poverty that would follow a reduction in world prices is much larger in less poor areas, since cocoa production is more intensive in coastal and forest areas.

Comparing Geographic, Proxy Means-Testing, and Community-Based Targeting

Two chapters in the study provide simulations to compare the potential performance of geographic targeting versus proxy means-testing or a combination of both. The first chapter assesses the potential targeting performance of the distribution of free school uniforms to close to two million students that is planned by the government for the fall of 2009. The program can be considered as a scheme to lower the private cost of schooling for households. As mentioned earlier (see table 2.2), the results suggest that proper geographic targeting could go a long way in making the program pro-poor. Proxy means-testing, which would make the free uniform available to some children but not others on the basis of the characteristics of their household, would not improve targeting performance, and it could also potentially generate stigma. One should stress that the targeting performance of the free school uniforms program presented here is simulated. Actual targeting performance could be lower. But the data suggests that geographic targeting could lead to good targeting performance for programs that do not aim to reach all districts. It would be important however to use the poverty map for geographic targeting or possibly the food insecurity map as opposed to the deprived education district map to target, given that the main objective of the program is to help poor households cope with the private cost of schooling, as opposed to improving the delivery of education services (which is what the deprived education district map is about).

It could be however that for some programs to gain political support and thereby sustainability, they need to be implemented in a large number of districts rather than only in the poorest areas of the country. The desire to reach a larger share of the poor through at least some of programs (to reduce errors of exclusion) may also make it necessary to implement those programs in a large number of areas, in which case geographic targeting cannot be used efficiently. The question then is whether in some areas geographic targeting performs better than proxy means-testing, while in others the reverse may be true. It may also be useful in some areas to combine geographic targeting with proxy means-testing. Simulations for the targeting performance of conditional cash transfers at the junior high level suggest that in less poor areas, proxy means-testing performs better than geographic targeting, while the reverse is observed in the poorest areas. Thus for some programs a combination of geographic targeting in some areas, proxy means-testing in others, and perhaps even a combination of both could lead to the best targeting.

While geographic targeting is easier to implement than proxy means-testing, LEAP has demonstrated that it is feasible to set up a well performing targeting mechanism, in this case by combining proxy means-testing and community-based targeting. Under LEAP, districts are first selected on the basis of their poverty incidence, rate of HIV/AIDS prevalence, rates of child labor, and lack of access to social services, although the large number of participating districts makes this selection less potent. Next, and more importantly, within selected districts committees identify the most vulnerable households in their communities. Third, social welfare officers administer a survey questionnaire to the households proposed by local communities to select those who are likely to be the poorest (proxy means-testing). The survey questionnaire implemented by LEAP has two parts. The first part includes about 40 questions on the housing conditions of the household, selected household characteristics including a series of assets, and the household roster. The second part includes about 30 questions on the characteristics of individual members of the household, including their demographic characteristics, their education and their employment status. The data on LEAP beneficiaries (as well as on households not selected into the program) are kept electronically in a single registry. The list of the proposed beneficiaries after taking into account results from proxy means-testing is sent back to each Community LEAP Implementation Committee (CLIC) for approval.

LEAP is probably today the best targeted program in the country, and the proxy means-testing component part of its overall targeting mechanism could be used to improve the targeting performance of other programs that are not as well targeted, or to confirm eligibility under some programs that are likely to be well targeted (such as the indigent exemption under the NHIS). As mentioned earlier, the good targeting performance of LEAP does not mean that there are no areas for improvement. The actual formula used by LEAP to determine eligibility based on the data collected on households is not fully clear. A more detailed assessment of the variables collected, the estimation model, and the threshold used for eligibility should be conducted to assess whether the mechanism can be further improved. At the same time, the mechanism has the merit of being in place, and it could thus be applied for example on a pilot basis to other programs. Using a common targeting mechanism to target different programs could over time reduce the administrative costs associated with targeting as a share of the total outlays provided on the basis of the mechanism. This simple idea has been implemented in middle income Latin American countries for many years, and it is flexible enough to allow for different eligibility thresholds for different programs. For example, the eligibility threshold for benefiting from the indigent exemption under the NHIS, an electricity connection subsidy, or a micro-credit could be set differently for each program than for the participation in LEAP, but the same information base would be used to target the various programs.

This also does not mean that the LEAP formula would need to be implemented for all programs, as in some cases targeting might not be appropriate, while for others, other mechanisms such as geographic targeting might be sufficient. One additional point worth emphasizing is that proxy means-testing can be implemented a priori to decide on program eligibility but it can also be implemented a posteriori through surveys of a sample of program beneficiaries to measure ex post the targeting performance of such programs. For example, it may be for some reason difficult to use proxy means-testing in a community to decide on eligibility to participate in a public works program. But a survey instrument can be implemented among program participants to assess targeting performance on an ongoing basis, so that the program's administrators can take corrective action if it appears that a program is not well targeted.

Using Targeting Mechanisms for Non-State Providers of Services and Programs

Good targeting is essential for government programs, but it should also be an objective for privately funded development aid. Estimates suggest that in the last four years, an average of $216 million per year was allocated by private actors to development activities. While this represents only 8 percent of the amount received from official development assistance, it is still significant, especially because a large part of private aid goes to the social sectors. The bulk of private aid comes from foreign transfers to international and local NGOs. Corporate entities are estimated to have contributed $35 million, while large foundations spent $31 million on average through support for global and vertical funds. Religious organizations also devote significant resources toward charitable causes but estimates of the value of these contributions are not available. This means that private flows of aid are even larger than estimated.

Targeting is probably even more important for programs and projects run by NGOs or FBOs (faith-based organization), because many of the NGOs and FBOs implementing programs do not aim to reach the population as a whole, and many also profess to target the poor in priority. Geographic targeting is certainly one option for privately funded programs, but proxy means-testing is also an option because it is easy to package a proxy means-testing mechanism in a user friendly excel spreadsheet that can be used at the local level by program's social workers. Finally, targeting assessment is also important for larger NGO or FBO networks that benefit from state funding, such as the Christian Health Association of Ghana. The data from the 2003 CWIQ survey, which thanks to a larger sample size is more reliable for this type of analysis than the GLSS5, suggests that CHAG serves the poor slightly better than public health facilities. This is in itself an important piece of information when discussing how to better reach the poor through health facilities.

Policy Recommendations

Decisions on which programs to fund in priority should not be based only on an assessment of the targeting performance of these programs. The impact of any given program in the medium-term is also essential, and some programs do not target the poor in priority. Still, targeting performance does matter, and the following tentative recommendations can be made on the basis of the findings from this study:

LEAP appears to be one of the best targeted programs in Ghana. An expansion of the program would thus generate substantial benefits for the poor and would also help in reducing the share of program costs currently devoted to administration and delivery. LEAP's targeting mechanisms should however be reviewed to assess if it could be improved in terms of both its proxy means-testing and community-based components. In addition, a LEAP-inspired household questionnaire could be used to assess eligibility for other programs (possibly on a pilot basis) and for assessing ex post the targeting performance of some programs such as public works. There is thus scope for building on LEAP's experience to progressively design targeting mechanisms that could be used for multiple programs, or at least for those programs that are not geographically targeted (for programs serving the north, geographic targeting is often enough).

The indigent exemption under the NHIS is also probably well targeted to the poor, although we have only limited data to make this assessment. Given low levels of enrollment under this exemption today as compared to the share of the population in extreme poverty, districts should be encouraged to make more extensive use of the indigent exemption. A first step could be to enable (most) LEAP households to benefit from the exemption. New applicants for the exemption could be screened with a LEAP-inspired questionnaire, and the procedure for verification of district enrollment under the indigent exemption once the share of indigents exceeds a certain threshold could also be based on a LEAP-inspired questionnaire that would be administered to a random sample of beneficiaries chosen within the district under review.

The distribution of free school uniforms should not be made on the basis of the map of educationally deprived districts, because this map relates too much to supply-side issues in the delivery of education. Instead, free school uniforms should be distributed according to the Ghana poverty map, the food security map, or a map of gaps in primary school completion at the district level. Free school uniforms should not be targeted individually—geographic targeting through public schools in poor districts is sufficient.

The government could consider testing on a pilot basis some type of a conditional cash transfer program possibly for primary or JHS students from poor families, with a proper baseline and follow-up survey so that we can measure impact. This should be done in priority in the northern districts using geographic targeting, but part of the pilot could take place in less poor districts using proxy means-testing. Possibly the program could be tested through LEAP, which has some conditionalities, but that are not really enforced.

Large subsidies that are not well targeted to the poor for food (rice), energy, and electricity, and possibly piped water should be reduced. This does not mean that all subsidies should be eliminated. Kerosene is for example a good that can be subsidized to protect the poor from fluctuations in world oil prices. Some subsidies for electricity or piped water can also be considered, but they need to be limited, and in general connection subsidies would tend to be better targeted than consumption subsidies.

The allocation procedure for school lunches at the district and school level should be revised given weak targeting performance. This should be done firstly to have a transparent allocation procedure, and secondly to propose a more systematic use of the geographic targeting information now available, following the poverty/food security maps rather than the educational deprived district maps.

The educational deprived district formula should continue to be used for the targeting of supply-side investments with transfers provided to districts and thereafter to schools. However the formula to identify the deprived districts should be revised from a rank-based to a level-based indicator. There should also be a process of reassessment, say every two years, to reorient on a dynamic basis the funds to districts in need given that some of the variables used in the formula change substantially over time.

Labor intensive public works and so-called productive safety nets should be targeted to the poorest areas of the country. This is because in a context where a large number of workers work for no or limited pay, self-targeting through low wages may not be enough to ensure good targeting performance. Proxy means-testing would not be needed for determining eligibility of public works participants if the program is geographically targeted, but a LEAP-inspired questionnaire could be used ex post on a sample of participants to monitor targeting performance and implement corrective measures as needed.

Social protection and service delivery strategies need to take into account the important role of privately funded or privately run (and publicly funded) partners. The same tools of targeting assessment can be used to measure how well NGOs and FBOs reach the poor through their programs in Ghana.

On fertilizer subsidies/vouchers, geographic targeting as well as a cap on the size of vouchers to be received by any one household would help to improve targeting performance. Many of these measures have already been taken by the government, but data collection and monitoring is needed to measure to what extent the fertilizer voucher program is reaching the poor.

This study does not provide recommendations regarding the allocation of funding for general services in education and health, as many other considerations must be taken into account. The assessment of benefit incidence provided here is simply an input for more detailed forthcoming analysis to be conducted for an Education Country Status Report, a Health Country Status Report, and a Poverty Assessment.

The data from the 2003 CWIQ survey was essential to various parts of the analysis conducted in this study, including the poverty map and the work on geographic targeting. The CWIQ was important because its large sample size provides statistical reliability at the district level. Ghana Statistical Service should be encouraged to field a new large sample CWIQ survey apart from the upcoming implementation of the GLSS6 to monitor district-level progress and assess directly participation in a range of programs at the district level. Both the new CWIQ and the GLSS6 should include new questionnaire modules aiming to measure program targeting (i.e., participation) as well as program impacts.

PART II
Targeting Performance of Social Programs

CHAPTER 3

Principles of Targeting:
A Brief Review

David Coady, Margaret Grosh, and John Hoddinot[1]

This chapter provides a brief overview of issues related with the decision to target programs to the poor as well as the methods used to do so. Program managers and policy makers have many methods available to target an antipoverty intervention. In developing an understanding of what methods are appropriate under what circumstances, it is helpful to begin by enumerating the benefits and costs of targeting. Decisions about whether to target, how precise to be, and what method to use, will depend on the relative size of these costs and benefits, which will vary by setting. An assessment of these benefits and costs requires the measurement of targeting performance, which is the third topic taken up here. Lastly, the chapter outlines a structure for classifying targeting methods.

Benefits of Targeting

Targeting is a means of increasing program efficiency by increasing the benefit that the poor can get within a fixed program budget. The case for targeting is tantalizingly simple. Imagine an economy with 100 million people, 30 million of whom are poor. The budget for a transfer program is $300 million. With no targeting, the program could give everyone in the population $3. If the program could be targeted only to the poor, it could give each poor person $10 and spend the full budget, or it could continue to give each poor person $3 for a budget of only $90 million. More generally, the motivation for targeting arises from the following three features of the policy environment: (1) **Objective:** the desire to maximize the reduction in poverty or, more generally, the increase in social welfare; (2) **Budget constraint:** a limited poverty alleviation budget; and (3) **Opportunity cost:** the tradeoff between the number of beneficiaries covered by the intervention and the level of transfers. These three features imply that targeting transfers at poor households has a potential return, namely, that the amount of the transfer budget going to those households deemed to be most in need of transfers can be increased.

This concept can be expressed graphically (figure 3.1). As a policy maker, suppose we have a fixed transfer budget just sufficient to eliminate consumption poverty. We have representative household survey data and, using this, we graph consumption levels of individual households before any transfers to them, ordering them from worst to best off. This ordering is represented on the x-axis as "original income," while a household's income after the transfer is given on the y-axis as "final income." The maximum

Figure 3.1: Targeting poverty alleviation transfer

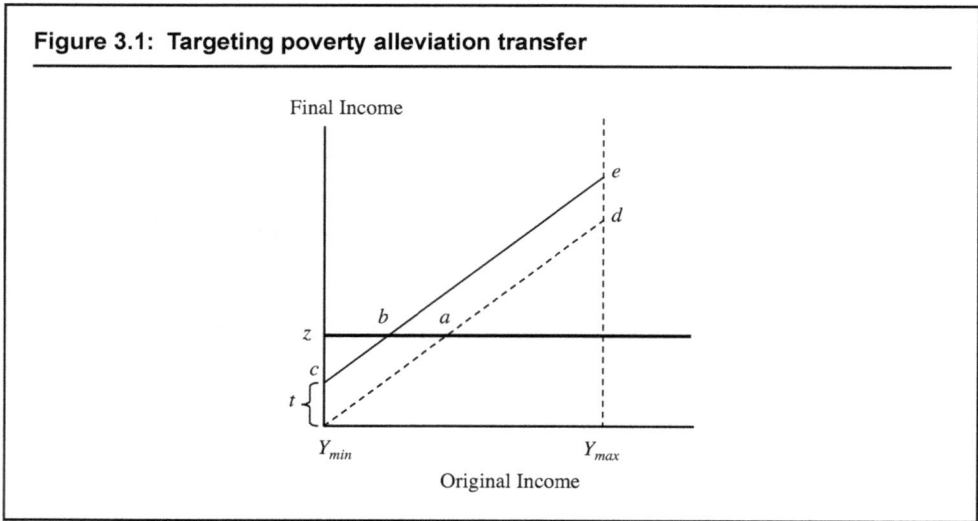

Source: Coady et al., 2004.

and minimum household incomes in the survey are y_{max} and y_{min}, respectively, and z is the poverty line. The line dy_{min} shows that, by definition, before the transfer program is in place households' final incomes are equal to their original incomes. The optimal transfer scheme is one that gives a transfer to all poor households only (i.e., those with income less than z), with transfer levels equal to their individual "poverty gaps," that is, the distance between their original income and the poverty line, za. This transfer program brings all poor households up to the poverty line; all nonpoor households have equal final and original incomes. The poverty budget is represented by the area zay_{min} and is the minimum budget required to eliminate poverty. Consider the case of a uniform transfer program, which gives the same transfer equal to t ($= c - y_{min}$) to all households, both poor and nonpoor.

Because of the leakage of transfers to nonpoor households, the transfers to poor households are no longer sufficient to eliminate their poverty. Two forms of "inefficiency" are associated with the uniform transfer: (1) Nonpoor households receive a transfer; and (2) some poor households (those in the line interval ba) receive transfers greater than their poverty gaps. As a result of these inefficiencies, the poverty impact of the uniform transfer scheme is less than that of the optimal transfer scheme, less by the area zcb. The total leakage of the budget (reflecting the two sources of inefficiency identified above) is given by the area $bade$, which for a fixed budget must also equal the area zcb, which equals the level of poverty after the uniform transfer program. Therefore, imperfect targeting results in a lower poverty impact for a given budget. Improved targeting involves screening some of the nonpoor households out of the program.

Costs of Targeting

The scenario outlined above illustrating the benefits of targeting assumed that it was possible to distinguish who is poor and who is not. In fact, there are costs to acquiring information about who is needy and, even then, such information is rarely perfect. These costs can be classified as follows.

Administrative Costs: These costs include the costs of collecting information, for example, conducting means testing of households or conducting a survey on which to base a poverty map. These costs mean that less of the budget is available to be distributed to beneficiaries. In general we expect that the costs of gathering information to target will increase with the precision of the targeting. It is possible that if finer targeting means that the total number of beneficiaries declines, the total administrative costs will decline, either absolutely or a share of total costs. This would result from two forces. First, a targeted program may serve a smaller number of people, so the overall scope of machinery to deliver benefits could be smaller. Second, if the tighter targeting allows a larger benefit per client, the share of administrative costs will be lower. Imagine a program that costs $1 per household to gather information about targeting and $5 per household for the administrative costs of delivering the benefit worth $100. If the program serves 1 million client households, then the total administrative cost would be $6 million, the total cost $106 million, and the share of administrative costs about 6 percent. Next imagine moving to much finer targeting, for example, from demographic targeting to a means test. The cost of gathering information for targeting might rise to $5 per household. The cost of getting the benefit into the client's hands remains $5. However, now the program serves only 250,000 families, so administrative costs are $2.5 million. If the benefit is kept at $100 per family, then the total budget will be $27.5 million and the share of administrative costs about 10 percent. If some of the resources freed through the finer targeting are used to raise the benefit to $200 per family, then the total cost would be $52.5 million and the share of administrative costs would be about 5 percent, lower in both absolute terms and as a share of the total program budget.

It is important to note, however, that from the perspective of targeting the relationship between the level of costs incurred because of the decision to target transfers to the poor and the improved targeting performance resulting from these extra costs is of particular interest. While from this perspective it is always desirable to reduce the level of nontargeting-related program administrative costs, higher targeting costs are acceptable if they lead to sufficiently better targeting of transfers. When interpreting the relative size of administrative costs across programs, it is also important to recognize that some costs are fixed (i.e., independent of the number of households included in the program and/or of the transfer levels given to households) so that relative the cost-effectiveness of programs is sensitive to the size of the program. Focusing on fixed targeting-related costs, this means that expensive targeting methods are only likely to be warranted for large programs, that is, programs with large transfer levels and/or a large number of beneficiaries).

Private Costs: Households also incur private costs involved in taking up transfers. For example, workfare programs involve households incurring an opportunity cost in terms of forgone income opportunities. Queuing involves similar, though usually much smaller, opportunity costs. Households may face cash costs for obtaining certifications required for the program, such as a national identity card or proof of residency or of disability, and for transportation to and from program offices. Private costs, which are often overlooked when evaluating programs, may be quite important, especially when self-selection methods are used or when access to the program is conditioned on actions (e.g., keeping children in school) by the household. Indeed, Duclos (1995), estimates that even for Great Britain's Supplemental Benefit—a means-tested cash transfer not particularly reliant on self-targeting—"approximately one-fifth of the total income support budget is lost to recipients in the form of various takeup inconveniences."

Incentive Costs: These are often referred to as *indirect costs.* They exist because the presence of eligibility criteria may induce households to change their behavior in an attempt to become beneficiaries. For example, a program open only to those below a minimum income may cause some households to reduce their labor supply and thus their earned incomes. This is one of the reasons why transfers that guarantee a minimum income irrespective of earnings are not considered desirable. Other examples of such "negative incentive effects" are higher consumption of subsidized commodities, crowding out of private transfers (Cox and Jimenez 1995; Jensen 1998), relocation/migration, or devoting resources to misreporting. Indirect effects may also be positive, for example, when transfers are conditioned on household behaviors such as the enrollment of children in school or attendance at health clinics. Though labor disincentive effects are an important concern in the development of many OECD countries' welfare programs (Moffitt 1992, 2003), they may be less important in developing country safety net programs for several reasons: (1) Direct means tests are not the most common targeting method and are especially rare in low-income countries; (2) Transfers are rarely graduated. Thus, only those around the cutoff point have an incentive to change their behavior so as to be deemed eligible for transfers. The smaller the transfer is, the lower is the number of people likely to be affected; and (3) Benefit levels are usually low, implying that recipients will maintain a strong incentive to choose additional earnings over additional leisure when they have a choice. Nonetheless, in principle, such labor-disincentive effects cannot be ignored or assumed not to exist.

One way of minimizing disincentive effects would be to keep the population relatively uninformed about the detailed eligibility criteria being used, for example, letting the population know that it is based on some concept of poverty but not providing the details of how this is actually measured. Such lack of transparency may in itself be seen as an undesirable characteristic of program design. Basing eligibility on information or characteristics collected prior to the program is another way to eliminate the problem, assuming that households were not answering strategically in anticipation of a program. However, the need for periodic recertification will require the eventual use of updated information on characteristics so that the incentive problem will arise.

Social Costs: These costs may arise when the targeting of poor households involves publicly identifying households as poor, which may carry a social stigma. If the poorest households do not take up the transfer as a result, then this decreases the effectiveness of the program at getting transfers into the hands of the poorest. Such issues obviously take on additional importance when one appeals to concepts of poverty such as Sen's "capabilities" (Sen 1988).

Political Costs: Excluding the middle classes may remove broad-based support for such programs and make them unsustainable if voter support determines the budget and is in turn determined by whether the voter benefits directly from the program. On the other hand, efficient targeting to ensure that only those in need receive benefits may actually increase political support from those who support it based on its indirect benefits to them of reducing poverty (such as a feeling of social justice, being hassled by fewer beggars, lower likelihood of property theft, increased political stability, or lower taxes). Of course, political support may come from interest groups who are suppliers to the program or advocates for its beneficiaries—farmers' and teachers' unions may support school lunch programs on these grounds.

The relative importance of the above costs will differ across targeting methods and also across different sociopolitical environments. For example, it is likely that administrative costs are more important when individual or household assessment is used. Incentive costs are likely to be less important when categorical targeting is used. Private costs are likely to be more important when self-selection is used. While the nature and importance of social costs may differ widely with the form of self-selection inherent in the program design, all of these costs need to be considered when evaluating the targeting effectiveness of programs.

Measuring Targeting Performance

In practice program officials do not have perfect information about who is poor because this information is difficult, time consuming, and costly to collect. Thus, when basing program eligibility on imperfect information, they may commit errors of inclusion—identifying nonpoor persons as poor and therefore admitting them to the program, or errors of exclusion—identifying poor persons as not poor and thus denying them access to the program. In a world of unlimited resources, such errors could be greatly minimized by collecting additional information. However, in a world of limited resources, policy makers and program managers need to know whether such costs are justified in terms of improved targeting. Further, governments will wish to determine how effective a given targeted intervention is. Both exercises require a measure of targeting performance. A common approach to evaluate the targeting performance of alternative transfer instruments is to compare undercoverage and leakage rates. **Undercoverage** is the proportion of poor households that are not included in the program (errors of exclusion). **Leakage** is the proportion of those who are reached by the program who are classified as nonpoor (errors of inclusion).

In general actions taken to reduce one kind of error may cause the other to increase. Introducing more stringent rules to to identify need so as to screen out the nonpoor will, for example, also make it more difficult for the poor to provide the necessary information. Thus, while meant to reduce errors of inclusion, it will also raise errors of exclusion. Similarly, raising the cut-off point in an (imperfect) proxy means score to reduce undercoverage will also tend to increase leakage. In practice, the inevitability of targeting errors affects the decision about whether to target, how precisely to target, and the method used for targeting. First, it reduces the potential benefit; the illustration in figure 3.1 assumed perfect targeting and thus exaggerated the benefit from targeting. Second, the fact that both types of targeting errors will occur and are generally inversely linked means that policymakers must decide how well they can tolerate each. An error of inclusion wastes program resources (e.g., by leaving less for "poor" households or by increasing the budget required to have the same poverty impact) and thus makes the program inefficient. An error of exclusion leaves that person without help and makes the program ineffective at reducing poverty. Both are undesirable, and different policy makers may have different views about which is worse.

This approach has several limitations (Coady and Skoufias 2001). First, it discards much distributional information. Surely it is better to give a transfer to someone just over the poverty line than to someone at the very top of the distribution, but both count equally as errors of inclusion. Similarly, benefits to the very poorest as opposed to those just below the poverty line count equally as success cases, although the former is presumably more desirable. Second, it focuses only on who gets the transfers and not on how much households get (i.e., the size of the transfer budget and the differentiation of transfer levels across households). Third, when comparing across programs it is often the case that those that do well on undercoverage simultaneously score badly on leakage. For example, universal programs would be expected to score relatively well on undercoverage but poorly on leakage, but the leakage/undercoverage approach does not address the issue of trade-off. The core problem is that a focus solely on leakage and undercoverage fails to make explicit how program managers, policy makers, or society itself weights the benefits of transferring resources to different groups, for example, the moderately versus extremely poor.

Three alternatives overcome these limitations. One approach is based on the **distributional characteristic** more commonly used in the literature on commodity taxation (Newbery and Stern 1987; Ahmad and Stern 1991; Coady and Skoufias 2001). This approach builds an index of society's welfare, summing across individuals and using explicit welfare weights for different kinds of individuals. The attraction of this index is that welfare weights are made more transparent and that it generalizes from familiar simple cases. For example, if poor households are given a welfare weight of one and nonpoor households a weight of zero, and if we further assume that all beneficiary households receive the same level of transfer, then this index collapses to the proportion of households receiving transfers that are classified as poor (or 1 minus the rate of leakage). If, in addition, we know the level of benefits received by beneficiaries, then it collapses to the share of the program budget received by poor households. Where the "poor" are defined as households falling within the bottom deciles (e.g., 20 percent or 40 percent) of the national income distribution, similar indices can be calculated. Generally, all that is required to calculate the distributional characteristic is mean incomes by decile and decile shares in transfers. The administrative cost side of the program can be easily incorporated by including this cost in the denominator along with total transfers.

An alternative to specifying welfare weights either implicitly or explicitly is to calculate the share of the program budget going to, for example, the various deciles or quantiles of the national income distribution. The numbers can relate to either proportions of beneficiaries or proportion of total transfers. One can focus on whatever part of the distribution that one wishes, although one should be clear that this implicitly involves specifying welfare weights. For example, focusing on the share of the transfer budget accruing to the bottom 20 percent of the distribution is equivalent to attaching a welfare weight of unity to these households and zero to others. If, in addition to the shares of total transfers received by each decile, one also presents mean incomes, then one provides sufficient information for the calculation of the distributional characteristic

A third approach reframes the issue. Rather than asking how effective the program is at identifying the poor, it asks how effective it is at reducing poverty. It proceeds by comparing the relative impacts of the alternative instruments on the extent of poverty subject to a fixed common budget or, equivalently, the minimum cost of achieving a given reduction in poverty across instruments (Ravallion and Chao 1989; Ravallion 1993). This explicitly incorporates into the previous approaches the size of transfers and the budget, in addition to how transfer levels are differentiated across households in different parts of the income distribution.

A final complication in evaluating targeting outcomes stems from the fact that the program analyst faces many of the difficulties in correctly measuring welfare that the program official faces. Not only is income difficult to measure for those with irregular incomes or entwined household and small business accounts; the household survey information that the analyst usually relies on may not use exactly the same concepts for income, time period, or unit of observation that the program does. Moreover, household welfare may have changed between the time the household sought entry to the program and when it was surveyed. Duclos (1995) expands this analysis and shows that analyst error can lead to substantial misestimates of take-up rates and targeting errors.

Classifying Targeting Methods

Targeting methods all have the same goal—to correctly and efficiently identify which households are poor or which are not. To understand the effectiveness of these approaches, it is useful to distinguish between **methods** and **actors**. **Methods** refer to the approaches taken to reach a target group. Below, we divide these into three groups: individual/household assessment, categorical targeting, and self-selection. **Actors** refer to the identity of the individuals who perform two roles: the implementation of the targeting method and the subsequent implementation of the intervention. **Individual/Household Assessment** is a method in which an official (usually a government employee) directly assesses, household by household or individual by individual, whether the applicant is eligible for the program. It is the most laborious of targeting methods. The gold standard of targeting is a **verified means test** that collects (nearly) complete information on a household's income and/or wealth and verifies the information collected against independent sources such as pay stubs or income and property tax records. This requires the existence of such verifiable records in the target population, as well as the administrative capacity to process this information and to continually update it in a timely fashion. For these reasons verified means tests are extremely rare in developing countries where the poorest households receive income from a myriad of diverse sources and formal record keeping is nonexistent. Other individual assessment mechanisms are used in the absence of the capacity for a verified means test. Three common ones are simple means tests, proxy means-tests, and community-based targeting.

Simple means tests, with no independent verification of income, are not uncommon. A visit to the household by a program social worker may help to verify in a qualitative way that visible standards of living (which reflect income or wealth) are more or less consistent with the figures reported. Alternately, the social workers' assessment may be wholly qualitative, taking into account many factors about the household's needs and means but not having to quantify them. These types of simple means tests are used for both direct transfer programs and for fee-waving programs, with or without the visit to the household. Jamaica's food stamp program, implemented in the 1980s, is an example (Grosh 1992).

Proxy means tests, while relatively rare, are being instituted in a growing number of countries. We use the term to denote a system that generates a score for applicant households based on fairly easy to observe characteristics of the household such as the location and quality of the dwelling, ownership of durable goods, demographic structure of the household, and the education and, possibly, occupations of adult members. The indicators used in calculating this score and their weights are derived from statistical analysis (usually regression analysis or principal components) of data from detailed household surveys of a sort too costly to be carried out for all applicants to large programs. The information provided by the applicant is usually partially verified by either collecting the information on a visit to the home by a program official, as in Chile's unified family subsidy (Sancho 1992) or by having the applicant bring written verification of part of the information to the program office, as done in Armenia (World Bank 1999).

Community-based targeting uses a group of community members or a community leader whose principal functions in the community are not related to the transfer program to decide who in the community should benefit. School officials or the parent-teacher association may determine entry to a school-linked program. A group of village elders may determine who receives grain provided for drought relief, or special committees composed of common community members or a mix of community members and local officials may be specially formed to determine eligibility for a program. The idea is that local knowledge of families' living conditions may be more accurate than the results of a means test conducted by a government social worker or a proxy means test.

Categorical targeting refers to a method in which all individuals in a specified category—for example, a particular age group or region—are eligible to receive benefits. This method is also referred to as **statistical targeting, tagging, or group targeting.** It involves defining eligibility in terms of individual or household characteristics that are fairly easy to observe, hard to falsely manipulate, and correlated with poverty. Age, gender, ethnicity, land ownership, demographic composition, or geographical location are common examples that are fairly easy to verify. Age is a commonly used category, with cash child allowances predominant in transition countries, supplemental feeding programs for children under five common in poor countries, and noncontributory pensions for the elderly common in many places. Geographic targeting is even more common, often used in combination with other methods. Unemployment or disability status is somewhat harder to verify, but cash assistance to these groups may be categorically targeted as well. In other chapters for this study, we will review results for the performance of geographic, demographic, and other categorical methods in Ghana.

Under **self-selection,** the program has universal eligibility, but the design involves dimensions that are thought to encourage the poorest to use the program and the nonpoor not to do so. This is accomplished by recognizing differences in the private participation costs between poor and nonpoor households. For example, this may involve: (1) use of low wages on public works schemes so that only those with a low opportunity cost of time due to low wages or limited hours of employment will present themselves for jobs; (2) restriction of transfers to take place at certain times with a requirement to queue; (3) transfer of in-kind benefits with "inferior" characteristics (e.g., low quality wheat or rice); (4) location of points of service delivery (e.g., ration stores, participating clinics or schools) in areas where the poor are highly concentrated so that the nonpoor have higher (private and social) costs of travel. Universal food subsidies can be viewed as a form of self-selection since they are universally available and households receive benefits by consuming the commodity. In practice, households can often determine not just whether to participate but also the intensity of their participation. Tunisia's reformed milk subsidy program, whereby milk subsidies are higher for reconstituted milk in inconvenient and small packages than for other grades and packaging of milk, is an example of a self-targeted intervention (Tuck and Lindert 1996), as is a public works program in Maharashtra State, India, called the *Employment Guarantee Scheme* (Datt and Ravallion 1994).

Whereas methods refer to "how" targeting is undertaken, actors refer to "who" targets and "who" implements these interventions. Actors can include central government officials; lower state, municipality, or district level officials; private sector contractors; and community members such as teachers, health clinic staff, and elders. The decision whether to decentralize both the identification of beneficiaries and the provision of the program will hinge on several factors: which actors can provide the most cost-effective source of information on individual, household or locality circumstances; which actors can deliver the intervention most cost-effectively; and whether different actors have the incentive to target and implement the intervention in the manner desired by those who fund the program.

In reviewing this menu of targeting options, policy makers should be mindful of two important considerations. First, individual targeting methods are not mutually exclusive and can be used in different combinations and sequences. A child allowance (categorical targeting) may be means tested (individual assessment). Subsidized coarse grain (self-targeting) may be available for sale only in food shops in poor neighborhoods (geographic targeting). In fact, the use of a single targeting method is not the norm; 60 percent of the interventions described in the next section used two or more methods. Second, when assessing whether a particular intervention reaches its intended beneficiaries, it is important to be cognizant of four dimensions: (1) type of interventions chosen—for example, a food-for-work program will, by design, exclude poor people who are physically unable to work; (2) targeting method chosen; (3) identity of the actor who undertakes this targeting; and (4) identity of the actor who provides the intervention.

Note

1. This paper is reproduced with minor modifications from David Coady, Margaret Grosh, and John Hoddinot (2004).

CHAPTER 4

A New Poverty Map for Ghana

Harold Coulombe and Quentin Wodon

Poverty maps have become a popular tool to assess the geography of poverty in developing countries and to target government programs to comparatively poorer areas. However, a weakness of standard Census-based poverty maps is the fact that the low frequency of implementation of Censuses (which are conducted typically every ten years, and in some cases at even larger time intervals) makes it sometimes difficult to have recent enough poverty maps on which to base policy decisions. This chapter documents the construction and presents results for a new poverty map of Ghana based on the GLSS 2005–06 and the CWIQ 2003 surveys. Since the levels of poverty are driven by the poverty estimates from the GLSS5, the map can be considered as representing the geography of poverty in Ghana in 2005–06. The methodology takes advantages of the large sample size of the CWIQ, which can be considered as statistically representative at the district level, which is the level at which the poverty map is constructed. Comparison of the results obtained with the new poverty map and a previous poverty map based on the GLSS4 for 1998–99 and the 2000 Census shows that for a very large majority of districts, the new estimates of poverty are statistically different from the previous census-based estimates.

Objective of the Poverty Map

Poverty profiles have long been used to characterize and monitor poverty. Based on information collected in household surveys, including detailed information on expenditures and incomes, those profiles present the characteristics of the population according to their level of monetary and non-monetary standards of living that can help assessing the poverty reducing effect of some policies and compare poverty level between regions, groups or over time. While these household-based studies have greatly improved our knowledge of welfare level of households in general and of poorer households in particular, the approach has a number of constraints. In particular, policy makers and planners may need more finely disaggregated information to implement anti-poverty schemes. For example, given that many social programs are targeted geographically, policy makers often need information for small geographic units such as city neighborhoods, towns or villages. Telling a Ghanaian policy maker that many among the poorest live in the savannah ecological zone is not enough as this information is too vague and already well-known. But knowing which district has the highest rate of poverty would be more useful. Even region-level information often hides the existence of pockets of poverty in otherwise relatively well-off regions, as well as pockets of relative wealth in poor regions, which could lead to poorly targeted schemes.

Following on work by Elbers et al. (2002, 2003) who have shown how to construct detailed poverty maps by combining census and household survey data, there has been a growing literature on the construction of these maps and their use for policy. The World Bank recently published a collection of papers showing how poverty maps can be used for policy (Bedi et al., 2007). In this collection, country studies include Albania (Carletto et al., 2007), Bolivia (Arias and Robles, 2007), Bulgaria (Gotcheva, 2007), Cambodia (Fujii, 2007), China (Ahmad and Goh, 2007a), Ecuador (Araujo, 2007), Indonesia (Ahmad and Goh, 2007b), Mexico (Lopez-Calva et al., 2007), Morroco (Litvack, 2007), Sri Lanka (Vishwanath and Yoshida, 2007), Thailand (Jitsuchon and Richter, 2007), and Vietnam (Swinkels and Turk, 2007). While the above set of countries does not include any country from sub-Saharan Africa, poverty maps have been constructed for Ghana (Coulombe, 2008), Madagascar (Mistiaen et al., 2002), South Africa (Alderman et al., 2002), and Uganda (Emwanu et al., 2006; Hoogeveen and Schipper, 2005).

However, an issue when using poverty maps for policy is that the maps can become rapidly outdated. In most countries census data are collected only every ten years, and in some sub-Saharan African countries, time span between two censuses can be even longer due to limited capacity and funding to implement such large scale data collection efforts. As a result, existing poverty maps can rapidly fail to represent appropriately the geography of poverty in a country especially when the country is undergoing rapid growth and structural change that leads to large increases or decreases in poverty over time.

Ghana is a case in point. The first poverty map for Ghana was constructed by Coulombe (2008) using the fourth round of the Ghana Living Standards Survey (GLSS4) implemented in 1998–99 and the Housing and Population Census of 2000. Yet the map probably fails to represent the geography of poverty today. This is because poverty has been reduced dramatically from 39.5 percent in 1998–99 to 28.5 percent in 2005/06 according to results based on the fifth round of the Ghana Living Standards Survey (GLSS5) presented in Ghana Statistical Service (2007) and Coulombe and Wodon (2007). Furthermore, the reduction in poverty has not been uniform in the country. The data suggest that there was an increase in poverty in the capital city of Accra, a sharp reduction in poverty in the coastal and forest areas, and a stagnation or only very limited progress towards poverty reduction in the northern savannah area.

One possibility to update poverty maps with a single census consists in using panel data, as documented by Emwanu et al. (2006) in the case of Uganda. However, panel data remain rare, again especially in sub-Saharan Africa. For example, in none of the 26 countries of West and Central Africa is there today a good and nationally representative panel data set with consumption data. Another possibility is to construct poverty maps with a regular survey with consumption data and another survey which would not include consumption data but would be of a sufficiently large sample size so as to permit the estimation of poverty measures at relatively low levels of geographic aggregation. This appears to be feasible in some West African countries which have implemented large scale surveys in recent years, including Ghana and Nigeria, two countries that have implemented large Core Welfare Indicators Questionnaire surveys (CWIQ), with approximately 50,000 households in Ghana and 70,000 in Nigeria. The Ghana survey is deemed representative by Ghana Statistical Services for each of 110 districts that existed in the country at the time of the implementation of the CWIQ in 2003, and the Nigeria survey is similarly deemed representative for each of 36 states in the country and three senatorials within each state.

This chapter presents a new poverty map for Ghana by combining data from the GLSS5 of 2005–06 and the large 2003 CWIQ household survey, and to compare the precision of the poverty estimates obtained at the district level with the estimates obtained from the previous map based on the GLSS4 of 1998–99 and the 2000 Census. We compute poverty indicators at district level, using the detailed information found in the GLSS survey and the geographical coverage of the CWIQ. Results at the region and district levels are presented, and a comparison with the previous Census-based poverty map for Ghana is provided.

Methodology for the Construction of the Poverty Map

As noted by Elbers et al. (2002, 2003), the basic idea behind the methodology is rather straightforward. Given our data, first a regression model of per adult equivalent expenditure is estimated in the GLSS5, limiting the set of explanatory variables to those which are common to both that survey and the 2003 CWIQ. Next, the coefficients from that model are applied to the CWIQ data set to predict the expenditure level of every household in the CWIQ survey. Finally, these predicted household expenditures are used to construct a series of welfare indicators (e.g., poverty level, depth, severity, and inequality) for different geographical subgroups. It should be noted that the questionnaire of the CWIQ is very detailed (much more so than a typical census questionnaire), which helps in yielding good predictions. At the individual level, the questionnaire covers demography, education and economic activities. At the household level, dwelling characteristics and ownership of durable goods are also well covered. Ghana's national territory is divided into 10 regions which are further divided down into districts. No districts overlap two or more regions. The districts are the lowest administrative level for which a formal geographical definition is currently available. At the time of implementation of the CWIQ survey in 2003, there were 110 districts. In 2004, a district remapping yielded 28 new districts, while another 32 districts were added in 2008, essentially by splitting a number of large districts into two separate districts (or in one case by combining two adjacent districts and splitting them into three districts). Our estimations remain based however on the original 110 districts, as this is the level at which the CWIQ survey is deemed representative (in other chapters in this study, we present results relying on the poverty map for data for 138 districts; in such cases, when one district has been split in two, both districts are assigned the poverty estimates from the poverty map, and when two districts are aggregated and split into three new districts, all three districts are assigned the poverty estimate obtained from the combination of the two previous districts).

Although the idea behind the poverty map methodology is simple, its proper implementation requires complex computations. Those complexities are due to the need to take into account spatial autocorrelation (expenditure from households within the same cluster are correlated) and heteroskedasticity in the development of the predictive model. Taking into account those econometric issues ensures unbiased predictions. A further issue making computation non-trivial is the need to compute standard errors for each poverty measure or welfare statistics. Those standard errors are important since they tell us how low we can disaggregate the poverty indicators. As we disaggregate results at lower and lower levels, the number of households on which the estimates are based decreases as well and therefore yields less and less precise estimates. At a certain point, the estimated poverty indicators would become too imprecise to be used with confidence. The computation of standard errors helps in deciding where to stop the disaggregation process. We will use these standard errors to compare the new estimates of poverty at the district level obtained with the CWIQ based poverty map to those obtained in the census-based map.

Reliability of the Poverty Map Estimates

To improve accuracy of poverty estimates the regression model was estimated at the lowest geographical level for which the GLSS survey was deemed representative. A household level expenditure model was developed for Accra and the three ecological zones (coastal, forest, and savannah) using explanatory variables which are common to both the GLSS and the CWIQ. The first task was to make sure the variables deemed common to both surveys were really measuring the same characteristics. For this, we first compared the questions and modalities in both questionnaires to isolate potential variables. We then compared the means of those (dichotomized) variables and tested whether they were equal using a 95% confidence interval. Restricting ourselves to those variables should ensure the predicted welfare figures would be consistent with GLSS-based poverty profile. We also deleted or redefined dichotomic variables being less that 0.03 or larger than 0.97 to avoid serious multi-collinearity problems in our econometric models.

That comparison exercise was done at the level of the four strata (Accra, coastal, forest, and savannah). The choice of the independent variables used in the predictive models was based on a backward stepwise selection procedure. All coefficients in the regressions were of expected sign. Regressions using the base model residuals as dependant variables were estimated as well, with the results used in the construction of the poverty map to correct for heteroskedasticity. The explanatory power (R^2) of the regressions varies from 0.25 to 0.49. Although this may appear to be on the low side, these statistics are typical of survey-based cross-section regressions and are comparable with results from other poverty maps. The relatively low R^2s for some of the models are mainly due to four important factors. First, in many areas households are fairly homogeneous in terms of observable characteristics even if their consumption levels vary. Second, a large number of potential correlates are simply not observable using standard closed-questionnaire data collection methods. Third, some good predictors have to be discarded at first stage of the procedure when their distributions did not appear to be identical. And finally, many indicators do not take into account the quality of the correlates.

The poverty estimates by strata obtained in the CWIQ are very similar to those obtained in the GLSS survey. By using the estimated parameters from the GLSS-based prediction model in the CWIQ data, we can generate poverty measures for all households in the census as well as by area. Table 4.1 presents estimated poverty measures for each stratum in the CWIQ and compares them with actual figures from GLSS. For each stratum and poverty indicators, the equality of GLSS-based and CWIQ-based indicators cannot be rejected (at the 95 percent confidence level). Although CWIQ-based poverty measures can only be compared with the ones provided by the GLSS survey at stratum level, equality of those poverty measures provides a reliability test of the methodology. Having established the reliability of the predictive models, we estimated poverty measures for the top two administrative levels: region and district.

Table 4.1: Poverty measures based on GLSS5 and CWIQ 2003, by strata

	Headcount Index		Poverty Gap		Squared Poverty Gap	
	GLSS5 (Actual)	CWIQ (Predicted)	GLSS5 (Actual)	CWIQ (Predicted)	GLSS5 (Actual)	CWIQ (Predicted)
Accra	0.136 (0.035)	0.130 (0.018)	0.038 (0.012)	0.031 (0.005)	0.015 (0.005)	0.011 (0.002)
Coastal	0.149 (0.019)	0.137 (0.013)	0.032 (0.005)	0.037 (0.005)	0.010 (0.002)	0.015 (0.002)
Forest	0.204 (0.016)	0.211 (0.011)	0.050 (0.005)	0.056 (0.005)	0.018 (0.002)	0.022 (0.002)
Savannah	0.537 (0.031)	0.541 (0.020)	0.223 (0.017)	0.219 (0.012)	0.121 (0.011)	0.116 (0.008)

Sources: Authors' calculation based on GLSS5 2005–06 and CWIQ 2003. Robust standard errors are in parentheses.

Since the precision of poverty estimates declines as the number of households by administrative unit decreases, one must identify at what level the map is reliable. To make an "objective" judgment on the precision of those estimates we computed coefficients of variation of the headcount ratio for both administrative levels under study (region and district) and then compared them with an arbitrary but commonly-used benchmark. Figure 4.1 presents the headcount ratio coefficients of variation of the region- and district-level estimates and compared them to a 0.2 benchmark. The lower curve (represented by Os) in figure 4.1 clearly shows that our region-level headcount poverty estimates does very well while the precision of district-level estimates fair well for most districts but badly for a small number of districts as shown by the upper curve (represented by Xs) on figure 4.1. Do those districts having higher coefficients of variations create problems in the application of the poverty map? Figure 4.2 plots coefficients of variation against poverty headcount for each district. It shows that amongst districts with higher coefficients of variation only a handful has also a poverty headcount level above the national level (28.5 percent). Since one of the main applications of the poverty map would be to target the poorest districts we believe that level of precision is acceptable and suitable for targeting purposes. It is clear that our poverty estimates at disaggregated levels would be good guides to policy makers.

Poverty measures for each of the 10 regions and 110 districts have been computed. In most cases, standard errors are small so that predicted poverty measures are reliable. The district results for poverty headcount are reproduced on the map in Figure 4.3. The map shows a very heterogeneous country in terms of poverty headcount. In particular, the four districts in the top northwest corner show poverty headcounts above 80 percent; while many districts in the southern districts of Ghana have poverty rates below 10 percent. Those results clearly show the usefulness of computing poverty indicators at disaggregated level given the rather heterogeneous district poverty pattern. How could these results be used? Among others, the results could be used to design budget allocation rules to be applied by different administrative levels toward their subdivisions: the central government toward the regions and the regions toward their districts. That map could become an important tool in support of the decentralization process currently undertaken in Ghana, or for the allocation of resources under different projects. Obviously such monetary-based target indicators could be used in conjunction with

Figure 4.1: Poverty headcount accuracy, by administrative level

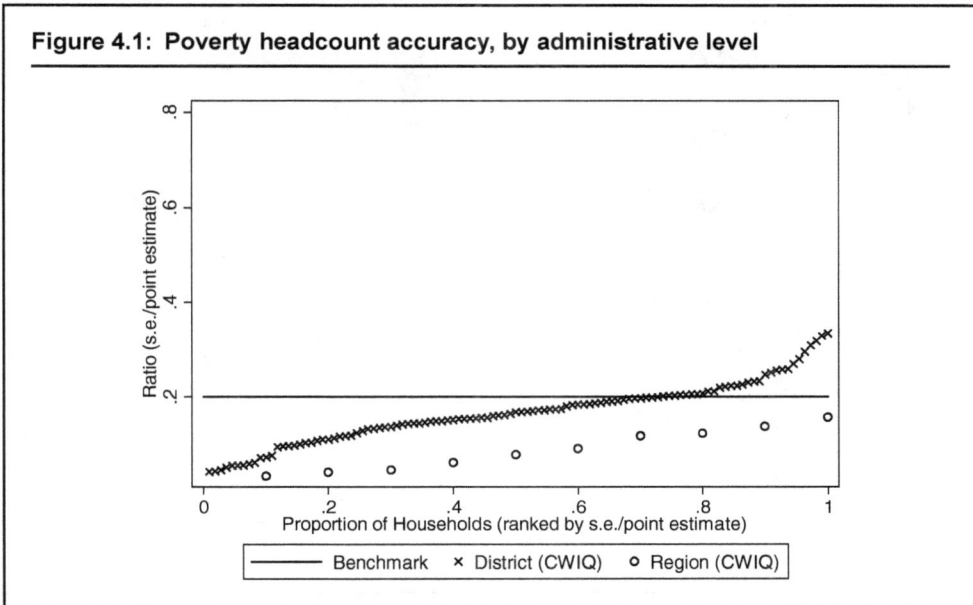

Source: Authors' calculation based on GLSS 2005–06 and CWIQ 2003.

Figure 4.2: Relationship between poverty headcount and coefficient of variation

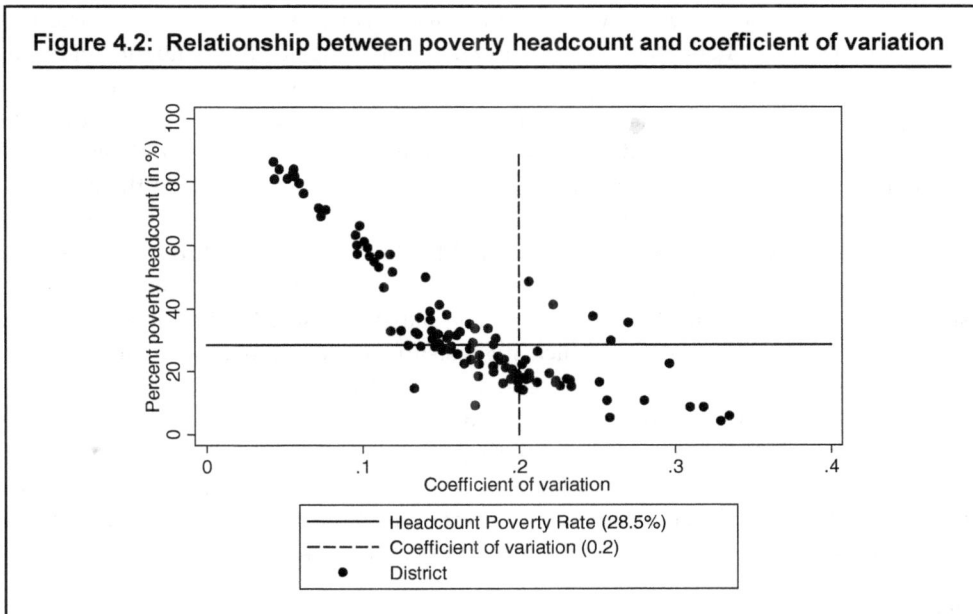

Source: Authors' calculation based on GLSS 2005–06 and CWIQ 2003.

Figure 4.3: District-level poverty headcount and poverty gap

Poverty headcount   Poverty gap

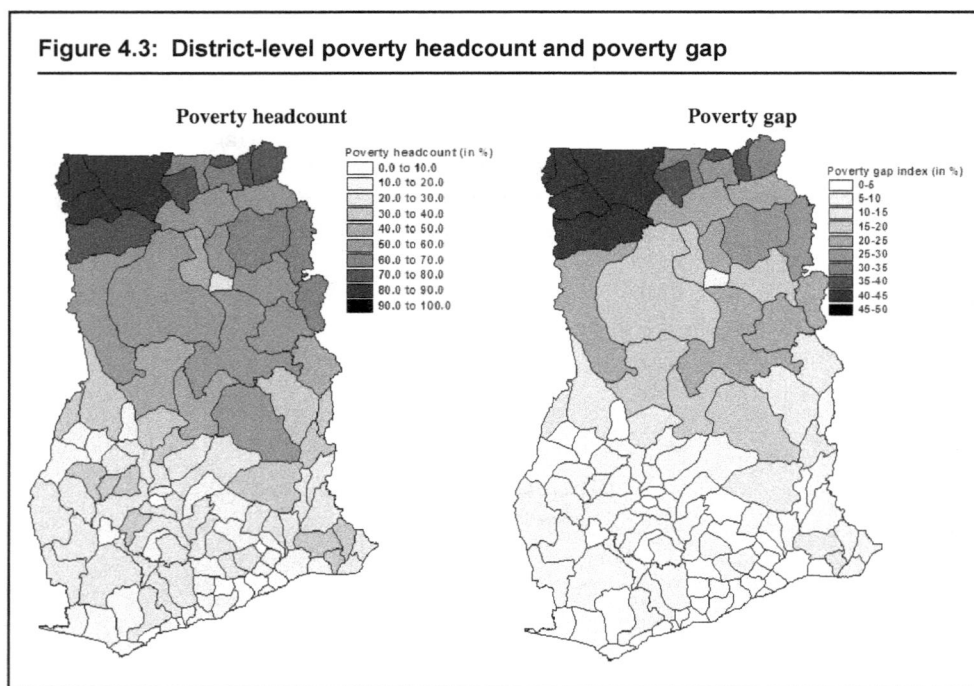

Sources: Authors' calculation based on GLSS 2005–06 and CWIQ 2003.

alternative measures of poverty based on education, health or infrastructure indicators. In particular merging the poverty map with education and health maps could yield useful targeting tools. Others uses of the poverty map could include the evaluation of locally targeted anti-poverty schemes (e.g. Social funds, Town/village development schemes), impact analysis, etc. And finally, researchers could use it in various ways to study the relationship between poverty distribution and different socio-economic outcomes.

How different are the district-level poverty measures obtained with the new poverty map from those of the census-based poverty map? A simple test of the equality of the poverty measures between the Census and the CWIQ can be performed by computing the difference between the two poverty estimates divided by the square root of the sum of the corresponding standard errors. The statistics is smaller than 1.96 in absolute value for only 16 of 110 districts, which suggests that most of the new district estimates of poverty obtained from the GLSS5 and the CWIQ are different from the estimates obtained from the GLSS4 and the census. Thus even though the precision of the poverty measures in the CWIQ can be shown to be slightly lower than in the Census, the combination of GLSS5 and the CWIQ data enables us to provide new and updated estimates of poverty at the district level that are fairly different from the older estimates based on the GLSS4 and the Census, confirming the usefulness of the new poverty map.

Conclusion

This chapter has documented the procedure used for the construction of a new poverty map for Ghana and the main results obtained from this procedure. This new map combines data from the 2005/06 GLSS5 survey with the 2003 CWIQ survey that has a very large sample size and is considered to be representative at the district level but does not have data on consumption or income. The map can be compared to a previous map combining data from the 1998/99 GLSS4 survey and the 2000 Census. The results suggest that the estimates of poverty at the district level obtained with the CWIQ on the basis of the consumption aggregate of the GLSS5 are less precise than those obtained with the Census and the consumption aggregate of the GLSS4 (this is discussed in Coulombe and Wodon, 2009). However, the CWIQ-based estimates are still sufficiently precise to identify important changes in district-level poverty measures between the two poverty maps. Indeed, the changes in poverty measures appear to be statistically significant for all but 16 of the 110 districts, which reflect the fact that the country experienced substantial poverty reduction between the GLSS4 and the GLSS5 survey years. This suggests that the new poverty map should be used for poverty-based geographic targeting in Ghana.

CHAPTER 5

A Food Insecurity Map for Ghana

Harold Coulombe and Quentin Wodon

While poverty maps have been used in some countries to target social programs, it is not clear whether they are the most appropriate geographic targeting tool for interventions that do not aim only or primarily to reduce monetary poverty. For example, one could target nutrition programs, school lunches and food aid according to a poverty map, but one could also rely on a food insecurity map to the extent that these programs aim to improve the nutrition and food intake of the population. The concept of food insecurity is at least as complex as that of poverty, and various authors have used different approaches to defining food insecurity. Due to data limitations, we consider here a set of simple variables to discuss the issues. Whether there is a strong correlation between poverty and food insecurity maps is an empirical matter, and this indeed will depend on how food insecurity is measured. This chapter documents the construction and presents results from a food insecurity map of Ghana based on the GLSS5 2005/06 and the CWIQ 2003 surveys. The map is based on estimates of the caloric intake of households in the GLSS5, and its construction in the CWIQ follows the poverty mapping technique described in the previous chapter. The map is also compared to other potential indicators of food insecurity available in the CWIQ, namely the subjective assessment by households as to whether they have difficulty in meeting their basic food needs, and with child malnutrition, some of which are directly related to food insecurity. The results suggest a very strong correlation between the poverty and food insecurity (i.e., caloric intake) maps, but weaker relationships between these maps and indicators of child malnutrition, subjective assessments of the capacity to meet food needs, and subjective assessments of the ability to cope with shocks.

Estimation of a Food Insecurity Map Based on Caloric Intake

This chapter documents the construction and presents results from a food insecurity map of Ghana based on the GLSS5 2005–06 and the CWIQ 2003 surveys. The map is based on estimates of the caloric intake of households in the GLSS5. The CWIQ also provides data on a series of indicators associated with food insecurity. In particular, we compare the caloric intake map with a subjective assessment by households as to whether they have difficulty in meeting their basic food needs. We also compare both maps with measures of child malnutrition that are also available in the CWIQ (i.e., stunting, wasting, and malnutrition). For these indicators, maps are based directly on the survey data, while for the caloric intake map, since consumption of food items is not available in the CWIQ, predictions are needed.

To construct the caloric intake map for Ghana using data from the GLSS5 of 2005–06 and the 2003 CWIQ household survey we use the poverty map methodology developed by Elbers et al. (2002, 2003). Results at the region and district levels are presented. As noted in the chapter on the poverty map, the basic idea behind the methodology is rather straightforward. Given our data, first a regression model of adult equivalent caloric intake is estimated in the GLSS5, limiting the set of explanatory variables to those which are common to both that survey and the 2003 CWIQ. Next, the coefficients from that model are applied to the CWIQ data set to predict the caloric intake of every household in the CWIQ survey. Finally, these predicted caloric intakes are used to construct a series of caloric intake deficiency indicators for different geographical subgroups. It should be noted that the questionnaire of the CWIQ is very detailed (much more so than a typical census questionnaire), which helps in yielding good predictions. At the individual level, the questionnaire covers demography, education and economic activities. At the household level, dwelling characteristics and ownership of durable goods are also well covered.

Ghana's national territory is divided into 10 regions which are further divided down into districts. No districts overlap two or more regions. The districts are the lowest administrative level for which a formal geographical definition is currently available. At the time of implementation of the CWIQ survey in 2003, there were 110 districts. In 2004, a district remapping yielded 28 new districts, while another 32 districts were added in 2008, essentially by splitting a number of large districts into two separate districts (or in one case by combining two adjacent districts and splitting them into three districts). Our estimations remain based however on the original 110 districts, as this is the level at which the CWIQ survey is deemed representative (we could also present results for 138 districts from the original 110 districts in the CWIQ 2003, by splitting a few districts in two, in which case both districts are assigned the food insecurity estimates from the food security map, or by aggregating two districts and splitting them into three new districts when needed, with all three districts being assigned the food insecurity estimates obtained from the combination of the two previous districts).

Although the idea behind the poverty map methodology is simple, its proper implementation requires complex computations. Those complexities are due to the need to take into account spatial autocorrelation (expenditure from households within the same cluster are correlated) and heteroskedasticity in the development of the predictive model. Taking into account those econometric issues ensures unbiased predictions. A further issue making computation non-trivial is the need to compute standard errors for each food insecurity statistics. Those standard errors are important since they tell us how low we can disaggregate the food insecurity indicators. As we disaggregate results at lower and lower levels, the number of households on which the estimates are based decreases as well and therefore yields less and less precise estimates. At a certain point, the estimated food insecurity indicators would become too imprecise to be use with confidence. The computation of standard errors helps in deciding where to stop the disaggregation process.

The computation of the caloric intakes itself in the household survey is challenging and its results should be used with caution. Part of the challenge comes from the fact that household survey typically record values but not quantities of food consumed. To obtain those food-specific quantities, we divided the annual expenditure of each food items by its prices. The prices used come from a price survey conducted at the same as the main GLSS5 questionnaires. For each item, we use the locality median prices. In the GLSS context the seven localities are defined as the three ecological zones (coastal, forest and savannah) split between urban and rural areas, and the capital Accra is set apart. Those quantities are then converted to calories using Ghana-specific conversion factors provided by the University of Ghana at Legon. Such conversion factors were found for almost all food items consumed in Ghana and certainly for all the main ones. However it is difficult to measure the calories contained in meals taken outside the home. For those "restaurant meals" we assumed that they had the same average caloric content as home food and we made the appropriate household-specific correction. Next, the number of calories is aggregated across all items for each household found in the GLSS survey. Finally, a last transformation yields a daily per equivalent adult level of calories, which was then normalized into caloric intake per capita. Households consuming less than 1800 calories per day per capita were considered as food insecure. All the measures used for assessing poverty (headcount, poverty gap, squared poverty gap) can be applied to food insecurity.

Reliability of the Food Insecurity Map Estimates

To improve accuracy of caloric intake deficiency estimates regression models were estimated at the lowest geographical level for which the GLSS survey was deemed representative. A household level caloric intake model was developed for Accra and the three ecological zones (coastal, forest and savannah) using explanatory variables which are common to both the GLSS and the CWIQ. The first task was to make sure the variables deemed common to both surveys were really measuring the same characteristics. For this, we first compared the questions and modalities in both questionnaires to isolate potential variables. We then compared the means of those (dichotomized) variables and tested whether they were equal using a 95 percent confidence interval. Restricting ourselves to those variables should ensure the predicted welfare figures would be consistent with GLSS-based estimates. We also deleted or redefined dichotomic variables being less that 0.03 or larger than 0.97 to avoid serious multi-collinearity problems in our econometric models. That comparison exercise was done for each of the four strata (Accra, coastal, forest, and savannah).

The choice of the independent variables used in the predictive model was based on a backward stepwise selection procedure. All coefficients in the regressions were of expected sign. Regressions using the base model residuals as dependant variables were estimated as well, with the results used in the construction of the caloric intake map to correct for heteroskedasticity. The explanatory power (R^2) of the regressions varies from 0.22 to 0.42. Although this may appear to be on the low side, these statistics are typical of survey-based cross-section regressions and can are comparable with results from other poverty maps. The relatively low R^2s for some of the models are mainly due to four important factors. First, in many areas households are fairly homogeneous in terms of observable characteristics even if their caloric intake levels vary. Second, a large number of potential correlates are simply not observable using standard closed-questionnaire data collection methods. Third, some good predictors have to be discarded at the first stage of the procedure when their distributions did not appear to be identical. And finally, many indicators do not take into account the quality of the correlates.

The caloric intake deficiency estimates by strata obtained in the CWIQ are very similar to those obtained in the GLSS survey. By using the estimated parameters from the prediction model in the survey in the CWIQ data, we can generate caloric intake measures for all households in the CWIQ as well as by area. Table 5.1 presents estimated caloric intake measures for each stratum in the CWIQ and compares them with actual figures from GLSS. For each stratum and caloric intake indicators, the equality of GLSS-based and CWIQ-based indicators cannot be rejected (at the 95 percent confidence level). Although CWIQ-based caloric intake measures can only be compared with the ones provided by the GLSS survey at stratum level, equality of those measures provides a reliability test of the methodology. Having established the reliability of the predictive models, we estimated caloric deficiency measures for the top two administrative levels: region and district.

Table 5.1: Caloric intake deficiency in GLSS5 (actual) and CWIQ 2003 (predicted), by strata

	Headcount index		Caloric intake gap		Squared caloric intake gap	
	GLSS (actual)	CWIQ (predicted)	GLSS (actual)	CWIQ (predicted)	GLSS (actual)	CWIQ (predicted)
Accra	0.336 (0.044)	0.345 (0.043)	0.113 (0.021)	0.105 (0.019)	0.053 (0.012)	0.045 (0.011)
Coastal	0.211 (0.022)	0.222 (0.014)	0.062 (0.008)	0.075 (0.006)	0.027 (0.005)	0.037 (0.003)
Forest	0.241 (0.016)	0.273 (0.014)	0.076 (0.007)	0.090 (0.006)	0.035 (0.004)	0.043 (0.004)
Savannah	0.439 (0.026)	0.429 (0.022)	0.158 (0.012)	0.161 (0.011)	0.080 (0.008)	0.082 (0.007)

Sources: Authors' calculation based on GLSS 2005–06 and CWIQ 2003. Robust standard errors are in parentheses.

Since the precision of caloric deficiency estimates declines as the number of households by administrative unit decreases, one must identify at what level the map is reliable. To make an "objective" judgment on the precision of those estimates we computed coefficients of variation of the estimates for both administrative levels under study (region and district) and then compared them with an arbitrary but commonly-used benchmark. Figure 5.1 presents the coefficients of variation of the region- and district-level estimates and compared them to a 0.2 benchmark. The lower curve (represented by "Os") in figure 5.1 clearly shows that our region-level caloric intake deficiency estimates do very well while the precision of district-level estimates fairs very well for most districts except for a handful of districts as shown by the upper curve (represented by Xs) on figure 5.1. Are those districts having higher coefficients of variations creating problems in the application of the caloric intake map? Figure 5.2 plots coefficients of variation against caloric intake deficiency headcount for each district. It shows that amongst the districts with higher coefficients of variation only a handful has also a caloric intake deficiency headcount level above the national level (30.0 percent). Since one of the main applications of the map would be to target the poorest districts in terms of caloric intake we believe that level of precision is acceptable and suitable for targeting purposes. Thus the estimates at disaggregated levels could be good guides to policy makers.

Figure 5.1: Caloric intake deficiency headcount accuracy, by administrative level

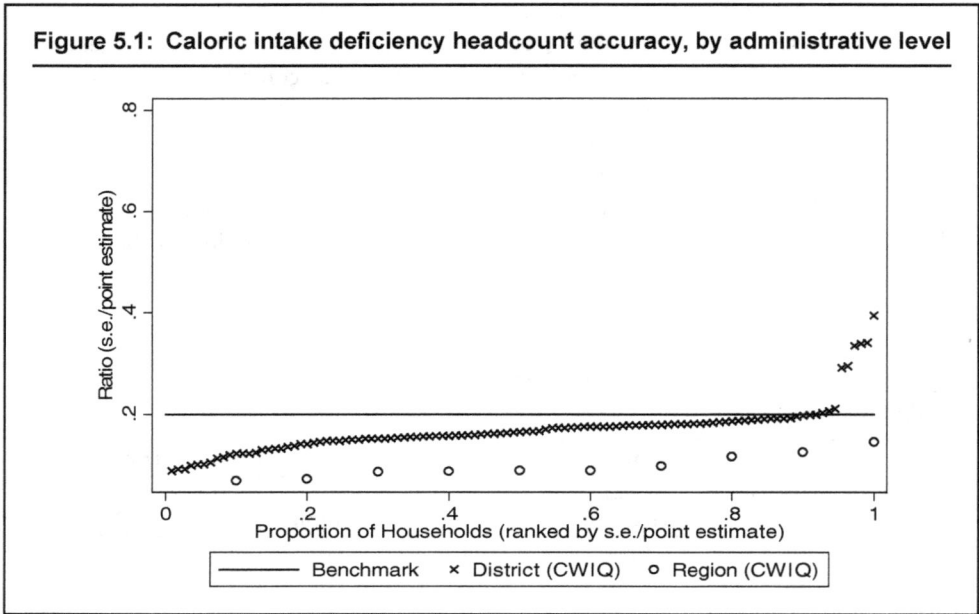

Source: Authors' calculation based on GLSS 2005–06 and CWIQ 2003.

Figure 5.2: Relationship between caloric intake deficiency headcount and coefficient of variation

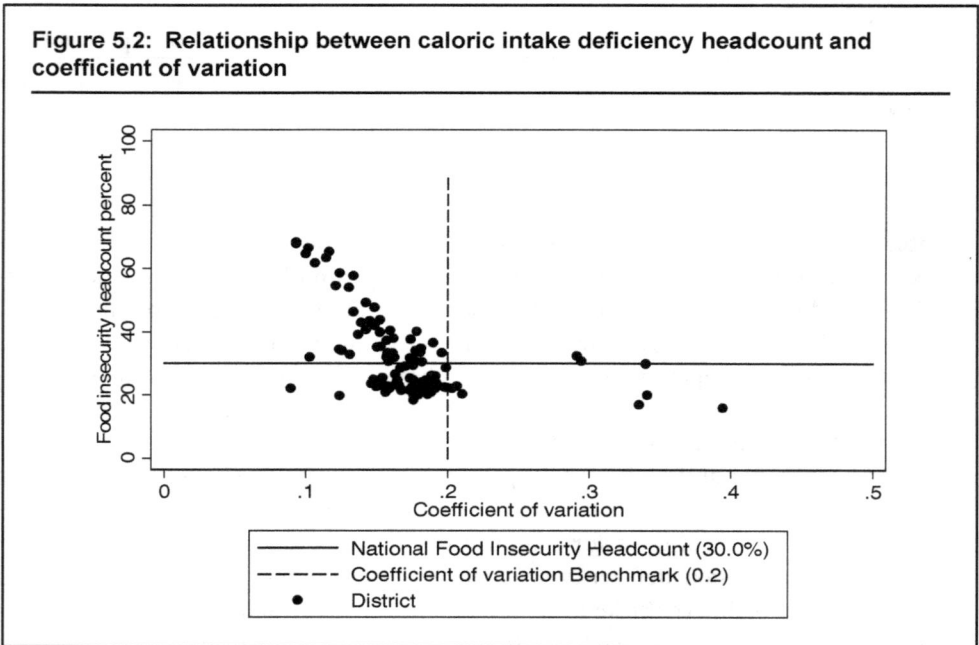

Source: Authors' calculation based on GLSS 2005–06 and CWIQ 2003.

Caloric intake measures for each of the 10 regions and 110 districts have been computed. In most cases, standard errors are small so that predicted caloric intake measures are reliable. The district results for caloric intake deficiency headcount are reproduced on the map in figure 5.3. Overall 30.0 percent of the population has a caloric intake below 1800 calories per day per person. Similarly to the poverty map presented in the previous chapter, the map shows a rather heterogeneous country in terms of caloric intake deficiency headcount. In particular, the ten northernmost districts along the Burkinabe border show caloric intake deficiency headcount above 50 percent.

Figure 5.3: Food insecurity maps based on caloric intake (1,800 kCal per person-day), Ghana

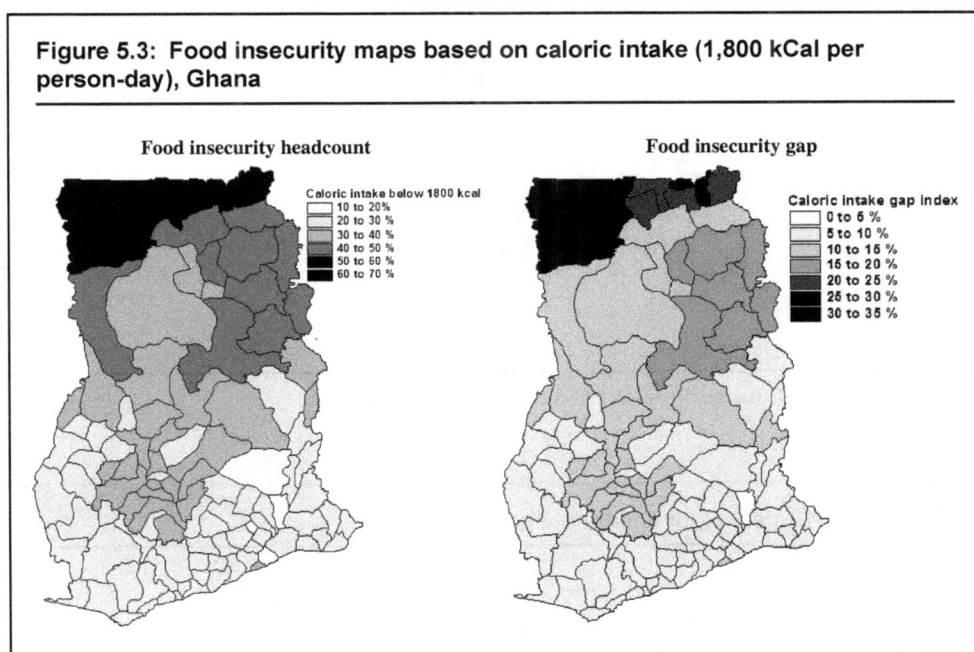

Sources: Authors' calculation based on GLSS 2005–06 and CWIQ 2003.

Alternative Measures of Food Security

The CWIQ permits for each household in the survey to make a subjective assessment of whether they have difficulty in meeting their basic food needs. Overall 13.4 percent of the population has *often* difficulty in meeting their basic food needs. The map in figure 5.4 shows that apart some isolated districts in the forest ecological zones and along the eastern border, the districts along the Burkinabe and northern Ivorian borders fare the worst. Those same districts also are the poorest in terms of expenditure and caloric intake. Another measure of food security is the state of child malnutrition in the different districts. Based on the CWIQ survey, we estimate that almost 26 percent of children aged less than 60 months were underweight (this proportion has declined since then according to the 2008 DHS). The map in figure 5.5 presents the percentage of underweight children by district. Contrary to the other food security indicators, it seems difficult to find any spatial pattern and hence any correlation with caloric intake, monetary poverty

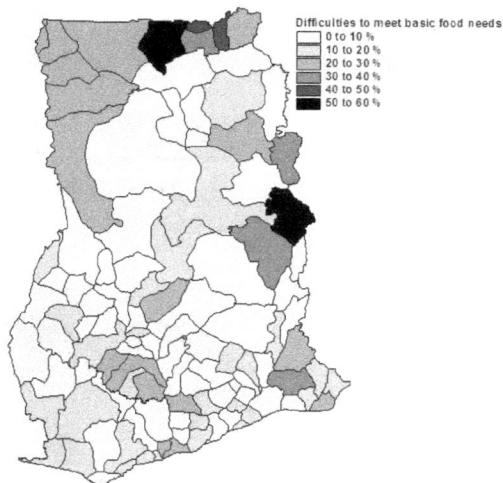

Figure 5.4: Subjective difficulty to meet basic food needs, Ghana

Difficulties to meet basic food needs
- 0 to 10 %
- 10 to 20 %
- 20 to 30 %
- 30 to 40 %
- 40 to 50 %
- 50 to 60 %

Sources: Authors' calculation based on GLSS 2005/06 and CWIQ 2003.

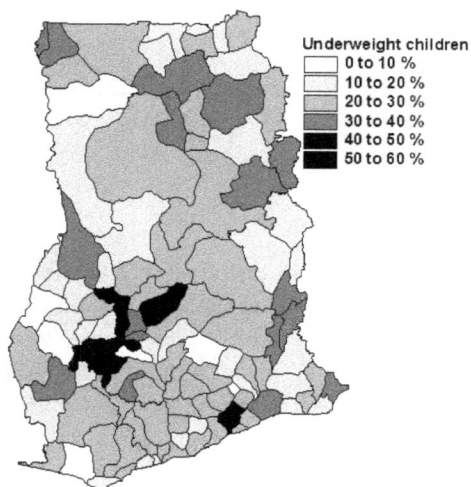

Figure 5.5: Underweight children, Ghana

Underweight children
- 0 to 10 %
- 10 to 20 %
- 20 to 30 %
- 30 to 40 %
- 40 to 50 %
- 50 to 60 %

Sources: Authors' calculation based on GLSS 2005/06 and CWIQ 2003.

or self-assessed difficulty in meeting basic food needs. Figure 5.6 presents the relationships between the different food security indicators as well as between these indicators and monetary poverty headcount. As suggested by the different maps, it appears that monetary poverty is strongly correlated with caloric intake deficiency and well correlated with the self-assessment indicators of food insecurity. However, child malnutrition as measured by the proportion of underweight children may have correlates not linked that much to expenditure or caloric intakes.

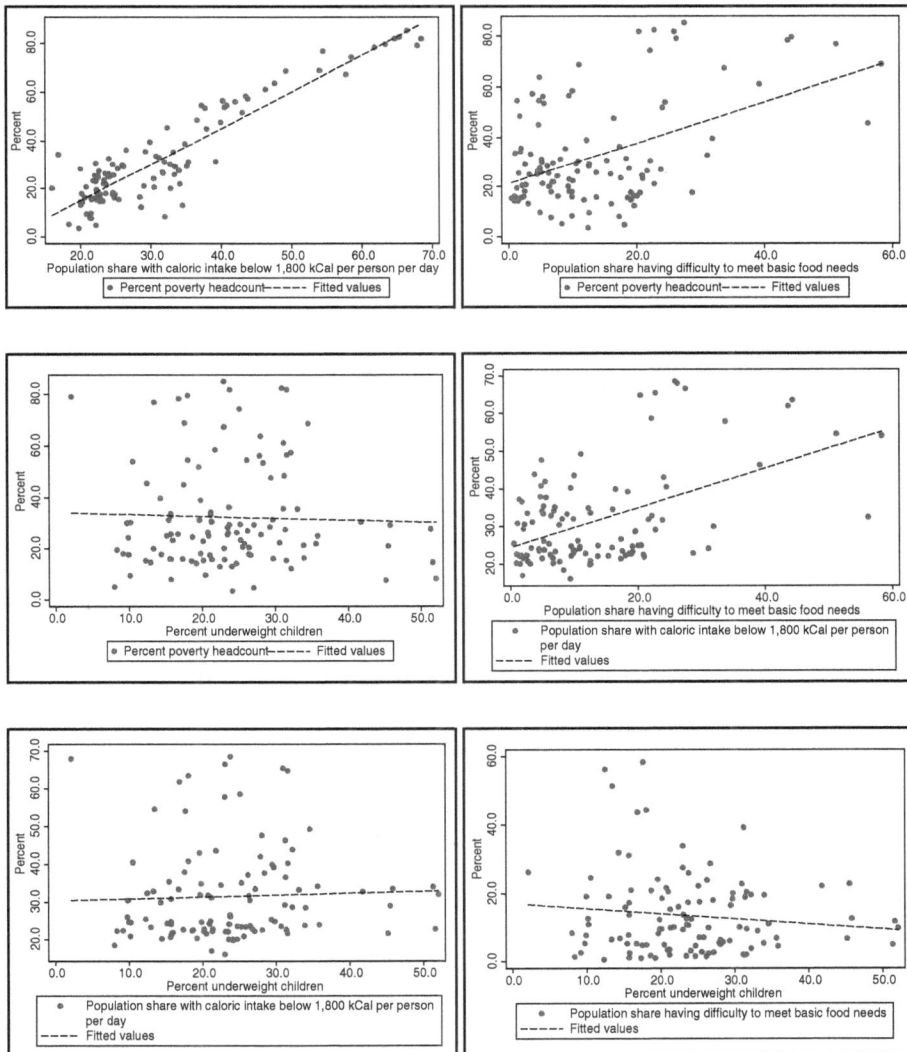

Figure 5.6: Relationships between different food security indicators

Sources: Authors' calculation based on GLSS 2005–06 and CWIQ 2003.

Conclusion

We presented a series of food security indicators at district level as estimated for the 110 districts at the time of the CWIQ survey in 2003. The results suggest a strong correlation between district-level measures of poverty and food insecurity when food insecurity is measured through caloric intake, and weaker but still substantial correlations between these maps and subjective assessments of the capacity to meet food needs. However our indicator of child malnutrition does not seem to be spatially correlated with the other indicators. Depending on which indicator a program is trying to influence, different maps might thus be of use, although more confidence should be placed on objective as opposed to subjective measures.

CHAPTER 6

The Geographic Impact of Higher Food Prices in Ghana

Harold Coulombe, Clarence Tsimpo, and Quentin Wodon

One key issue faced by policy makers when implementing or expanding a safety net or social program at a time of economic crisis is whether to target households that are affected the most by the crisis, or households that are the poorest (or the most insecure or the least educated) before or after taking into account the impact of the crisis. In the case of geographic targeting, this may imply a choice between targeting areas that are likely to suffer from a large increase in poverty following a shock, or areas with an initial or final high level of poverty. In principle, from a social welfare point of view, one could argue that one should always target the areas with the highest level of poverty. But governments are also under pressure to respond to the impact of crises on specific groups of households. To the extent that the increase in poverty is going to be higher in already poor areas, the dilemma faced by policy makers is reduced. In this chapter, we first provide estimates of the potential impact that the recent increase in food prices may have had on Ghana. The results suggest that poverty in Ghana is likely to have been less affected than in other West and Central African countries, but that the impact was nevertheless substantial. Next, using the poverty mapping technique, we analyze where higher food prices are likely to have had the largest impact on the poor in Ghana. The results suggest that contrary to popular belief the poorest areas of the country are likely to have been the most affected by the increase in food prices, which warrants targeting these areas through emergency safety nets.

Impact of Higher Food Prices on Poverty

To assess the potential impact of rising food prices on poverty, one needs to look at the impact on both food producers who could benefit from an increase in prices and food consumers who lose out. In most West and Central African countries, including in Ghana, the sign (positive or negative) of the impact of a change is not ambiguous because a substantial share of food consumption is imported, so that the negative impact for consumers is typically larger than the positive impact for net sellers of locally produced foods. Yet even if the sign of the impact is clear, its magnitude is not. Using a set of recent household surveys, this chapter summarizes findings from an assessment of the potential impact of higher food prices on the poor in Ghana and a dozen other West and Central African countries. Rising food prices for rice, wheat, maize, and other cereals as well as for milk, sugar, and vegetable oils probably led to a substantial increase in poverty in many of the countries, but the impact in Ghana was smaller than elsewhere. In addition to assessing overall impacts, the chapter also discusses where the impacts on poverty are likely to have been the largest.

In the absence of new survey data on household consumption after the price increase in most countries, simulation techniques are necessary to assess the potential impact on the poor of the increase in food prices. We consider here only the short term impact on poverty of higher food prices, as estimated by looking at the consumption and production of food by households. This means that we do not take into account potential medium- to long-term impacts arising, for example, from the fact that an increase in food prices may lead to higher wages for farm workers (findings from studies on medium-term impacts suggest that wage gains compensate only in a very limited way only for the initial impact of food price shocks).

For the sake of simplicity, a number of assumptions have been used to provide the estimates or are implicit in the analysis. First, we assume that the cost of an increase in food prices for a household translates into an equivalent reduction of its consumption in real terms. This means that we do not take into account the price elasticity of demand which may lead to substitution effects and thereby help offset part of the negative effect of higher prices for certain food items. Similarly, an increase for producers in the value of their net sales of food translates into an increase of their consumption of equivalent size, and we again do not take into account the role that the price elasticity of supply may play here. As for food auto-consumed by producers (which represents a large share of total consumption), it is not taken into account in the simulations since changes in prices do not affect households when food is auto-consumed. Poverty measures obtained after the increase in prices are then compared to baseline poverty measures to assess impacts. This implicitly means that we do not take into account the potential spill-over effects of the increase in food prices for the food items included in the analysis on the prices for items not included. Finally, for comparability purposes, all our simulations are based on the same price increases for all countries and all food items. In the more detailed country case studies, more information is provided to be able to look at the impact of different price increases, for example through interpolations.

A difficult question is whether increases in consumer prices do translate into increases in producer prices. At least two factors may dilute the impact of rising food prices on the incomes of farmers. First, production costs for farmers as well as transport costs are likely to be rising due to higher costs for oil-related products. Second, market intermediaries may be able in some cases to keep a large share of the increase in consumer prices for themselves without paying farmers much more for their crops. Because it is difficult to assess whether producers will benefit substantially from higher food prices, especially in the short term, we consider our estimates obtained when considering only the impact on consumers as an upper bound of the impact of the rise in prices on poverty, and we interpret the results obtained when factoring in a proportional increase in incomes for net sellers or producers as a lower bound of the impact.

Table 6.1 provides data on a number of countries for which the estimations have been prepared. The data have been collected from the most recent available household survey for each country. The survey years range from 2003 in Guinea to 2007 in Liberia, so the data can reasonably be considered as accurately capturing the current (or recent) consumption patterns of the population in the respective countries. Table 6.1 included the list of food items considered for the analysis in each country. The analysis is for the most part focused on rice, flour and bread, maize, vegetable oil, sugar, and milk, because these are food items that tend to be imported to a substantial extent, so that likely poverty impacts may be substantial (since there are no compensating impacts on the producer side). In some countries however, we consider also additional items, such as cassava and plantain in the Democratic Republic of Congo. As shown in table 6.2, the share of total consumption represented by the various goods ranges from 6.5 percent in Togo to 28.3 percent in the Democratic Republic of Congo and even 41.0 percent in Niger. Yet for two thirds of the countries, the food items included in the simulations account for less than 15 percent of total consumption.

Table 6.1: Food items considered for simulating the impact of higher food prices on poverty

Country	Household survey	Food items taken into account for simulations
Burkina Faso	QUIBB, 2003	Rice, bread, vegetable oil and butter, sugar, milk
Congo, Dem. Rep.	123 Survey, 2005	Rice, cassava, maize, palm oil, plantain, wheat, sugar, milk
Ghana	GLSS, 2005–06	Rice, bread, flour, maize
Gabon	CWIQ, 2005	Rice, cassava, maize, wheat, palm oil and groundnut oil
Guinea	EIBEP, 2002–03	Rice
Liberia	CWIQ, 2007	Rice (locally produced and imported)
Mali	ELIM, 2006	Rice, millet, maize, wheat
Niger	QUIBB, 2005	Rice (locally produced and imported), millet, sorghum
Nigeria	NLSS, 2003–04	Rice, corn, maize, wheat flour and bread, cassava
Senegal	ESPS, 2006	Rice, vegetable oil, sugar, bread, milk
Sierra Leone	SLLS, 2003	Rice
Togo	QUIBB, 2006	Rice, vegetable oil, sugar, bread, milk

Source: Authors' estimation using respective household surveys.

Table 6.2 provides the summary data on the impact on the share of the population in poverty (i.e., the headcount index) of the higher food prices using two levels of price increase: 25 percent and 50 percent. The results for the headcount are those provided in the first part of table 6.2. As mentioned earlier, the lower-bound impact on poverty is obtained by combining the consumer and producer impact, while the upper-bound impact factors in gains for net sellers of food. In two countries, due to lack of appropriate data in the surveys, we compute only the upper-bound estimates. Consider the increase in the headcount index stemming from a 50 percent increase in prices. At the national level the upper-bound estimates suggest that the increase in the headcount index of poverty varies from 1.8 percentage point in Ghana to 9.6 points in Senegal. The differences in impacts are due in part to the fact that the sets of goods considered for the simulations in the various countries represent different shares of total consumption. In Ghana the goods account for 7.7 percent of total consumption versus 20.5 percent in Senegal. If we look at the impact on poverty per percentage point of consumption accounted for by the food items included in the analysis, the impact varies from 0.17 points in the Democratic Republic of Congo to 0.47 points in Senegal. Thus, while Ghana was affected by the increase in food prices, it was probably less affected than most other West and Central African countries.

In figure 6.1, the upper-bound impacts for the increase in the price of rice alone are provided. This is the only commodity which was included in all of the sets of food items

Table 6.2: Potential impact on poverty of higher food prices in Africa (%)

Country	Share in consumption	Baseline headcount	Upper-bound impact (Consumption) 25% increase	Upper-bound impact (Consumption) 50% increase	Lower bound impact (Consumption & production) 25% increase	Lower bound impact (Consumption & production) 50% increase
		Impact of food price shock on poverty headcount index				
Burkina Faso	6.8	**46.4**	47.5	48.4	—	—
Ghana	7.7	**28.5**	29.6	30.4	29.2	29.7
Liberia	22.8	**63.8**	67.1	69.8	66.6	69.4
Senegal	20.5	**50.8**	55.9	60.4	—	—
Sierra Leone	11.7	**66.4**	67.8	69.6	67.2	68.5
Togo	6.5	**61.6**	62.7	63.7	62.5	63.0
Congo, Dem. Rep.	28.3	**71.3**	73.9	76.2	72.6	73.7
Guinea	13.0	**49.1**	50.7	52.1	50.0	50.7
Gabon	10.7	**32.7**	34.5	36.7	34.3	36.2
Mali	13.4	**47.5**	50.1	52.8	49.2	50.9
Niger	41.0	**62.1**	66.1	70.0	65.9	69.6
Nigeria	9.80	**54.68**	56.20	57.77	55.19	55.65
		Impact of food price shock on poverty gap				
Burkina Faso	6.8	**15.6**	16.1	16.7	—	—
Ghana	7.7	**9.6**	9.9	10.3	9.7	9.9
Liberia	22.8	**24.4**	26.3	28.3	26.2	28.1
Senegal	20.5	**16.4**	18.8	21.5	—	—
Sierra Leone	11.7	**27.5**	28.6	29.7	28.1	28.7
Togo	6.5	**22.9**	23.5	24.2	23.5	24.1
Congo, Dem. Rep.	28.3	**32.2**	32.4	32.7	32.3	32.5
Guinea	13.0	**17.2**	17.9	18.6	17.3	17.6
Gabon	10.7	**10.0**	10.8	11.7	10.7	11.5
Mali	13.4	**16.7**	17.6	18.8	17.1	17.8
Niger	41.0	**25.9**	26.6	29.6	26.5	29.4
Nigeria	9.80	**22.5**	23.3	24.2	16.6	17.0
		Share of increase in poverty gap due to deeper poverty among those already poor				
Burkina Faso	n.a.	n.a.	96.7	93.4	—	—
Ghana	n.a.	n.a.	96.2	92.3	92.5	86.3
Liberia	n.a.	n.a.	94.9	90.2	94.8	90.2
Senegal	n.a.	n.a.	93.3	86.9	—	—
Sierra Leone	n.a.	n.a.	97.1	94.9	95.9	92.8
Togo	n.a.	n.a.	98.4	96.8	98.3	96.6
Congo, Dem. Rep.	n.a.	n.a.	95.1	90.4	111.0	136.0
Guinea	n.a.	n.a.	94.4	89.3	70.7	60.9
Gabon	n.a.	n.a.	95.4	90.7	95.1	90.1
Mali	n.a.	n.a.	89.9	82.3	81.1	71.3
Niger	n.a.	n.a.	70.6	75.9	65.3	74.6
Nigeria	n.a.	n.a.	96.0	91.8	94.1	88.7

Source: Wodon et al. (2008).
Notes: — = not available, n.a. = not applicable.

Figure 6.1: Upper-bound estimates for the impact of a price increase in rice

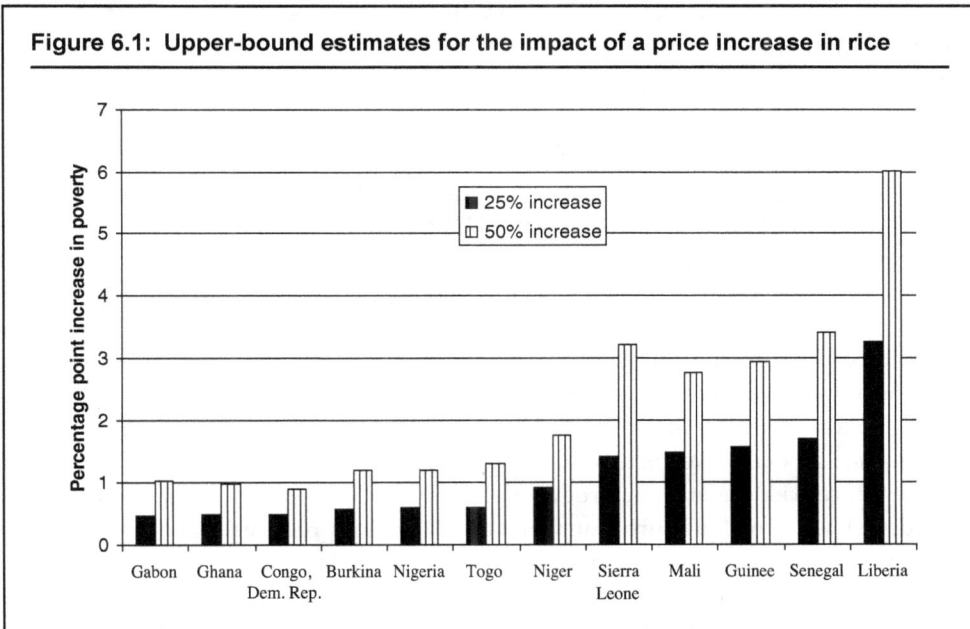

Source: Wodon et al. (2008).

considered for the twelve countries. It is an important commodity, especially in Liberia, Senegal, Guinea, and Sierra Leone where it represents a very large share of the food basket of the population. Rice is also important because West and Central African countries are typically net importers (and in some countries such as Senegal, virtually all the rice consumed is imported), and the price of rice increased very substantially in 2007–08. Rice also matters because this is the commodity for which most countries implemented a reduction in import taxes in an effort to dampen the impact of the increase in international prices on the poor. Finally, available data suggests that in those countries where both local and imported rice are consumed, the price of both types of rice move very closely together, so that an increase in the price of imported rice does translate into an increase in the price of locally produced rice. As is clear from the data presented in figure 6.1, a 50 percent increase in the price of rice alone could lead to an increase in the headcount of poverty of 2.2 percentage points in the countries in the sample, and much more in some cases. Importantly, the lower bound estimates for the impact of rice shocks are not much lower than the upper bound because much of the locally produced rice is self-consumed in the countries that do produce rice.

Table 6.2 also provides the impact of the increase in food prices on the poverty gap, as well as the share of the increase in the poverty gap that is due to an increase in how much poorer those who were already poor before the shock are becoming as a result of the shock, as opposed to the increase in the poverty gap that comes from household who have become poor as a result of the shock, but were not previously poor before the shock. The findings are revealing: an overwhelming majority of the increase in the poverty gap (and the squared poverty gap, although this is not shown here) are due to higher levels of poverty among households who were already poor before the shock.

This suggests in turn that the areas that are likely to be most affected by the shock are probably those that were already very poor before the shock (this is discussed in more detail below).

Geographic Impact of the Increase in Food Prices

In this section, the poverty mapping technique is used to estimate the impact of higher food price at the district level. Mistiaen (2003) conducted similar work to estimate the impact of a change in the price of rice in Madagascar. His idea consists in estimating a new poverty map using a revised consumption aggregate in the survey with the consumption data. This revised consumption aggregate takes into account the impact of the shock. By comparing the initial poverty map with the revised poverty map based on the new consumption aggregate, we obtain estimates at a disaggregated geographical level of the impact on poverty of the shock. This is also the procedure used here. In the case of a food price shock, the key is to assess impacts on both the consumer side (higher food prices reduce welfare) and the producer side (higher food prices increase incomes for producers), while making sure than when a food item is produced and auto-consumed, neither effects are taken into account since prices are irrelevant.

We simulate here the impact of an increase in the price of five food items (rice, maize, bread, maize flour, and flour) of 50 percent. To construct the revised consumption aggregate in the GLSS5, a number of assumptions are used. As before, we assume that the cost of an increase in food prices for a household translates into an equivalent reduction of its consumption in real terms. This means that we do not take into account the price elasticity of demand which may lead to substitution effects and thereby help offset part of the negative effect of higher prices for certain food items. Similarly, an increase for producers in the value of their net sales of food translates into an increase of their consumption of equivalent size, and we again do not take into account the role that the price elasticity of supply may play here. As for food self-consumed by producers (which represents a large share of total consumption for some goods), it is not taken into account in the simulations since changes in prices do not affect households when food is auto-consumed. We also do not take into account the potential spillover effects of the increase in prices for the food items included in the analysis on the prices for items not included. Finally we consider only the short-term impact on poverty of higher food prices, as estimated by looking at the consumption and production of food by households. Thus we do not take into account potential medium- to long-term impacts arising, for example, from the fact that an increase in food prices may lead to higher wages for farm workers (findings from studies on medium-term impacts suggest that wage gains compensate only in a very limited way for the initial impact of food price shocks).

Are the hardest hit areas the poorest? The relationship between initial poverty and the change in poverty by area is visualized in figure 6.2. The scatter plots provide on the horizontal axis the initial level of poverty (measured through the headcount index and the poverty gap) and on the vertical axis the change in poverty due to the increase in food prices. When using the headcount index, we find evidence of an inverted-U relationship between the change in poverty and the initial level of poverty. For areas with very low poverty measures, the impact of the food crisis is not very large, as most households are not poor and able to cope with the shock. For the very poor districts, the impact is also not very large, not so much because many households are protected from the increase in prices because they are net sellers of food or rely in large part on auto-

Figure 6.2: Increase in poverty with a 50 percent increase in rice prices

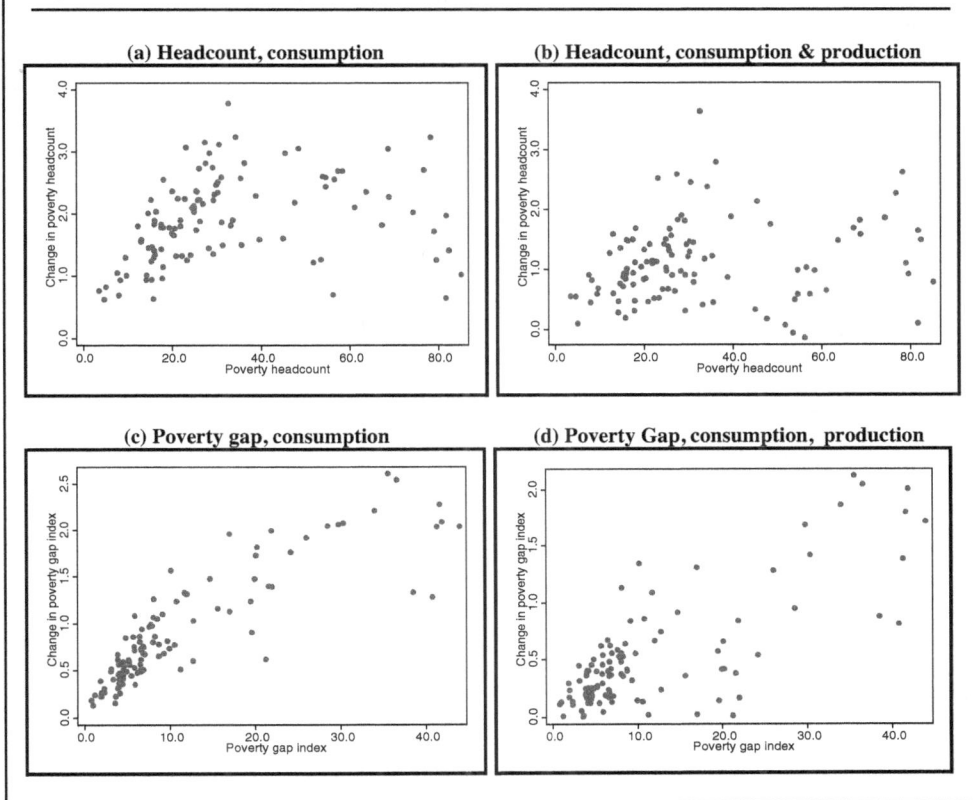

(a) Headcount, consumption

(b) Headcount, consumption & production

(c) Poverty gap, consumption

(d) Poverty Gap, consumption, production

Source: Authors' estimations using GLSDS5 and CWIQ 2003.

consumption to meet their basic food needs, but instead because in those districts high levels of poverty reduce the likelihood that more households will become poor due to the higher prices. The most affected areas are those that are in the middle ground with initial poverty levels in the 30 to 60 percent range.

The results are very different with the poverty gap. There is a clear positive relationship between the initial level of poverty and the increase in poverty, suggesting that the areas that were the poorest before the food price crisis were also on average the areas affected the most by the increase in food prices. The relationship is especially strong when considering the upper bound impacts of the crisis that take into account only the impact of the crisis on the consumer side. Thus while it has often been assumed that urban areas were hit hardest by the food price increases because urban households do not produce their own food, the results show that the poorest areas of the country were probably those affected the most.

Conclusion

In a context of crisis, should safety nets target areas that are affected the most by the crisis, or areas that are initially the poorest or that are the poorest after taking into account the impact of the crisis? In principle, from a social welfare point of view, one could argue that one should most of the time target in priority the areas with the highest level of poverty. But governments are also under pressure to respond to the impact of crises on households so as to offset part of that impact. To the extent that the increase in poverty is going to be highest in already poor areas, the dilemma faced by policy makers is reduced.

The results in this chapter suggest that the impact on poverty of higher food prices is likely to have been lower in Ghana than in other West and Central African countries, but that the impact was nevertheless substantial. Using poverty mapping techniques, we also analyzed where geographically higher food prices are likely to have had the largest negative impact. The results suggest that contrary to popular belief the poorest areas of the country are likely to have been the most affected by the increase in food prices, which would then warrant targeting these areas through safety nets independently of whether one considers that the priority is to reach poor areas or to help offset the impact of the shock.

CHAPTER 7

Targeting Free School Uniforms in Ghana

Juan Carlos Parra Osorio, Clarence Tsimpo, and Quentin Wodon

This chapter is the first of two papers aiming to compare the potential performance of geographic targeting versus proxy means-testing. The assessment of the potential targeting performance of both targeting mechanisms is conducted using simulations for programs that are under consideration or could be considered for implementation in Ghana. In this chapter, we assess the potential targeting performance of the distribution of free school uniforms to close to two million students that is planned by the Government for fall 2009. The program can be considered as a scheme to lower the private cost of schooling for households. We first provide a brief introduction regarding the issue of the costs faced by household when enrolling their students in school. Next, we simulate how well targeted to the poor the planned school uniform program could be if various targeting mechanisms were used. Three mechanisms are considered: geographic targeting (at both the district and local levels), proxy means-testing, and a combination of both. The results suggest that proper geographic targeting could go a long way in making the program pro-poor. Proxy means-testing, which would make the free uniform available to some children but not others on the basis of the characteristics of their household, would not improve targeting performance, and it could also generate stigma (this does not mean that proxy means-testing would not be appropriate for other types of programs, as discussed in other chapters). One should stress that the targeting performance of free school uniforms program presented here is simulated. Actual targeting performance could be lower. But the data suggest that geographic targeting could lead to good targeting performance.

Private Education Costs and School Uniforms

The cost of schooling remains an issue for many children not attending school. The GLSS5 does not have a question on why children do not attend school, but such a question is asked in the 2003 CWIQ. Table 7.1 shows that the cost of schooling is cited as the main reason for not being enrolled in both the sample of children aged 6 to 11 who are not in school, and that of children aged 12 to 17. Surprisingly, the issue of cost is mentioned by children from all five quintiles as the main reason for not enrolling. Note that the CWIQ was implemented before the school reform that led to the abolition of school fees. Even though the CWIQ data is somewhat dated, and even though measures have

Table 7.1: Main reasons for not attending school, 2003 CWIQ (%)

	Residence Area		Welfare Quintiles					
	Urban	Rural	Q1	Q2	Q3	Q4	Q5	Total
	Children aged 6–11							
Not of school age	0.0	2.2	1.4	4.0	0.0	0.0	0.0	1.5
Too far away	0.9	7.3	9.1	2.7	5.7	2.5	2.6	5.2
Too expensive	57.9	34.8	29.1	47.6	48.4	47.0	52.9	42.4
Is working (home or job)	4.4	5.1	6.1	4.9	3.9	5.5	2.3	4.9
Useless/uninteresting	28.1	38.6	46.1	25.6	34.3	32.9	31.9	35.2
Illness	5.2	5.6	4.8	6.9	5.0	7.7	1.1	5.5
Other specify	4.8	11.2	11.9	9.7	7.6	2.9	9.9	9.1
	Children aged 12–17							
Completed school	27.9	23.3	15.0	27.0	26.9	26.2	32.2	25.2
Too far away	0.3	2.0	2.4	1.5	1.0	0.3	1.1	1.3
Too expensive	25.6	21.9	25.2	21.5	22.2	25.5	23.9	23.5
Is working (home or job)	7.4	9.7	9.7	7.6	7.5	7.8	12.7	8.7
Useless/uninteresting	19.6	31.0	37.6	28.9	24.3	20.0	17.4	26.2
Illness	1.4	3.4	4.1	3.6	1.2	2.3	1.4	2.6
Having a child/pregnancy	3.1	3.1	2.3	3.1	3.4	4.0	2.6	3.1
Failed exams	3.4	4.2	4.8	3.9	3.6	3.7	3.2	3.9
Apprenticeship	20.4	13.1	10.5	15.5	17.8	20.0	17.4	16.2
Other reason, specify	3.1	3.7	3.4	2.3	4.0	3.8	4.5	3.5

Source: Authors' estimations using 2003 CWIQ.
Note: Reasons affecting less than 1 percent of the children not enrolled have been dropped from the table.

since been taken to reduce the cost of schooling, the data still suggest that lower private costs of schooling could help boost enrollment rates.

Data from the GLSS5 on private expenditure for schooling confirm that cost may indeed be an issue, and these data were collected just after the abolition of school fees in the academic year 2004–05 (this later led to the adoption of pilot capitation grants for schools to compensate for lost revenues, first in deprived schooling districts, and ultimately nationally). The average share of total consumption allocated by households to education expenditures is high at 9.3 percent in urban areas and 5.0 percent in rural areas (table 7.2). For the poor, the costs of education are far from negligible, and many among the poor may decide not to go to school, or not to pursue their education because of cost. The share of households receiving scholarships is rather low. School fees, as well as food, boarding, and lodging at school are the highest costs, but these average costs are heavily influenced by children who go to private schools, as opposed to public schools. Other costs include dues for PTAs (Parent Teacher Associations), school uniforms and sports clothes, books and school supplies, transport, extra classes, and other expenses (or expenses that households could not allocate to specific categories during the survey interview).

School uniforms represent only 4.8 percent of total education expenditure, but for the poorest quintile of the population, they account for 11.0 percent of total spending on

Table 7.2: Percentage of budget shares of various education expenditures, 2005–06 (%)

	Educational scholarship (received)	School fees	PTA fees	Uniforms and sports clothes	Books and school supplies	Transport	Food, board, and lodging at school	Extra classes	In-kind expenses	Cannot give break down	% of total cons.
Location											
Urban	0.3	23.9	0.9	3.5	7.9	6.0	28.3	5.4	0.4	23.8	9.3
Rural	0.4	14.7	1.4	7.6	7.9	4.0	46.2	4.5	0.8	13.0	5.0
Locality											
Accra (GAMA)	0.1	25.4	0.6	2.7	7.2	7.8	23.5	5.3	0.4	27.2	11.0
Urban coastal	1.0	20.9	1.1	4.0	10.0	3.8	35.9	4.1	0.3	19.9	7.4
Urban forest	0.3	24.1	1.2	3.8	7.7	4.5	30.6	6.0	0.4	21.7	8.9
Urban savannah	0.9	16.8	1.8	8.2	9.8	3.6	38.1	5.2	0.7	15.8	6.0
Rural coastal	0.4	11.9	1.3	7.5	8.3	5.8	48.1	4.9	1.1	11.1	4.5
Rural forest	0.4	15.3	1.3	6.5	7.3	3.9	46.7	4.8	0.7	13.6	6.3
Rural savannah	0.3	16.0	2.0	13.0	9.9	2.1	41.1	2.1	0.8	12.9	2.7
Quintile											
Q1 (poorest)	0.4	14.6	1.9	11.0	9.1	1.9	45.5	3.1	0.4	12.5	6.4
Q2	0.4	16.1	1.3	7.9	8.2	2.2	45.7	4.5	0.7	13.3	7.3
Q3	0.6	19.1	1.2	5.6	7.7	3.0	41.7	4.9	0.5	16.3	8.4
Q4	0.2	20.5	1.3	4.4	7.5	5.4	35.7	5.9	0.4	18.8	8.2
Q5 (richest)	0.3	24.0	0.7	3.2	7.9	7.4	25.4	5.1	0.6	25.6	6.7
Total	0.4	21.1	1.1	4.8	7.9	5.4	33.7	5.1	0.5	20.5	7.3

Source: Authors using GLSS5.

education (table 7.2). Among all categories of education expenditures, school uniforms are clearly the category of expenditure that affects the poor much more than others, in the sense that school uniforms represent much larger share of total education expenditures for the poor than for other groups. This can also be seen in figure 7.1 which provides consumption dominance (CD) curves of the second order for the various categories of spending. CD curves of the second order represent the share of total spending (on the vertical axis) that is accounted for by the population before a certain level of well-being (on the horizontal axis), with a value of one on that axis representing the poverty line. To reach the poor, of all categories of private education spending that could be targeted for subsidies, school uniforms should be the top candidate, since the CD curve for school uniforms is above all others. The fact that providing free school uniforms could if implemented well benefit the poor more than other groups is one of the reasons why the Government of Ghana is putting in place a program that will provide free school uniforms to up to two million children in public primary schools (details of the implementation of the program are still being discussed).

Targeting Performance Simulations for School Uniforms

Free school uniforms could be distributed in many different ways. One possibility would be to target the uniforms geographically and primarily to educationally deprived districts. These districts tend to have fewer educational facilities, facilities that are in poorer conditions, lower enrollment rates, and lower test scores than other districts in

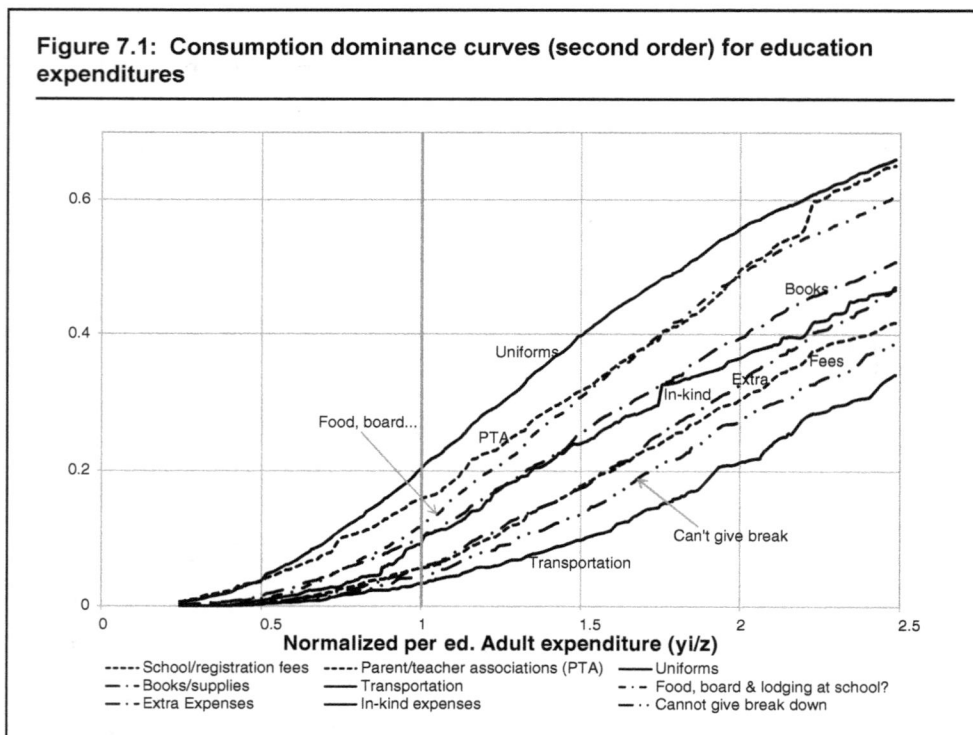

Figure 7.1: Consumption dominance curves (second order) for education expenditures

Source: Authors using GLSS5.

the country. Another possibility would be to target the uniforms geographically to poor areas, in which case the share of the benefits that would accrue to the poor is likely to be higher. Still another alternative is to rely on a proxy means-testing mechanism such as that used by LEAP. In this section we use GLSS5 data to simulate the targeting performance of school uniform distributions under three different targeting mechanisms: geographic targeting, proxy means-testing, and a combination of both. We assume that two million school uniforms are distributed (one uniform per child) at a unit cost of $5. This value was chosen because the average expenditure on uniforms for children attending public primary schools and for which households declare an expenditure on school uniforms is $5.63 in the GLSS5.

To select the students who may receive the school uniforms, we proceed as follows. First, to be eligible, a child must first be enrolled in primary school, and s/he must attend a public school (under the assumption that children attending private school are likely to come from better off households). A total of 3.1 million children attend public primary schools according to the GLSS5, and 36 percent of them are poor. Next, for geographic targeting of the school uniforms distribution, we consider two options: geographic targeting at either the district or local level. Specifically, we use the GLSS5 data to rank districts and enumeration areas (these are so-called primary sampling units in which there are typically 20 households that have been randomly selected from a small area such as a village or part of a city) according to their level of poverty, using the headcount index for the ranking (we could also use higher order poverty measures such as the poverty gap and squared poverty gap, which would be more appropriate to target the poorest among the poor, but the results are not very sensitive to this assumption. There are 110 districts and 580 enumeration areas identified in the GLSS5 data. The number of districts is only 110 because the data predate the expansion in the number of districts first to 138, and later to 170.

Note that the poverty estimates at the district and enumeration area levels use for geographic targeting in the GLSS5 have high standard errors due to small sample sizes at those levels in the GLSS5. Yet for the simulations presented here in the aggregate, this is not problematic because the reliability of the aggregate targeting performance indicators is good, since it is based on estimates for many different areas. Note also that while we consider the targeting performance estimates obtained with the district level data as potentially achievable in practice (because we have good estimates of poverty at the district level through the poverty map presented in chapter 4 of this study), the targeting performance obtained through targeting at the level of enumeration areas may be difficult to achieve since it is not easy to obtain valid poverty estimates for very small areas (the CWIQ-based poverty map is valid only at the district level). We provide enumeration area targeting performance for comparison purposes to show that the gain obtained from further targeting at that level are limited, so that district-level geographic targeting is good enough.

It is also worth noting that the poorest districts in the GLSS5 data need not be all the same as the poorest districts in the new and more robust poverty map based on the GLSS5 and the 2003 CWIQ, although there is a high degree of correlation between both sets of districts. The reason for not using the poverty map for the simulations presented here is that we want to compare the performance of geographic targeting and proxy means-testing in a single data set, and the poverty map cannot be used for simulating proxy means-testing because the consumption data that would be used to simulate proxy means-testing within the CWIQ data themselves have been obtained using a predictive model.

The children who benefit from the school uniforms under geographic targeting in the simulations are those who live in the poorest districts or enumeration areas. That is, all children in public primary schools living in the poorest district or enumeration area are selected for participation in the distribution program. Next all children in the second poorest district or enumeration area are selected, and so on up to having selected a total of two million children by progressively including less poor districts or enumeration areas.

For proxy means-testing (PMT), we use a regression model to estimate the expected level of consumption of the household in which a child enrolled in a public primary school lives. For the pure PMT we select as beneficiaries of the programs the children who live in the poorest households, as classified by the result of the prediction from the regression. This assumes that PMT is implemented nationally, and we simply choose the poorest children as beneficiaries of the programs (i.e., two million children in public primary schools are selected). For the combination of geographic targeting and PMT, whereby PMT is applied to select beneficiary children in areas identified as poor, the PMT eligibility criteria is set at a level of consumption per equivalent adult equal to 150 percent of the poverty line. Then, the poorest children according to the PMT prediction are selected within the set defined by both geographical eligibility (poor districts) and PMT eligibility.

It is important to highlight the fact that the PMT technique used here does not rely on community-level information from those who live in poor communities. In the targeting mechanism used by LEAP, performance appears to be especially good (and better than the estimates presented here) because the targeting mechanisms used by LEAP combines unique information available at the community level (but typically not available to government officials) together with proxy means-testing.

Table 7.3 presents the performance resulting from the various targeting mechanisms, by computing the percentage of the target population in each poverty status according to the poverty line, and their predicted status under each program and scheme. Inclusion errors are defined as the total number of nonpoor eligible children predicted poor as a share of the total number of eligible children predicted poor. Exclusion errors are defined as the total number of poor eligible children that are predicted nonpoor as a share of the total number of poor eligible children. It is desirable to have low levels of both errors, but given a limited budget, inclusion errors matter the most because they drive the share of benefits accruing to nonpoor households, while the objective is to maximize the share of benefits accruing to the poor.

Reading the first row in table 7.3, corresponding to the school uniforms program targeted geographically at the district level, 32.2 percent of the eligible children are poor according to the poverty line and correctly predicted poor by geographic targeting; 4.3 percent of the eligible children are poor according to the poverty line but predicted nonpoor by geographic targeting; 31.2 percent are nonpoor according to the poverty line and correctly predicted nonpoor by geographic targeting, and the other 32.3 percent of the eligible children are nonpoor according to the poverty line and incorrectly predicted poor by geographic targeting. The share of the predicted poor population by geographic targeting that is nonpoor according to the poverty line, which is the inclusion error, is equal to 50.1 percent. Thus half of the benefits would go to the poor (this is also apparent in the share of the benefits accruing to the poor listed at the bottom right of the table; this

Table 7.3: Simulated targeting performance of free school uniforms (%)

	Indicators of Targeting Performance					
	Poor, predicted poor	Poor, predicted nonpoor	Nonpoor, predicted nonpoor	Nonpoor, predicted poor	Error of inclusion	Error of exclusion
Geographic targeting						
District	32.2	4.3	31.2	32.3	50.1	11.8
PSU	35.8	0.7	34.8	28.7	44.5	2.0
Proxy means-testing	31.5	5.0	30.5	33.0	51.2	13.7
PMT within geographic						
District	32.9	3.6	31.9	31.6	49.1	10.0
PSU	33.0	3.5	32.0	31.5	48.8	9.6
	Share of the benefits that go to each quintile and to the poor					
	Q1	Q2	Q3	Q4	Q1	Poor
Geographic targeting						
District	36.2	27.4	19.1	11.7	5.6	49.9
PSU	39.1	31.7	17.2	8.5	3.5	55.5
Proxy means-testing	35.2	28.9	21.7	11.0	3.3	48.8
PMT within geographic						
District	36.7	30.0	20.8	8.8	3.6	50.9
PSU	36.8	29.5	20.5	10.1	3.1	51.2

Source: Authors' estimations using GLSS5 data.

is one minus the error of inclusion). This share might not seem that impressive, but it is much higher than the performance of most if not all other programs reviewed here (i.e., food subsidies, fertilizer subsidies, oil related subsidies, electricity subsidies, and school lunches). This share is also substantially higher than the benefit accruing to the poor from public education spending.

Table 7.3 suggests that shifting from district-level geographic targeting to targeting at the level of enumeration areas would increase targeting performance further, as expected, but not by a wide margin. Proxy means-testing would work almost as well as geographic targeting, but it would be more complicated to implement, and probably not appropriate from a political point of view in the case of the distribution of school uniforms (because it might generate either stigma or envy if some children in the same school get a uniform, and others do not, and the risk of stigma or envy is not worth it given the relatively low value of the transfers provided through the free uniforms). Finally, PMT within geographic targeting actually reduces targeting performance, essentially due to the imperfect prediction of consumption, too many poor households living in poor areas are being denied eligibility (we could however change the threshold of rejection depending of the district in which a household lives, but the point is that the complication arising from implementing PMT within geographic targeting would probably still not bring much, if any benefits in terms if improving overall targeting performance).

Table 7.4 provides data on the potential impact on poverty of the school uniform program assuming that the in-kind transfer of $5 represented by a uniform represents an equivalent increase in the consumption level of program beneficiaries. The impacts are small, because program outlays themselves are small in comparison to what would be needed to eradicate poverty in Ghana. Under the reference targeting mechanism (district level geographic targeting), the headcount index of poverty would be reduced by 0.34 percentage point, the poverty gap by 0.22 points, and the squared poverty gap by 0.15 points. Normalized poverty impacts are also provided under the other targeting mechanisms (the normalization simply consists in expressing the poverty reduction under the alternative mechanism as a ratio of the poverty reduction under the baseline mechanism in percentage terms). As expected, differences in poverty impacts are small between the different options considered here (this is not surprising given that the various mechanisms have similar orders of magnitude in terms of targeting performance in table 7.3).

Table 7.4: Normalized poverty reduction impact of school uniforms under alternative targeting (%)

	Headcount ratio	Poverty gap	Squared poverty gap
No program (rates)	28.53	9.59	4.60
Poverty impact under district targeting	−0.34	−0.22	−0.15
Geographic targeting–Normalized impact			
District	100.0	100.0	100.0
PSU	117.5	111.2	106.7
Proxy means testing–Normalized impact	96.4	97.8	98.0
PMT within geographic–Normalized impact			
District	99.7	102.2	101.3
PSU	99.7	102.7	101.3

Source: Authors' estimations using GLSS5 data.

Conclusion

In this chapter we provided an assessment of the potential targeting performance of the distribution of free school uniforms to close to two million students that is planned by the Government for fall 2009. We first suggested that targeting school uniforms to reduce the private cost of schooling for household was a good idea given that this is the area of private spending for education that hurts the poor the most proportionately to the amounts spent. Said differently, a much larger share of the total private spending for school uniforms is paid by the poor than for any other private education expenditure that can be identified in the household survey data. Next, we suggested that geographic targeting would work as well as, if not better, than proxy means-testing to target the beneficiaries of the free school uniforms. Given that geographic targeting is simpler and less costly to implement than proxy means-testing, and that it is also less likely to generate any stigma, it should be recommended to target the program. Targeting within districts would result in some gains in targeting performance and poverty impacts, but even simple targeting at the district level would already achieve good targeting performance.

CHAPTER 8

Simulating Conditional Cash Transfers for Education in Ghana

Juan Carlos Parra Osorio and Quentin Wodon

If from a political economy point of view it is acceptable to target social programs geographically, and thus to cover only the poorest areas of a country, geographic targeting may often perform as well as if not better than proxy means-testing. In such a context, geographic targeting is preferable since it is easier and less costly to implement. However, when governments are under pressure to implement at least some programs nationally (which seems to be the case in Ghana), and/or when governments want to reach a larger share of the poor through at least some of their programs (to reduce errors of exclusion), it becomes necessary to implement those programs in a larger number of areas, in which case geographic targeting may not be sufficient anymore. The question then is whether in some areas geographic targeting performs better than proxy means-testing, while in others the reverse may be true. It may also be possible in some areas to combine geographic targeting with proxy means-testing to achieve better targeting performance. After a brief review of Mexico's experience with conditional cash transfers (CCTs), this chapter looks at these issues by simulating the potential targeting performance of a CCT program for junior secondary education under geographic targeting, proxy means-testing, and a combination of both. The results suggest that in less poor areas, proxy means-testing performs better than geographic targeting, while the reverse is observed in the poorest areas. One should stress that the targeting performance of the program presented here is simulated. Actual targeting performance could be lower. But the data suggest that for programs such as conditional cash transfers that would aim to promote a better transition from primary to junior secondary school among poor households nationally, a combination of geographic targeting and proxy means-testing could lead to the best targeting.

Conditional Cash Transfers: Mexico's Experience[1]

Conditional cash transfers have proven effective in many countries to reduce poverty both today and in the future through investments in the education and health of younger generations (for a detailed review of the international experience to-date with conditional cash transfers, see Fiszbein and Schady 2009). The most famous (and one of the first) example of CCTs is Mexico's *Oportunidades*, previously known as PROGRESA (*Programa de Educación, Salud y Alimentación*). Confronted with rising poverty after the economic crisis of 1995, the Mexican government progressively changed its poverty reduction strategy by ending costly universal tortilla subsidies and instead funding new investments in human capital through PROGRESA. The program gives cash grants to poor rural households, provided their children attend school for 85 percent of school days and the household visits public health clinics and participates in educational workshops on health and nutrition. Founded in 1997, within two years PROGRESA covered 2.6 million families: 40 percent of all rural families and one in nine families nationally. Operating in 31 of the 32 states, in 50,000 localities and 2,000 municipalities, its 1999 budget was about 0.2 percent of Mexico's gross domestic product. This funding for PROGRESA, and reduced funding for other programs, was a deliberate policy choice to favor programs that are better targeted to the poor and that involve co-responsibility by beneficiaries, promoting long-term behavioral changes.

In education, the Mexico program provides bi-monthly cash transfers to households with children in school. The amounts rise with grade level, both to compensate for hypothetical lost earnings from child labor and to improve retention of children at the secondary level. Evaluations showed that the program raised school enrollment rates, with children from participating households receiving on average 0.64 year of schooling more than others. In health care, the program provides free basic health care to beneficiaries, prenatal care for pregnant women, growth monitoring of babies, nutritional supplements for children, monetary grants for purchasing food, and education on hygiene, nutrition and reproductive health. These benefits come with conditions, including regular visits to the health center, attendance at educational sessions, and helping to maintain schools and clinics. Evaluations found increased attendance at health clinics and reduced morbidity among beneficiary children aged 0 to 2 years. The cash payments to household for education and health also contribute to reducing monetary poverty.

PROGRESA used a three-stage targeting mechanism (Skoufias et al. 1999). First, using census data, poor rural localities were selected on the basis of their level of marginality. Specifically, PROGRESA used data from the 1990 population census and the 1995 population count (Conteo) to create a marginality index for 105,749 localities. The index was developed using a principal component analysis, based on seven variables, the first four of which came from the 1995 population count (Conteo) and the remaining three from the 1990 population census. The seven variables were: (1) Share of illiterate adults (>14 years) in the locality; (2) Share of dwellings without water; (3) Share of dwellings without draining systems; (4) Share of dwellings without electricity; (5) Average number of occupants per room; (6) Share of dwellings with dirt floor; and (7) Share of population working in the primary sector. The first component of the principal component analysis was used to classify localities into five groups, with corresponding levels of marginality (see Appendix B in Skoufias et al. 1999, for details). For small localities representing less than 3 percent of the country's population, some variables were not available to compute the marginality index with the above method, so that regressions were used instead to estimate this index.

Among the 76,098 localities characterized as having a high, or very high level of marginality (the localities covered 15 million people, out of Mexico's total of 90 million in 1995), only 48,501 were eligible to benefit from the program, because eligibility required the presence of a primary school, a secondary school, and a clinic (to enable the program to function properly). Some more localities were dropped from the sample of potentially eligible localities because they had too few inhabitants, or because they were too isolated, or lacked access (this was done in part to reduce operation costs). Still, at the end of the process, the available evidence suggests that PROGRESA's methodology for selecting eligible localities performed well compared to a consumption-based model fitted using national surveys. However, the index lost some power of distinction between localities with medium (i.e., non-eligible) and high (i.e., eligible) levels of marginality, which may have led to some degree of arbitrariness in the selection or exclusion of some of the localities (Skoufias et al. 1999: 11–14).

The second stage in the targeting process consisted of selecting eligible families within participating communities. For this, PROGRESA collected data on all households living in participating communities and a multivariate discriminant analysis was used to classify households as poor (i.e., beneficiaries) or nonpoor (i.e., non-beneficiaries). More specifically, socio-economic information on all households in the communities was first gathered through the ENCASEH local census. The census questionnaire and the procedure to determine eligibility were standardized at the national level. Then, a per capita income indicator was constructed by summing all individual incomes and subtracting the income from children. This income was compared to a Standard Food Basket to create a binary variable for poor and nonpoor status. In each region, a discriminant analysis was then performed to identify the variables which best separate the poor and nonpoor, and a second index was computed (i.e., the discriminant score) to capture differences between the poor and the nonpoor. It is this index, and thus the related variables, which served for the classification of the households as poor or nonpoor (or eligible and noneligible). The reason to use this index, rather than the per capita income of the household, was that the index was deemed to better capture multiple dimensions of poverty. The evaluation of this second step in the targeting procedure suggested that while the targeting mechanism was fairly good at identifying extremely poor households, its accuracy was again lower at moderate rates of poverty (25th to 52nd percentiles; for details, see Skoufias et al. 1999: 14–21 and Appendixes C to E).

The third stage in the targeting process consisted of incorporating the eligible families into the program, and taking this opportunity to check the selection of the beneficiaries within the community. This was done through a community meeting for all beneficiaries and local authorities. Each community was given the list of program participants, and it was still feasible at this stage to change the selection, for example by suggesting a second visit by PROGRESA staff if it was believed that some poor families should be reclassified as nonpoor or vice versa. The proportion of households whose selection was disputed turned out to be, however, very small (0.1 percent of the selected households), which may be a good sign to avoid political interferences in the process.

Once the targeting mechanism was complete, eligible households were registered and a PROGRESA hologram ID with an identifying number was given to the household's main woman. A supply of health and school reporting forms was provided to schoolmasters and doctors. These forms were collected bimonthly and sent back to PROGRESA's central office, which in turn, issued listings with the amounts of transfers to be granted to the families. These listings were sent to state offices and Telecom offices. Telecom then issued cash for bimonthly transfers upon presentation of the individual hologram eligibility card and ID. Telecom gave the transfers only to the card bearer. Disputed amounts were discussed with PROGRESA staff and promotoras, who were volunteer community women in charge of the program in their community. Among other tasks, promotoras held meetings with beneficiary women in their communities and reported monthly on health and education services.

Simulating Conditional Cash Transfers for Ghana

Conditions may be present in Ghana to recommend or at least consider the implementation of CCTs for junior secondary school students. On the education side, completion of primary school is now higher than it was previously thanks to a large increase in school enrollment brought about among others by the capitation grants and the elimination of school fees. But for the poor the transition to junior secondary school remains more difficult, and the completion of senior secondary school is still very limited, especially again among the poor. On the labor market side, one of the advantages of CCTs is that they generate investments by households in the human capital of their children. Human capital is mobile and it can be used by children when they reach adulthood wherever they decide to live and/or work. The large geographic disparities observed in Ghana in terms of poverty and human development are unlikely to be resolved rapidly, so that migration to urban areas and coastal areas is expected to continue. By improving the education of younger generations who now live in poverty, CCTs may enable these generations to be better equipped for the labor market even if they migrate to other areas of the country after the completion of their studies. This does not mean that concurrently, investments in the physical capital of poor areas are not needed. But CCTs do have an advantage of portability which is important in a changing economy.

To analyze the potential impact on poverty of CCTs, this section follows a similar approach to the analysis conducted for school uniforms in chapter 7. Although we use the same techniques as those employed in that chapter, some of the methodological explanations are repeated here again for the benefit of readers who may have not read the chapter. We use GLSS5 data to simulate the targeting performance of conditional cash transfers (CCTs) under three different targeting mechanisms: geographic targeting, proxy means-testing, and a combination of both. For comparison with the school uniforms simulations we assume that $20 per child is provided to half a million children, so that the total cost of the program is identical to the cost of the simulated free school uniform program, at $10 million. The choice of $20 per child per year is somewhat arbitrary (and admittedly a relatively low transfer) and simulations could be redone with different amounts. But for comparison purposes, it is useful to keep the cost of the two programs equal.

To select the students who receive the CCT, we proceed in a fashion similar to what was done for school uniforms, with various scenarios. In a first set of simulations, we provide the CCT to students attending public junior secondary schools (denoted as JSS 1 in tables 8.1 and 8.2) under the assumption that children attending private school are likely to come from better off households, and therefore would not be eligible for the CCTs. Next, we also consider as additional potential beneficiaries of the program students with a completed primary education but unfinished junior secondary who are below 17 years of age (denoted as JSS 2). The assumption is that some of those children might have pursued their education if CCTs had been available (there also could be a pull effect from the CCT that would lead to higher primary school completion, and therefore even higher enrollment at the junior secondary level, but this is more difficult to simulate without increasing the sample of potential beneficiaries dramatically and probably too much).

Next, for geographic targeting, we consider two options: geographic targeting at either the district or local level, as was done for school uniforms. Specifically, we use the GLSS5 data to rank districts and enumeration areas (these are so-called primary sam-

Table 8.1: Simulated targeting performance of CCTs at the national level (%)

	Indicators of targeting performance					
	Poor, predicted poor	Poor, predicted nonpoor	Nonpoor, predicted nonpoor	Nonpoor, predicted poor	Error of inclusion	Error of exclusion
Geographic targeting						
JSS 1						
District	20.6	6.4	42.0	31.0	60.1	23.8
PSU	25.8	1.2	47.3	25.7	50.0	4.5
JSS 2						
District	20.6	6.5	42.2	30.7	59.9	24.2
PSU	25.8	1.3	47.5	25.4	49.5	4.6
Proxy means-testing						
JSS 1	20.5	6.5	42.0	31.0	60.2	24.1
JSS 2	20.4	6.7	42.0	30.9	60.2	24.8
PMT within geographic						
JSS 1						
District	21.7	5.3	43.2	29.8	57.8	19.6
PSU	22.1	4.9	43.6	29.4	57.1	18.1
JSS 2						
District	21.7	5.4	43.3	29.6	57.7	20.0
PSU	22.1	5.0	43.8	29.1	56.9	18.6
	Share of the benefits that go to each quintile and to the poor					
	Q1	Q2	Q3	Q4	Q1	Poor
Geographic targeting						
JSS 1						
District	28.4	29.2	21.1	15.5	5.8	39.9
PSU	32.7	36.8	17.8	8.9	3.8	50.0
JSS 2						
District	28.4	29.0	21.3	15.5	5.8	40.1
PSU	32.9	37.1	17.5	8.9	3.6	50.5
Proxy means-testing						
JSS 1	27.0	31.7	25.1	13.2	3.0	39.8
JSS 2	27.1	31.7	25.0	13.1	3.0	39.8
PMT within geographic						
JSS 1						
District	28.9	33.1	23.5	11.4	3.2	42.2
PSU	29.1	33.1	23.0	12.0	2.8	42.9
JSS 2						
District	29.0	33.2	23.1	11.6	3.2	42.3
PSU	29.3	33.1	22.6	12.2	2.8	43.1

Source: Authors' simulations using GLSS5 data.

pling units in which there are typically 20 households that have been randomly selected from a small area such as a village or part of a city) according to their level of poverty, using the headcount index for the ranking (we could also use higher order poverty measures such as the poverty gap and squared poverty gap, which would be more appropriate to target the poorest among the poor, but the results are not very sensitive to this assumption). There are 110 districts and 580 enumeration areas identified in the GLSS5 data. The number of districts is only 110 because the data predate the expansion in the number of districts first to 138, and later to 170.

As was the case for school uniforms, poverty estimates at the district and enumeration area levels used for geographic targeting in the GLSS5 have high standard errors due to small sample sizes at those levels in the data. Yet for the simulations presented in the aggregate, this is not problematic because the reliability of the aggregate targeting performance indicators is good, since it is based on estimates for many different areas. Note also that while we consider the targeting performance estimates obtained with the district level data as potentially achievable in practice (because we have good estimates of poverty at the district level through the poverty map presented in chapter 4), the targeting performance obtained through targeting at the level of enumeration areas may be difficult to achieve since it is not easy to obtain valid poverty estimates for very small areas (the CWIQ-based poverty map is valid only at the district level). We provide enumeration area targeting performance for comparison purposes to show that the gain obtained from further geographic targeting at that level are limited.

The children who benefit from the CCTs under geographic targeting in the simulations are those who live in the poorest districts or enumeration areas. Thus, all children already in public junior secondary schools living in the poorest district or enumeration area are selected for participation in the distribution program under the first set of simulations (JSS 1). Next all children in the second poorest district or enumeration area are selected, and so on up to having selected a total of half a million children by progressively including less poor districts or enumeration areas. For proxy means-testing (PMT), we use a regression model to estimate the expected level of consumption of the household in which a child enrolled in a public primary school lives. For the pure PMT we select as beneficiaries of the programs the children who live in the poorest households, as classified by the result of the prediction from the regression. This assumes that PMT is implemented nationally, and we simply choose the poorest children as beneficiaries of the programs. For the combination of geographic targeting and PMT, whereby PMT is applied to select beneficiary children in areas identified as poor, the PMT eligibility criteria is set at a level of consumption per equivalent adult equal to 150 percent of the poverty line. Then, the poorest children according to the PMT prediction are selected within the set defined by both geographical eligibility (poor districts) and PMT eligibility.

Table 8.1 presents the performance resulting from the various targeting mechanisms, by computing the percentage of the target population in each poverty status according to the poverty line, and their predicted status under each program and scheme. Inclusion errors are defined as the total number of nonpoor eligible children predicted poor as a share of the total number of eligible children predicted poor. Exclusion errors are defined as the total number of poor eligible children that are predicted nonpoor as a share of the total number of poor eligible children. It is desirable to have low levels of both errors, but given a limited budget, inclusion errors matter the most because they drive the share of benefits accruing to nonpoor households, while the objective is to maximize the share of benefits accruing to the poor.

Reading the first row in table 8.1, nationally 20.6 percent of the eligible children are poor according to the poverty line and correctly predicted poor by geographic targeting; 6.4 percent of the eligible children are poor according to the poverty line but predicted nonpoor by geographic targeting; 42.0 percent are nonpoor according to the poverty line and correctly predicted nonpoor by geographic targeting, and the other 31.0 percent of the eligible children are nonpoor according to the poverty line and incorrectly predicted poor by geographic targeting. The share of the predicted poor population by geographic targeting that is nonpoor according to the poverty line, which is the inclusion error, is

Table 8.2: Normalized poverty reduction impact of CCTs under alternative targeting (%)

	Headcount ratio	Poverty gap	Squared poverty gap
No program (rates)	28.53	9.59	4.60
School Lunch Benchmark	−0.34	−0.22	−0.15
Geographic targeting			
JSS 1			
District	59.8	78.5	70.7
PSU	126.6	96.4	80.7
JSS 2			
District	62.1	78.5	70.7
PSU	129.0	96.9	80.7
Proxy means-testing			
JSS 1	79.6	77.6	68.7
JSS 2	79.6	77.6	68.7
PMT within geographic			
JSS 1			
District	88.8	82.5	72.0
PSU	97.3	83.4	72.7
JSS 2			
District	88.8	82.5	72.0
PSU	97.3	83.9	72.7

Source: Authors' estimations using GLSS5 data.

equal to 60.1 percent. Thus less than half of the benefits would go to the poor (this is also apparent in the share of the benefits accruing to the poor listed at the bottom right of the table; this is one minus the error of inclusion). This share is lower than what was obtained from the analysis of school lunches separately, essentially because enrollment rates gaps in junior secondary schools are higher among poor versus better off households than is the case for primary school. The targeting performance of this scheme might not seem that impressive, but it is still higher than the performance of many other programs, and it is also much higher than the benefit accruing to the poor from public education spending.

Table 8.1 suggests that shifting from district-level geographic targeting to targeting at the level of enumeration areas would increase targeting performance further, as expected. Proxy means-testing would work as well as geographic targeting on average, but it would be more complicated to implement (note that the potential issue of stigma would probably not be as present here as with school lunches given that CCTs are typically not provided within the school). PMT within geographic targeting increases targeting performance by only a small margin (but at least, in this case, it does not lead to a reduction in targeting performance as had been observed with school lunches).

Table 8.2 provides data on the potential impact on poverty of the CCTs assuming that the cash transfer of $20 leads to an equivalent increase in the consumption level per equivalent adult of beneficiary households. The impacts are normalized versus the estimated potential impact of school lunches, to facilitate comparisons. The impacts are small, because program outlays themselves are small in comparison to what would be needed to eradicate poverty in Ghana. As a reminder, under the school lunch reference district-level geographic targeting mechanism, the headcount index of poverty would be reduced by 0.34 percentage point, the poverty gap by 0.22 point, and the squared poverty gap by 0.15 point. The normalized poverty impacts presented for

Table 8.3: Simulated targeting performance of CCTs at the regional level (%)

	Indicators of Targeting Performance					
	Poor, predicted poor	Poor, predicted nonpoor	Nonpoor, predicted nonpoor	Nonpoor, predicted poor	Error of inclusion	Error of exclusion
Geographic targeting						
Overall program	**19.3**	**17.1**	**48.7**	**14.9**	**43.4**	**47.0**
Accra	0.0	22.8	77.2	0.0	0.0	100.0
Urban coastal	2.1	6.0	84.8	7.0	76.8	73.9
Urban forest	2.7	7.7	84.7	5.0	65.4	74.3
Urban savannah	21.8	16.2	48.6	13.4	38.0	42.6
Rural coastal	17.0	14.2	49.4	19.4	53.3	45.6
Rural forest	15.3	20.0	46.4	18.3	54.4	56.6
Rural savannah	40.5	21.0	21.7	16.9	29.5	34.1
Proxy means-testing						
Overall program	**21.7**	**14.8**	**51.1**	**12.4**	**36.3**	**40.5**
Accra	2.9	19.9	77.2	0.0	0.0	87.1
Urban coastal	0.0	8.2	91.8	0.0	0.0	100.0
Urban forest	1.8	8.5	88.0	1.6	47.4	82.6
Urban savannah	11.5	26.5	55.2	6.8	37.0	69.7
Rural coastal	9.4	21.9	59.7	9.1	49.3	70.0
Rural forest	14.5	20.8	53.8	10.9	42.9	58.9
Rural savannah	57.9	3.5	11.1	27.4	32.2	5.7
	Percentage of benefits going to each quintile and to the poor					
	Q1	Q2	Q3	Q4	Q5	Poor
Geographic targeting						
Overall program	**43.9**	**24.4**	**19.4**	**8.8**	**3.6**	**56.6**
Accra	n.a.	n.a.	n.a.	n.a.	n.a.	n.a.
Urban coastal	0.0	23.2	9.0	44.5	23.2	23.2
Urban forest	23.9	10.7	29.7	21.2	14.5	34.6
Urban savannah	38.4	30.8	14.0	2.7	14.1	62.0
Rural coastal	35.6	24.9	30.4	7.2	1.9	46.7
Rural forest	29.9	33.0	24.0	10.8	2.3	45.6
Rural savannah	61.3	17.4	12.4	6.5	2.4	70.5
Proxy means-testing						
Overall program	**48.9**	**25.3**	**17.5**	**6.2**	**2.1**	**63.7**
Accra	49.4	50.6	0.0	0.0	0.0	100.0
Urban coastal	n.a.	n.a.	n.a.	n.a.	n.a.	n.a.
Urban forest	52.6	0.0	32.9	0.0	14.6	52.6
Urban savannah	39.6	35.5	17.5	7.3	0.0	63.0
Rural coastal	28.6	31.7	29.6	4.3	5.8	50.7
Rural forest	41.4	25.5	25.7	6.6	0.8	57.1
Rural savannah	54.6	24.2	12.7	6.4	2.1	67.8

Source: Authors' estimations using GLSS5 data.
Note: n.a = not applicable.

the CCTs are obtained simply by expressing the poverty reduction obtained under the various targeting mechanisms as a ratio of the poverty reduction obtained under the baseline district level geographic targeting mechanism for school lunches in percentage terms. The impacts of the CCTs tend to be lower than the impact of the school lunches in large part because we target junior secondary education, where enrollment by the poor is lower than at the primary level. There are some exceptions to this generic statement for the headcount index, but these should not be considered as too important given that the headcount is a less valuable measure of poverty than the poverty gap or squared poverty gap (changes in headcount are influenced by what happens in the vicinity of the poverty line, while social programs should aim to target poorer households when feasible).

The fact that CCTs at the junior secondary school level achieve in the simulations a smaller immediate impact on poverty through the cash transfer provided than school lunches should not be interpreted as an argument to dismiss such CCTs. Indeed, to the extent that CCTs would generate higher levels of education among beneficiaries, the long term benefits from the program could be very large in terms of higher future expected earnings for participants that would lead to future poverty reduction. Thus, if CCTs generate larger school gains than school lunches, they might be a good addition to a well targeted school lunch program. In this chapter, we focus however solely on the targeting performance of various targeting mechanisms, and thus only on the immediate gains from the cash transfers.

Comparing Geographic Targeting and Proxy Means-Testing at the Regional Level

Proxy means-testing does not add much to the performance of geographic targeting at the national level. Thus, if from a political economy point of view it is acceptable to target CCTs geographically and to cover only the poorest areas of the country, geographic targeting would work fine. However, in Ghana as in other countries, the government is under pressure to implement many of its programs nationally or at least in a large number of districts. For a program such as CCTs for junior secondary school which has the potential to significantly contribute to a higher level of education for future generations the government may also want to reach a larger share of the poor to reduce errors of exclusion. In such circumstances it may be interesting to implement the program in a larger number of areas, in which case geographic targeting may not be sufficient anymore because it may not perform well in some areas.

This section provides results from running again the simulations presented in the previous section, but at the regional level rather than at the national level, under the assumption that the CCT program must be implemented in all regions. For simplicity, we compare geographic targeting and proxy means-testing, but not proxy means-testing within geographic targeting as was done by the Mexican government for PROGRESA. As discussed earlier, the most important statistics for a cost-benefit analysis of poverty programs is the error of inclusion, since this gives the share of spending that does not reach the poor. Table 8.3 suggests that if the CCT program were to be implemented at the regional level, proxy means-testing would perform better than geographic targeting in most of the regions that do not have very high levels of poverty, with the differences in performance being substantial in some cases.

Conclusion

Two main results emerge from the analysis conducted in this chapter. First, CCTs could be an attractive option to improve school enrollment at the junior high level in Ghana, and to also reduce poverty. Second, from the point of view of the analysis of targeting mechanisms, while at the national level it may not be useful to implement proxy means-testing to target CCTs, at the regional level this may make sense because in better off regions, proxy means-testing tends to work better to identify the poor than geographic targeting. The Mexico experience combined geographic targeting and proxy means-testing. In Ghana the LEAP program combines some geographic targeting with community-based targeting and proxy means-testing. The suggestion from this chapter is not that proxy means-testing should necessarily be used to implement CCTs, but rather than it could be an appropriate choice especially if the program were to be implemented in many different parts of the country including those with lower poverty. One other advantage of proxy means-testing is that the administrative structure to implement the mechanism can potentially be used for several different programs, which reduces administrative costs. We will come back to this issue when discussing the targeting performance of LEAP.

Note

1. This section is adapted from Wodon et al. (2003).

CHAPTER 9

Tax Cuts for Rice and Fertilizer Subsidies in Ghana

Clarence Tsimpo and Quentin Wodon

In part due to a lack of well developed safety net programs, the first response of many African governments to the food price crisis has consisted in implementing broad-based tax cuts and/or subsidies for basic food staples such as rice. Governments have also implemented programs designed to increase food production by subsidizing seeds and fertilizers. This chapter provides evidence that in Ghana the nonpoor benefited the most from tax cuts on imported foods. Most of the fertilizer subsidies provided by the government have probably also benefited the nonpoor, but the program is likely to have been more pro-poor than rice tax cuts. Given the additional production impact of fertilizers, they appear to be a better option than the import tax cuts on rice.

Who Benefits from Tax Cuts on Rice and Other Imported Foods?

Confronted with rising food prices for cereals such as imported rice in 2007–08 many governments including that of Ghana implemented reductions in import and other taxes levied on basic foods. The implicit assumption was that a reduction in taxes would be passed on by intermediaries to consumers, thus reducing market prices as well. However, even if there were such a pass-through or trickle down, it is not clear if a reduction in indirect taxes is good policy for helping the poor.

Why have so many governments implemented tax cuts on imported foods? At least two variables are often used by policy makers to assess to what extent a shock in the price of food items are likely to have a large effect on the standard of living of the population, and thereby to determine whether it is necessary for the government to reduce taxes on these food items. The first variable is the share in total consumption represented by the items. This information is provided in the second column of table 9.1. The larger the share is, the more likely it will be that a government will feel pressure to reduce the tax on the commodity in a time of food price crisis. A second important piece of information is the share of the population that is likely to be affected by the price shock. This share maters from a political economy point of view because when a larger share of the population is affected, it is more likely that policy makers will be under pressure to respond to the crisis. This information is provided in the third column of the table. In the case of rice, we see that in many countries more than 90 percent of the population consumed it (this is the case in Gabon, Guinea, Liberia, Mali, Senegal, Sierra Leone,

Table 9.1: Basic statistics and benefit incidence of reduction in indirect taxes on imported food

Food item	Share in total consumption (%)	Proportion consumers (%)	Share consumed by bottom 40%	Share consumed by bottom 60%
Burkina faso (2003 survey); Base share in poverty at 46.4%				
Rice	3.6	60.2	13.4	25.6
Bread	0.7	35.6	8.3	18.1
Vegetable oil, butter	1.1	74.9	16.1	31.6
Sugar	0.9	67.4	19.7	35.3
Milk	0.6	18.1	10.3	19.8
Congo, Dem. Rep. (2005 survey); Base share in poverty at 71.3%				
Rice	3.2	57.3	15.5	31.7
Palm oil	4.0	96.2	19.7	36.2
Wheat	1.8	35.1	7.1	17.4
Sugar	1.4	57.4	10.6	24.6
Milk	0.7	23.0	4.1	11.6
Gabon (2005 survey); Base share in poverty at 32.7%				
Rice	3.0	91.4	31.7	51.1
Maize	0.3	40.0	14.9	31.7
Wheat	3.9	93.5	27.9	46.8
Palm oil and groundnut oil	1.7	90.6	30.1	48.6
Ghana (2006 survey); Base share in poverty at 28.5%				
Rice	3.1	74.6	16.4	33.0
Bread	1.9	84.6	14.2	29.5
Flour	0.0	2.8	45.0	60.4
Guinea (2003 survey); Base share in poverty at 49.1%				
Rice	13.0	90.7	23.1	42.8
Liberia (2007 survey); Base share in poverty at 63.8%				
Local rice	9.6	60.1	27.5	47.8
Imported rice	13.2	84.9	22.3	41.2
Total rice	22.8	99.0	24.5	44.0
Mali (2006 survey); Base share in poverty at 47.5%				
Rice	7.2	95.1	11.1	25.1
Corn	4.2	91.0	14.4	33.1
Wheat	1.5	74.0	19.5	36.7
Niger (2005 survey); Base share in poverty at 62.1%				
Rice imported	4.4	54.7	14.8	31.4
Rice local	1.7	15.4	20.1	35.9
Maize	4.3	30.4	18.2	34.3

(Table continues on next page)

Table 9.1: (continued)

Food item	Share in total consumption (%)	Proportion consumers (%)	Share consumed by bottom 40%	Share consumed by bottom 60%
Senegal (2006 survey); Base share in poverty at 50.8%				
Rice	6.8	96.3	28.0	47.9
Vegetable oil	4.5	95.8	22.8	42.1
Sucre	3.0	99.2	27.1	46.6
Bread	4.0	92.7	14.8	32.6
Milk	2.1	79.6	10.0	23.4
Sierra Leone (2003 survey); Base share in poverty at 66.4%				
Rice	11.7	96.4	32.0	53.9
Togo (2006 survey); Base share in poverty at 61.6%				
Rice	3.5	92.2	23.0	40.4
Bread	0.6	27.0	5.8	15.5
Milk	0.7	31.1	7.6	18.4
Vegetable oil	1.1	81.3	21.3	39.5
Sugar	0.7	72.3	20.1	36.7
Nigeria (2004 survey); Base share in poverty at 54.7%				
Rice	4.1	73.4	14.0	30.2
Wheat flour and bread	1.5	70.4	12.5	27.0

Source: Authors' estimation using respective household surveys.

and Togo), and the proportion remains high in other countries (the minimum share of the population consuming rice is 57 percent in the Democratic Republic of Congo). For other imported foods such as bread, sugar, or milk, the proportion is lower on average, although bread and sugar in some countries are consumed by many.

However, what matters for poverty reduction is rather the share of a good's consumption that is accounted for by the poor in the population. The share of the population that is poor varies between countries, from 28.5 percent in Ghana to 71.3 percent in the Democratic Republic of Congo, so that for cross-country comparisons, it is easier to consider the share of total consumption accounted for by the bottom 40 percent or 60 percent of the population. Consider, for instance, the share of food consumption in the bottom 40 percent. For rice, this share varies from 11.1 percent in Mali to 32.0 percent in Sierra Leone. This means that if we consider the bottom 40 percent as the poor, only about 20 cents on average will benefit the poor out of every dollar spent by a government for reducing indirect taxes on rice. This is a low proportion, and also assumes that tax reductions do trickle down to lower prices for consumers, which is not necessarily true.

According to table 9.1, in Ghana only 16.4 percent of the tax cuts on rice are likely to have benefited the bottom 40 percent of the population, and this does not factor in the potential negative effect that a reduction in import taxes may have had on producer prices for local rice producers. Said differently, this policy was not well targeted from the point of view of poverty reduction although there may have been strong pressures to reduce import taxes on rice to avoid any likelihood of unrest similar to those that took place in other countries when food prices increased rapidly, from the point of view of poverty reduction this policy was not well targeted.

Who Benefits from Subsidies for Fertilizers?[1]

Another key policy implemented by the Government of Ghana at the time of the food price crisis consisted in a pilot fertilizer voucher scheme introduced in 2008. As noted in World Bank (2009), the value of the voucher was equivalent to (a) the increase in the import price of fertilizer from July 2007 to July 2008; plus (b) the cost of transporting fertilizer from the main ports to the farmers. Since the more remote areas are also those with the highest poverty rates the policy objective was not just to compensate farmers for recent global fertilizer price increase but also to promote pan-territorial pricing. Although no formal protocols were adopted efforts were made to target the scheme. First, the specific fertilizer formulations included were those for maize and other cereal production and excluded those most appropriate for cocoa and horticulture production. Second, more vouchers were printed for the poor districts in the northern areas of Ghana than elsewhere, and in excess of typical fertilizer use. Third, the staff responsible for fertilizer distribution were instructed to limit the number of vouchers per farmer (larger farmers also tend to purchase directly from importers and are outside the extension mechanism). Vouchers are redeemed through the private sector distribution system with payments made from MoFA (Ministry of Food and Agriculture) to importers in Accra. Thus importers essentially pre-finance the scheme and bear a risk of non-payment.

Of the $20 million of vouchers issues in FY2008, less than 50 percent were redeemed (redemption rates vary by compound and region), but initial results were nevertheless encouraging. Preliminary production figures for major staple foods for the 2008 season from the three northern regions showed significant increases compared to the five-year average. At the same time, the absence of clear rules determining targeting and administration of the voucher program have led to perceptions of mismanagement and leakages. Three reviews have been undertaken (an assessment of the modalities of the program by IFPRI, a small survey of beneficiaries sponsored by the Peasant Farmers Association of Ghana, and an internal workshop among MoFA staff involved in the program). Each has raised a number of concerns over the efficiency and efficacy of the program. The strengths of the program are: (a) the lead of the private sector and the Government's non-interference in the distribution of subsidized fertilizers; (b) the freedom for farmers to decide from which store to purchase fertilizers; and (c) the decision to exclude the most commonly utilized type of fertilizer in the cocoa subsector from the subsidy program, thereby ensuring adequate targeting of the program towards the food grain subsector. Apparent weaknesses include: (a) lack of an explicit beneficiary targeting mechanism; (b) lack of observance of a strict cap on the maximum number of vouchers per beneficiary; (c) heavy involvement of fertilizer importers in the implementation of the program, thereby excluding independent dealers from participating in the program; and (iv) poor communications resulting in de-facto practiced rule that dealers did not sell fertilizers to farmers without a voucher. It is also felt that by not tying in the fertilizer program to efforts to enhance the supply of improved seeds to farmers, there was a missed opportunity to boost the effectiveness of the program.

Data from GLSS5 can be used to assess who is likely to have benefited from the fertilizer program, if we are willing to assume that the distribution of the benefits from the voucher programs is somewhat similar to the distribution of the use of fertilizers in the GLSS5. Given the efforts that were made to provide more vouchers in the northern

Table 9.2: Comparing the benefit incidence of rice tax cuts and fertilizer subsidies, Ghana 2005–06

	Positive expenditure on rice, %	Positive expenditure on fertilizers, %	Amount spent on rice (all) GHc	Amount spent on fertilizers (all) GHc	Amount spent on rice (>0) GHc	Amount spent on fertilizers (>0) GHc
Residence area						
Urban	74.7	6.8	723,482	46,618	968,201	689,147
Rural	74.4	23.7	479,794	173,381	644,536	730,980
Locality						
Accra (GAMA)	65.3	0.3	729,702	1,644	1,116,862	567,611
Urban coastal	82.4	2.0	827,154	5,255	1,003,843	261,673
Urban forest	80.5	9.9	716,806	77,596	890,215	784,189
Urban savannah	71.6	21.4	584,368	128,965	816,611	602,626
Rural coastal	75.4	18.3	485,517	89,160	643,939	487,134
Rural forest	84.5	19.4	577,108	206,087	683,136	1,061,941
Rural savannah	57.7	34.4	320,274	180,858	554,843	525,006
Region						
Western	87.6	18.1	820,997	253,289	937,397	1,401,104
Central	84.7	16.0	623,365	116,092	736,132	725,281
Greater Accra	66.2	2.1	698,535	6,124	1,055,189	290,480
Volta	77.1	8.0	472,331	48,616	612,931	607,731
Eastern	78.1	13.9	574,072	106,991	734,665	770,964
Ashanti	81.2	12.3	633,554	80,050	780,625	653,301
Brong Ahafo	74.3	24.3	441,221	189,270	593,853	779,961
Northern	58.5	39.6	418,148	190,606	714,681	480,755
Upper east	60.8	40.6	326,755	195,446	537,581	481,468
Upper west	33.2	32.2	183,995	260,890	554,922	811,153
Quintile						
Q1 (poorest)	54.5	21.7	239,630	95,683	440,027	441,708
Q2	73.7	19.8	421,570	103,582	571,949	521,919
Q3	77.5	21.5	533,724	145,453	688,696	678,017
Q4	78.9	14.5	663,336	131,902	840,796	907,920
Q5 (richest)	78.3	11.0	777,354	110,726	992,589	1,005,254
Total	74.6	16.4	585,045	118,630	784,634	723,525

Source: Authors' estimation using GLSS5.

part of the country and the fact that some large users may purchase their fertilizers directly from importers, one could conjecture that the benefit incidence of the voucher program may have been more pro-poor than the patterns of use in the GLSS5. Table 9.2 provides the basic data on fertilizer use from the GLSS5 and a comparison with rice consumption. The share of households using fertilizers is much smaller than the share of households consuming rice, and the amounts spent on fertilizers are also lower than the amounts spent on rice, but for those using fertilizers, the amounts spent on them are of a similar order of magnitude to the amounts spent on rice. For benefit incidence what matters is the average amount spent on rice and fertilizers in each quintile. For rice, the average amounts are clearly increasing with the well-being of households, with the spending in the top quintile being three times higher than in the bottom quintile. For fertilizer, the amount spent in the top quintile is similar to that in the bottom quintile, and the highest amounts observed for the third and fourth quintiles are only somewhat larger than the amounts the amounts spent in the bottom quintile. This suggests that fertilizer subsidies are likely to have been better targeted to the poor than rice subsidies.

Comparing Rice Tax Cuts and Fertilizer Subsidies Using CD Curves

As shown by Makdissi and Wodon (2002) and Duclos et al. (2008), consumption or program dominance curves (CD curves) are a visual way to assess the impact of balanced budget marginal tax or subsidy reforms on poverty, and they can also be used to rank goods in terms of the impact of tax cuts and subsidies on poverty. The advantage of the technique of the CD curve is that if the curve for one good is above that for another good, then we can say that for a wide range of poverty measures as well as for any poverty line chosen by the analyst, it is better to reduce the tax (or increase the subsidy) for the good that has the higher CD curve than to reduce the tax (or increase the subsidy) for the other good. Also, if a government wants to implement a balanced budget tax reforms, if one CD curve is above another, then reducing a tax (or increasing a subsidy) on the good with the higher CD curve while increasing a tax (or reducing a subsidy) for the good with then lower CD curve can be shown to be poverty reducing. Different CD curves must be used to assess the impact of reforms on different classes of poverty measures. CD curves of the first order deal with measures such as the headcount index of poverty. CD curves of the second order deal with measures such as the poverty gap. CD curves of the third order deal with measures such as the squared poverty gap. In practice, it is often enough to look at the CD-curve of the second order, and these curves are also the easiest to interpret.

Figure 9.1 provides CD curves of the second order for rice and fertilizers in Ghana using GLSS5 data. The horizontal axis represents consumption per equivalent adult normalized by the poverty line, so that a value of one corresponds to the poverty line. The vertical axis gives the share of total consumption of a good accounted for by the population with a level of total consumption below the value of the horizontal axis. Thus at a value of one on the horizontal axis, we obtain on the vertical axis the share of total consumption of a good that is accounted for by the poor. The value on the vertical axis for a unit value on the horizontal axis is only slightly above 10 percent for rice. For fertilizers, the corresponding value is slightly above 20 percent. While this is not very high, it is still much better than the results obtained for rice, suggesting that the poor receive a share of fertilizer subsidies twice as large as the share of rice subsidies.

In figure 9.1, apart from CD curves, TD and AD curves are also provided. Following Duclos, Makdissi and Wodon (2005), TD curves simply represent the share of the beneficiaries of a tax cut or subsidy that are below a certain level of well-being. AD curves are obtained by subtracting the TD curve from the CD curve for the same good, so that AD = CD - TD. If the AD curve is below (above) the horizontal axis,

Figure 9.1: Consumption dominance curves for rice and fertilizers, second order

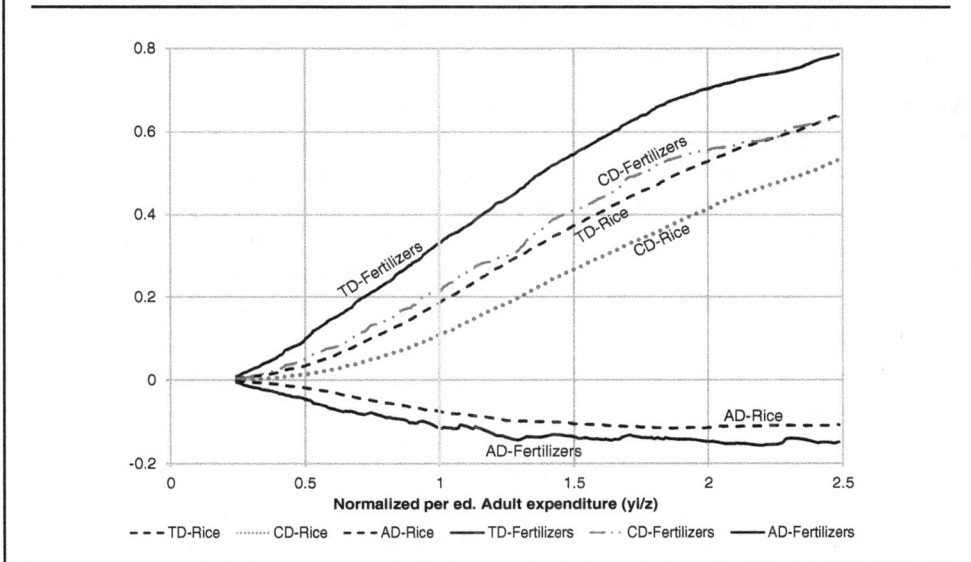

Source: Authors' estimates using GLSS5.

it simply means that the allocation effects of the tax cut or subsidy is such that it reduces (increases) targeting performance. It can be seen that the allocation effects, namely the differences in the amounts of tax cuts or subsidies received by different beneficiaries, are below the horizontal axis for both rice and fertilizers, suggesting that better off households among beneficiaries tend to benefit from larger amounts of subsidies or tax cuts simply because they consume much more of the good. The AD curve for fertilizers is below the AD curve for rice, suggesting even more inequality in consumption among fertilizer subsidy beneficiaries than among rice tax cut beneficiaries. However, the TD curve for fertilizers, which shows how poor beneficiaries are, is much higher than the TD curve for rice. Thus it is because of better beneficiary targeting that the fertilizer subsidies are more poverty reducing than the rice tax cuts.

The Government of Ghana is planning to continue the voucher scheme in 2009 and extend it through 2015. While the original aim was to prevent reduction in the use of fertilizers due to high prices, the intention now appears to be to stimulate its use. This is a good idea given that fertilizer use per hectare in Ghana is low in absolute terms, that the majority of farmers have little experience in using fertilizers (as shown in table 9.2, only one in four rural households was using fertilizers in 2005–06), and that the use of fertilizer, along with use of improved seeds, is an important determinant of productivity/ha. The results from the benefit incidence analysis however suggest that there is scope for improving the targeting of the program to the poor. This could be done by ensuring that poorer areas benefit from a larger share of the subsidies/

vouchers, and that a cap is enforced on the maximum amount of vouchers that could be received by single farmers.

Medium Term Effects: Comparing Rice Tax Cuts with Agricultural Productivity Gains

Although not very well targeted to the poor, fertilizer subsidies are likely to still be better targeted to the poor than tax cuts on imported foods such as rice. They also have potentially beneficial medium-term effects, while rice tax cuts have potentially negative medium term effects. In the case of the rice tax cuts, the potential negative effect is due to the fact that the tax cuts reduce the price of rice in the country, and thereby dampen incentives for local farmers to increase their production. Fertilizers have the opposite effect, because they can lead to an increase in productivity and thereby in incomes for farmers.

The medium term effects of tax cuts versus initiatives such as fertilizers that aim to improve productivity can be illustrated through results obtained by Nouve and Wodon (2008) with a dynamic CGE model for Mali. Rice production is captured in the model through two activities: food crop production whereby the paddy is produced, and cereal milling whereby the crop is transformed into rice actually sold on markets. The value of local rice production (milling) amounted to US$ 140 million or 3.1 percent of the GDP in 2004, with nearly 80 percent of the value of rice production coming from the purchase of intermediate inputs, mainly paddy. Still, only about half of the rice consumed in Mali is produced locally, with the rest being imported.

The question dealt with by the authors is as follows: what could be the impact of the increase in the world price for rice on rice production, rice consumption, rice prices, and poverty in Mali with and without policy responses? Two policy responses are considered. The first measure consists in the elimination of the import tax on rice to help offset part of the negative impact on the poor of the increase in international prices. The second policy response is the government's "rice initiative" that aims to boost domestic production. Through this initiative land should be set aside and agricultural equipment and inputs would be provided to increase the production of paddy by 50 percent to reach 1.6 million tons per year, which would provide one million tons of marketable rice (including some production that could be exported). The increase in local rice production requires higher productivity.

The CGE model is used to simulate the potential impact of both policy responses, and to compare the effectiveness of each not only in the short run, but in the medium term as well. Six scenarios are considered. The base scenario is business as usual. Rice prices, rice taxes, and rice productivity all remain unchanged. The second scenario is based on an increase in the international price of rice of 80 percent (the increase that took place between July 2007 and July 2008 in Franc CFA). The third scenario considers an increase in international rice prices of 110 percent, corresponding to the increase in US dollar terms in the price of rice. Next, the authors consider four other scenarios based on the two policy responses from the authorities (the policies are examined individually and jointly). Under the second scenario, the average price of rice (which covers both imported and locally produced rice) increases by 21 percent in 2008 against the base scenario. This is a much lower increase than the 80 percent increase in the international price of rice in large part because a majority of the rice consumed is produced domestically, and this proportion increases when the price of imported rice shoots up. This estimated increase in the price of rice is very much in line with what has been observed in the country. According to a USAID Mali (2008) brief, the price of rice increase by about 25 percent. If Mali had not been partially protected from higher rice prices thanks to the appreciation of the Euro and the CFAF versus the U.S. dollar, the increase in the average price of rice of the country would have been slightly higher.

In the CGE model, the removal of import tax duties on imported rice does not seem to have a large effect on the average price of rice, since depending on the year the reduction in the price increase thanks to the tax cuts is only of one to two percentage points. This is perhaps less than expected, but stems from the fact that imported and domestic rice are imperfect substitutes, and from the fact that the removal of taxes is relatively small as compared to the exogenous increase in international prices for rice. The scenarios under which productivity is increased (which can be associated to the fertilizer policy in the case of Ghana) have a much larger impact on rice prices, with a downward pressure on prices of about seven percent. The model also predicts a substantial supply response and a sharp decrease in imported rice to the benefit of domestic rice following the increase in the international price of rice. Under the scenario corresponding to the 80 percent increase in international prices, rice production increases by 24 percent in the first year, and up to 28 percent by 2012. Under the additional measures taken by the authorities, including measures to boost productivity, the increase is larger, reaching 32 percent in the first year, and up to 43 percent by 2012. These are very large increases in production, but they are still below the announced (and ambitious) objectives of the Government of Mali to increase rice production by 50 percent. As production of rice increases, imports decrease. The total demand for rice (imported and domestic) decreases by three to seven percentage points depending on the scenarios and years.

The most important results are those obtained for poverty. Under the first baseline scenario, the headcount index of poverty increases by 0.7 percentage points in the first year versus the baseline, and the overall increase after five years is 0.89 points. Given that Mali's population is at around 12 million people, this means that 107,000 people would fall into poverty. If Mali had not been protected by the appreciation of its currency, so that the international price of rice would have increased by 110 percent and the average price in the country by 26 percent, the increase in poverty would have reached 0.99 percentage points under the second scenario by the year 2012. Under the policy scenarios, the beneficial impact of the import and other tax cuts on rice is very limited, with these policies generating a gain in poverty reduction of only a tenth of a percentage point for most scenarios and simulation years. By contrast, the impact of an increase in productivity is much larger, since as of the year 2009, this increase in productivity is such that poverty is actually reduced following the initial international price shock.

Conclusion

The first response of many African governments to the food price crisis has consisted in implementing broad-based tax cuts and/or subsidies for basic food staples such as rice, but these subsidies tend to be poorly targeted. This has been confirmed in the case of Ghana, because the nonpoor tend to consume the largest share of the food items on which tax cuts were implemented. Fertilizer subsidies, while still not likely to be well targeted, at least better reach the poor than tax cuts for imported foods. In addition, as illustrated in the case of research for Mali, measures to increase agricultural productivity, for example through higher fertilizer use, tend to have a much larger beneficial impact for poverty reduction because farmers are able to increase their incomes substantially, while the increase in production also puts pressure down on prices paid by consumers. Thus fertilizer subsidies are better than import tax cuts as a policy response mechanism at a time of crisis both in the short run in terms of their benefit incidence for the poor, and in the medium run in terms of supply response. But in the case of Ghana, measures (such as geographic targeting or other mechanisms to reach comparatively poorer farmers) should probably also be taken to ensure that fertilizer subsidies reach the poor in priority.

Note

1. Background on the fertilizer program was written by Chris Jackson and is reproduced with permission of the World Bank (2009).

CHAPTER 10

Electricity Subsidies in Ghana

Clarence Tsimpo and Quentin Wodon

Ghana is currently facing a severe power crisis which could have significant macroeconomic repercussions. The prevailing tariff structure does not enable the sector to be financially sustainable, yet there are legitimate concerns about raising tariffs. In the case of residential customers, prevailing tariffs include subsidies for households who consume small amounts of electricity. It is feared that an increase in tariffs could exacerbate poverty. Yet while prevailing subsidies are supposed to be targeted to the poor, this may not necessarily be the case, because many among the poor simply do not have access to electricity. This chapter provides an analysis of the targeting performance of electricity consumption subsidies in Ghana as well as other African countries. On the basis of data from the GLSS5 and the tariff structure in place in 2005/06, it appears that only about 9 percent of the electricity subsidies reach the poor in Ghana, and similar findings are observed elsewhere. Connection subsidies by contrast could be much better targeted to the poor. It would therefore be preferable to shift from consumption to connection subsidies, while at the same time restoring the financial sustainability of the utilities.

Issues with Maintaining Electricity Residential Consumption Subsidies

In Africa it is tempting to subsidize residential electricity services. As the population is often poor, the need to make service affordable appears to be paramount in a large majority of countries. Electricity is more and more considered as a basic necessity, it is widely perceived to have important externalities for education and health outcomes, and to contribute in a decisive way to economic growth. However, the cost of a standard electricity bill would not be affordable for many households. For households connected to the network, electricity often represents from 3 to 5 percent of total consumption, and sometimes more. Considering that in many cases 60 percent of a household's budget must be devoted to food to cover nutritional needs, this makes it difficult for households connected to the electricity network to pay for electricity without sacrificing other basic necessities. As for those households who do not have a connection to the electricity network today, the share of total expenditure that they would have to allocate to electricity if they were connected to the network could even be even higher than 3 to 5 percent (since these households tend to be poorer), especially for the poor in rural areas.

The desire to make electricity affordable combined to the high levels of poverty in sub-Saharan countries, including in urban areas, has led governments and regulatory agencies to maintain tariffs at an artificially low level. The tariffs have often not followed the general increase in the cost of living, nor have they factored in the recent increases in oil prices. As a result, most utilities are not able today to properly maintain their network, yet alone expending it. At the same time, increasing tariffs is politically difficult for governments and regulatory agencies. First, such increases in tariffs would be highly visible for electricity customers who will feel it right away (especially as bills are paid only once a month, for relatively large amounts for the poor), while they may not know much about the cost structures of their utilities and the need for such tariffs increases. In addition, such increases in tariffs affect urban populations disproportionately, but these are the populations that are most likely to demonstrate in the streets against such increases, thereby threatening the hold on power of their elites.

While the temptation to keep subsidizing electricity tariffs for residential customers is high (as well as in many cases for commercial and industrial customers, but for other reasons), the cost of doing this is high for the economy and the population as a whole, and especially the poor. The cost of generating, transmitting and delivering electricity is high, in part because the populations served by the electricity network are often small (at least in the smaller countries of West and Central Africa), which prevents, to some extent, the utilities to reap the full benefit of economies of scale. In addition, many countries are landlocked, with high transportation costs, and limited hydroelectric power, which also contributes to high generation costs due to the need to rely on thermal power. Thus, due in part to high and increasing generation costs, subsidies that may appear to be limited at the household level tend to actually be very expensive at the macroeconomic level, especially when compared to the limited resources available to governments through taxation and foreign aid. Said differently, under strict budget constraints, subsidizing electricity has a direct cost in terms of crowding out today or in the future (typically through the accumulation of debt for the utilities but guaranteed by governments) resources for public interventions aimed at poverty reduction, be it through programs for employment creation or through improvements in education and health service provision.

In addition, there is a perverse incentive that derives from the inability of utilities to cover their costs due to low tariffs. When utilities are operating at a loss, or at least cannot properly fund their maintenance and investment costs, they have no incentives to expand the network, since expanding the network would probably imply increasing their losses. At the margin, new customers may be poorer than existing customers, thereby increasing the cost of delivery and also increasing the risk of non-payment. Furthermore, when investments are not sufficient, expanding the network to new customers is also problematic because of the limited generation capacity installed, which already translates into repeated cuts during the day. Finally, adding consumption through an expansion of the network often tends to further increases the average cost of generating electricity, since at the margin, even when countries have access to cheap hydroelectric power, the additional demand must be met through costly fuel generation.

The consequence of the above is that many utilities are trapped in a vicious circle. It can be shown that for the poor, the benefits of network extension are substantially larger than the benefits from the subsidization of electricity consumption. At the same time, without enough revenues to cover their operating and maintenance costs fully, utilities cannot seriously think about network expansions, as this might exacerbate their losses. In addition, poor quality of service, which is in part the consequence of the lack of revenues, limits the willingness of customers to pay a higher price for a service that is considered by them as deficient, for example, due to repeated cuts during the day. As to regulatory agencies and governments, given substantial price increases for oil, and thereby the cost of generating power, they are under pressures to reduce existing subsidies, especially in the context of their broader commitment to implement poverty reduction strategies. However, the fear of a backslash from the population makes such a reduction in subsidies difficult to implement. All three parties are in a situation that does not benefit them.

In the above context, the contribution of this chapter is to try to demonstrate a simple fact: that electricity subsidies are among the least well targeted subsidies that governments can implement, and that therefore the argument regarding the need to preserve these subsidies to make the services affordable for the poor, while valid for the small fraction of the poor connected today to the network, does not hold when considering what is required to accelerate poverty reduction more broadly. Said differently, even if some poor households would be hurt by a removal or substantial reduction in the electricity subsidies that are prevailing in many countries, the gains that could be achieved in terms of poverty reduction by reallocating the resources now allocated to these subsidies could be very large, with many other poor households benefiting, and with a restoration of profitability in the sector also conducive to growth itself.

The analysis of the targeting performance of electricity consumption subsidies in this chapter is based on nationally representative surveys from many countries, including the GLSS5 for Ghana. We find that in Ghana only about 10 percent of utility subsidies reach the poor. Following Angel-Urdinola and Wodon (2007a, 2007b), we also look at the determinants of the targeting performance of electricity subsidies by relying on a simple decomposition that allows us to analyze both "access" and "subsidy-design" factors that affect the overall targeting performance of subsidies.

Do the Poor Benefit from Inverted Block Tariff Structures?

Residential electricity tariffs tend to be below utility costs in Africa, so that customers receive substantial subsidies. These subsidies are implicit in the inverted block tariff structure used. The tariff structure for Ghana at the time of the GLSS4 and GLSS5 surveys is provided in table 10.1. Three points are worth emphasizing. First, prices per kWh are typically lower for the lower brackets of consumption in kWh per month (assuming that the customers in the lower brackets are close to the upper threshold of consumption of that bracket). The objective is to try to make electricity more affordable for the poor, under the assumption that the quantity consumed by a poor household is typically lower than that consumed by a richer household. Note however that the prices follows an Inverted Block Tariff (IBT) structure whereby even those who consume large amounts of electricity benefit from subsidies for part of their consumption. That is, everybody pays the same price between 50 kWh and 300 kWh, even if the total consumption of a household is above 300 kWh. If prices for lower levels of consumption were accessible only to households whose total consumption is below that level, then we would have a so-called Volume Differentiated Tariff (VDT), whereby only those consuming between 50 kWh and 300 kWh would benefit from the price associated to that bracket. Presumably the subsidies would be better targeted to the poor under a VDT than an IBT, but this depends on the consumption profile of households. The working assumption in this chapter is that the price per kWh in the highest bracket of consumption in the tariff schedule can be used as a first approximation of the cost of providing the service (this simplifies cross-country comparisons but the assumption is not crucial because the estimates of targeting performance are not very sensitive to that assumption).

Table 10.1: Tariff structure for residential customers of electricity

	1998/99 (GLSS4)	2005/06 (GLLS5)
Prime fixe	2000 GHc	13000 GHc
0–50 Kwh	—	—
50–300 Kwh	50 GHc	610 GHc
300–600 Kwh	75 GHc	1065 GHc
> 600 Kwh	180 GHc	1065 GHc

Source: Ghana PURC.
Note: — = not available.

We use a simple framework not only to analyze the targeting performance of electricity subsidies in about 20 African countries, but also to understand what affects targeting performance through access (who uses electricity) and subsidy design factors (who benefits from subsidies and by how much among users). The targeting performance indicator used, denoted by Ω (Omega), is simply the share of the subsidies received by the poor divided by the proportion of the population in poverty. In other words, a value of one for Ω implies that the subsidy distribution among the poor is proportional to their share in the overall population. If the poor account for 30 percent of the population, then a neutral targeting mechanism would allocate 30 percent of the subsidy to the poor. A value (lower) greater than one implies that the subsidy distribution is (regressive) progressive, since the share of benefits allocates to the poor is (lower) larger than its share in the total population. For instance, suppose that 30 percent of the population is poor and that they obtain 60 percent of the subsidy benefits. In such case, Ω would equal to two, meaning that the poor are receiving twice as much subsidies as the population on average. As shown in figure 10.1, in none of the countries is the targeting indicator superior to one, and it is often well below one. While there are some comparability issues between countries, the message is clear: utility subsidies tend to be poorly targeted, with on average the poor benefiting only from a fourth to a third of what a household randomly selected in the population as a whole would get. In Ghana, the value of Ω is 0.31. Given that in the GLSS5, 28.5 percent of the population is considered as poor, this means that 9 percent of the subsidies reach the poor.

While most indicators of targeting performance are silent as to why subsidies are targeted the way they are (they only give an idea a whether the subsidies reach the poor or not and to what extent), the framework used here allows for analyzing both "access" and "subsidy design" factors that affect targeting performance. Access factors as those related to the availability of electricity service in the area where a household lives and to the household's choice to connect to the network when service is available. These access factors have a strong influence on targeting performance but are usually difficult to change in the short run. Subsidy factors are more susceptible to policy design, such as changes in tariff structures affecting who is targeted to receive the subsidies, as well as the rates of subsidization and the quantities of electricity consumed by the households who benefit from the subsidies. It turns out that most electricity subsidy mechanisms are poorly targeted, essentially because most of the poor lack access to the electricity network and therefore cannot benefit from electricity subsidies, but also because the existing tariff structures are not designed in a way to target subsidies to the poor.

This can be seen in figure 10.2, which decomposes the value of the targeting indicator into access and subsidy design factors, so that $\Omega = $ (Access Factors) × (Subsidy Design

Figure 10.1: Targeting performance (Ω) of electricity subsidies, African countries

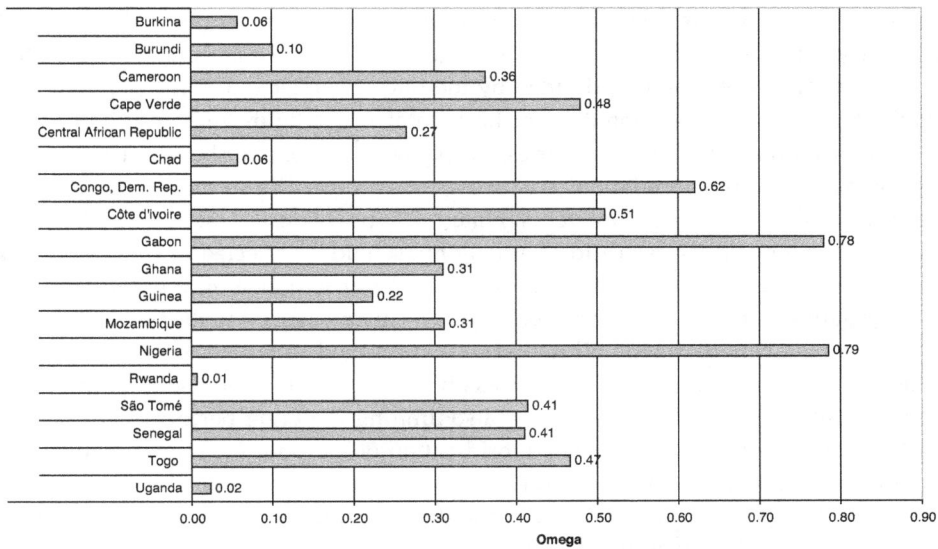

Country	Omega
Burkina	0.06
Burundi	0.10
Cameroon	0.36
Cape Verde	0.48
Central African Republic	0.27
Chad	0.06
Congo, Dem. Rep.	0.62
Côte d'Ivoire	0.51
Gabon	0.78
Ghana	0.31
Guinea	0.22
Mozambique	0.31
Nigeria	0.79
Rwanda	0.01
São Tomé	0.41
Senegal	0.41
Togo	0.47
Uganda	0.02

Source: Wodon et al. (2009).

Figure 10.2: Access factors and subsidy design factors affecting targeting performance

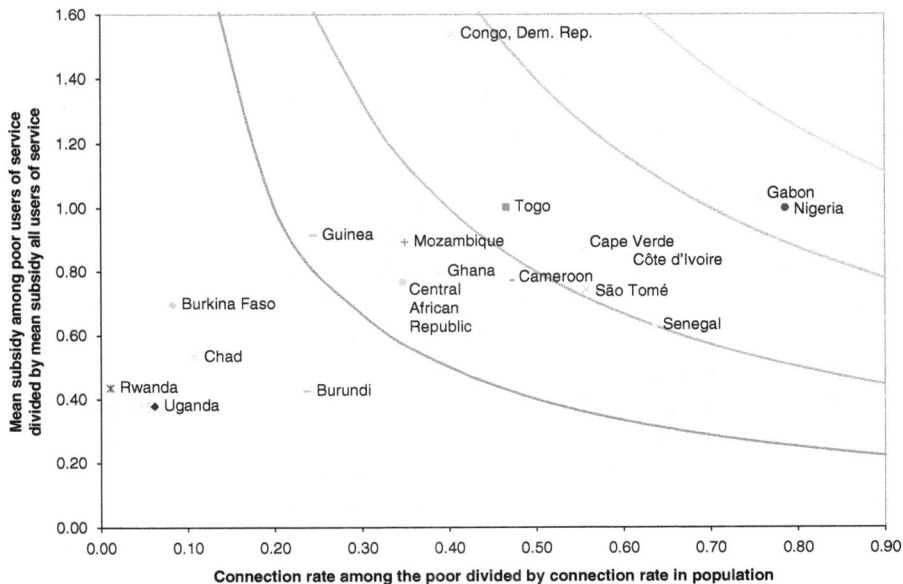

Source: Wodon et al. (2009).

Factors). The two access factors are first, whether a household lives in an area served by the electricity network, and second, whether a household in such an area is actually connected or not to the network, i.e., whether the household actually "takes up" the service. The value of the Access Factors is simply the rate of connection among the poor to the network (which depends on access at the neighborhood level and uptake by households in areas where there is access) divided by the rate of connection in the population as a whole. This variable is presented on the horizontal axis in figure 10.2, and as expected, it is much lower than one for all countries, simply because the poor have much lower connection rates than the population as a whole, on average. The second variable affecting the value of the targeting parameter is related to subsidy design factors which take into account who benefits from subsidies among households connected to the network, and how large the subsidies are. What the vertical axis represents is simply the ratio of the average subsidy among all poor households who are connected to the network, divided by the average benefit among all households connected to the network, whether poor or nonpoor. In many countries, the values on the vertical axis representing the subsidy design factors are below unity, thereby also limiting targeting performance. The main explanation is that while the rate of subsidization of the poor (i.e., the discount versus the full cost of providing electricity for the utility) is often larger than for the population as a whole that is connected to the network, the quantities consumed by the population as a whole tend to be larger than those consumed by the poor, so that the overall subsidy received by the poor is lower on average than that received by the population as a whole.

Connection Subsidies as an Alternative to Consumption Subsidies

It is clear from the empirical analysis of the targeting performance of electricity subsidies presented above that consumption subsidies for electricity appear to be poorly targeted in African countries, including in Ghana. One alternative to consumption subsidies would be to provide instead connection subsidies, assuming that the generation or production capacity is sufficient to expand the network. Figure 10.3 provides the potential targeting performance of connection subsidies under three scenarios. First, we assume that connection subsidies will be distributed in the same way as existing connections. This is a pessimistic assumption from a distributional point of view since it tends to favor better off households, but it could be realistic if access rates to the network are low. Second, we assume that new connections could be distributed randomly among households who are currently not connected, but live in a neighborhood where connections are available. Third, we assume that new connection subsidies could be randomly distributed among all households who do not currently have access. This is a very optimistic assumption given that many of these households do not live in neighborhoods where access is available.

As shown in figure 10.3, the value of Ω is largest under the assumption that new connections benefit households who are selected randomly from the population without access. In all countries, Ω is larger than one under this assumption. Yet the assumption is not realistic. The second scenario assumes that households who benefit from new connections are selected from non-served households living in those areas where there is already access to the network. The values of Ω, while often lower than one, are still much better than those for consumption subsidies. In the third scenario, targeting performance

Figure 10.3: Potential targeting performance of connection subsidies under various scenarios

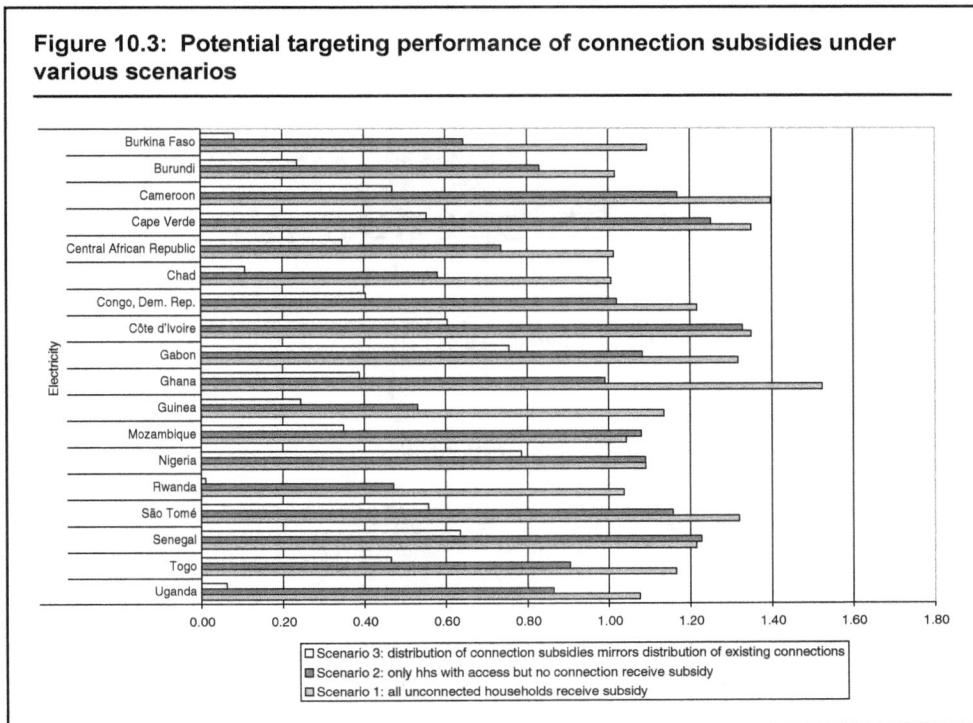

Scenario 3: distribution of connection subsidies mirrors distribution of existing connections
Scenario 2: only hhs with access but no connection receive subsidy
Scenario 1: all unconnected households receive subsidy

Source: Wodon et al. (2009).

remains poor. Thus, if connection subsidies could be designed to reach the majority of households not connected today but living in areas where service is provided, the targeting performance of those subsidies would be better than that of consumption subsidies. In addition, connection subsidies help in reducing the cost of service for users (as compared to using candles for lighting for example), while also bringing in positive externalities in areas such as education and health.

Conclusion

To conclude, this chapter has provided an analysis of the targeting performance of electricity consumption subsidies in Ghana as well as other African countries. Only about 10 percent of the electricity subsidies reach the poor in Ghana. Connection subsidies by contrast could potentially be much better targeted to the poor. Both from the point of view of poverty reduction and from the point of view of budget sustainability, it would therefore be preferable to shift from consumption to connection subsidies, while at the same time restoring the financial sustainability of the utilities.

CHAPTER 11

Benefit Incidence of Public Education Spending in Ghana

Harold Coulombe, Caroline Ly, and Quentin Wodon

Public funding for education accounts for a substantial share of the government's annual budget. This chapter provides a benefit incidence analysis of who benefits from public spending for education. The analysis is carried for all major levels of education (primary education, junior secondary education, senior secondary education, vocational and technical education, teacher training, and tertiary education). Unit costs are computed by comparing public spending using 2007 administrative data and district level school enrollment from the 2003 CWIQ survey to be able to estimate district-level unit costs of provision. The results suggest that despite an increase in funding for primary education in 2007, the poorest quintiles of children in age of schooling still benefit only from a relatively small share of total education spending (12 percent).

Principles of Benefit Incidence Analysis

Benefit incidence analysis is extensively used by national governments and international organizations to assess who benefits from public spending in areas such as education, health, and basic infrastructure services, often with recommendations on how the allocation of public spending could be improved to reduce poverty. However, the assumptions used in most empirical applications of the tool are often problematic. First differences between areas in the costs of service delivery of public services are rarely taken into account when assessing who benefits from public spending for such services. Second, differences in needs between various household groups also tend to be overlooked. In this chapter we provide a benefit incidence analysis of public spending for education in Ghana that takes differences in costs and needs into account. We start in this section with methodological considerations.

As noted by Demery (2003), the starting point in conducting a benefit incidence analysis lies in assessing the use of government services by households, typically by relying on data from a nationally representative household survey. This information is then combined with data on the cost for the government to provide the services, so that one can estimate the share of public spending that is allocated to different groups of households, for example classified according to quintiles of well-being. In most case studies of benefit incidence analysis embedded in poverty assessments and public expenditure reviews prepared by international organizations or national governments, data on unit cost are provided at an aggregate level. Denote by S_i the net government spending on education level i, with i =1, 2, 3 representing the level of education (primary, secondary and tertiary). The value S_i should represent net costs for the government after having deducted fees and receipts from cost recovery mechanisms. Denote by E_{ij} the number of children enrolled in school of group j at education level i, and by E_i the total number of children enrolled at that level. Only students attending government-subsidized (i.e., typically public) schools should be taken into account in the estimation. Then, S_i/E_i can be considered as the average unit cost for the government of providing education services at level i. A group's benefit share of total public spending is equal to the weighted sum of the group's share of total enrollment at each level of education, with the weight defined by the shares of the total budget allocated to the various levels of education.

As noted by Wodon and Ye (2009), a problem with this approach is that if there are differences in unit costs between areas, there may be a bias in the estimates of benefit incidence. Specifically, areas with higher (lower) unit costs than the average unit costs will appear in the analysis as benefiting from a smaller (larger) share of education benefit than their true share. A second issue discussed by Wodon and Ye (2009) relates to how aggregate results are presented in traditional benefit incidence analysis. To make comparisons between groups, or to assess whether the share of total benefits received by any given group can be considered as equitable, it is standard to compare the share of the benefits received by a group to the group's population share in the total population. The issue however is that public services often target specific groups, rather than the population as a whole, so that when comparisons are made using groupings related to the population as a whole we may again observe a bias. Assume for example that one presents the estimates of total education funding received by five quintiles of the population defined according to well-being (defined in Ghana on the basis of consumption per equivalent adult). Each quintile may receive 20 percent of total funding, in which case it could be concluded that funding is equally benefitting all groups in the population in terms of well-being. But the poorest quintile of population accounts for more than 20 percent of the children in age of schooling, simply because poorer families tend to have more children. In this case, the proportion of education funding received by child in age of schooling will be lower in the poorest quintile than in higher quintiles. To assess the fairness of the distribution of public spending for education, it is necessary to present the data according to the target population group, which in the present case would mean estimating the share of funding that goes to the various quintiles of children in age of schooling, rather than the various population quintiles. We will compare in this chapter the estimates obtained in both the traditional and needs-based approach.

Data on Public Spending for Education and Estimation of Unit Costs of Schooling

An effort was made by the Government of Ghana to increase public spending for primary schools over the last few years. Table 11.1 provides data on the shares of public spending for education allocated to various levels from 2004 until 2008. The benefit incidence analysis presented in this paper is based on the data for 2007 which represents actual expenditures instead of allocations. The shares in table 11.1 include both recurrent and investment spending, but our analysis for the benefit incidence analysis focuses on recurrent spending. The share of total education spending allocated to pre-school education decreases from 4.0 percent in 2004 to 3.4 percent in 2007. The share allocated to

Table 11.1: Trends in the percentage share of total expenditure per level of education (%)

	2004 Expenditure	2005 Expenditure	2006 Expenditure	2007 Allocation	2007 Expenditure	2008 Allocation
Pre-school	4.0	3.4	3.9	4.3	3.4	4.5
Primary	31.6	29.9	27.6	37.9	35.0	36.7
JHS	16.0	17.8	16.8	18.5	16.3	18.6
SHS	19.9	20.8	15.8	9.1	12.6	13.1
TVET	1.1	1.2	0.9	2.4	0.6	1.9
SPED	0.4	0.4	0.4	0.5	0.3	0.8
NFED	1.6	1.9	0.7	0.6	0.4	0.6
Teacher education	3.7	3.9	3.5	3.4	2.6	3.8
Tertiary	21.0	19.6	22.5	20.1	23.0	19.3
Management & subvented	0.5	1.0	7.7	3.0	5.5	0.8
HIV-AIDS	0.2	0.1	0.3	0.0	0.2	—
Total	**100**	**100**	**100**	**100**	**100**	**100.0**

Source: Ministry of Education.
Note: — = not available.

primary education first decreased until 2006, then increases sharply with expenditure in 2007 equal to 35.0 percent of the total budget. The proportion of expenditure assigned to JHS fluctuates between 16 percent and 18 percent, while there was a sharp decrease in the share allocated to SHS over time. The share allocated to tertiary education increased from 21 percent in 2004 to 23 percent in 2007.

Most of the education spending is used for teacher salaries and is transferred to the districts. We were able to use detailed information on district-level spending to compute district-level unit costs at the primary, junior secondary and senior secondary levels. We also estimated unit costs at the regional and at the national level to assess whether going down to the district level made a difference in results (in addition, at higher levels of schooling, it is better to rely on regional or national unit costs estimates because of the relatively small numbers of students in the poorest districts attending these levels of schooling; furthermore, at the tertiary level, funding is typically not directly allocated to districts).

The district-level estimates of unit costs were obtained by dividing total spending per level of education at the district level in 2007 by the number of students at that level in any given district, with this number of students estimated using the 2003 CWIQ survey. The reason for using the CWIQ survey is that it enables us to assess to which quintile of well-being every student belongs, while administrative data on school enrollment by district do not contain information that can be used to assess the location in the distribution of well-being of the household to which a student belongs. The assignment of the students to various quintiles of well-being was made on the basis of the predicted consumption per equivalent adult obtained in the construction of the new poverty map for Ghana.

The use of the 2003 CWIQ as opposed to the 2005–06 GLSS or administrative data to assess the number of students at various levels of schooling has pros and cons. On the positive side, the advantage of the CWIQ survey is that its sample size makes it representative at the district level, while the GLSS5 is representative only at the regional level. In addition, the larger sample size of the CWIQ makes the results more robust, especially for higher levels of schooling such as technical and vocational education where the number of observations in the GLSS5 is limited. The disadvantage of using the 2003 CWIQ data as opposed to administrative data is that enrollment rates increased between 2003 and 2007. To the extent that the poorest districts benefited from a larger increase in enrollment rates between 2003 and 2007 than the richest districts (the increase in enrollment was due in part to the introduction of the new capitation grants which initially targeted deprived districts), by using the 2003 CWIQ data instead of administrative data we would overestimate the unit costs for the poorest district in comparison to the unit costs for better off districts. This would probably not lead to a bias in our benefit incidence analysis however. Indeed what we rely on when constructing the quintiles of well-being is the total number of children in age of schooling in each district. If we had data on enrollment rates by quintile in 2007, we would obtain lower unit costs in the poorest districts where enrollment is likely to have increased the most between 2003 and 2007. However, the total amount of funding allocated to the poorest districts, and thereby to the population in age of schooling in those districts would remain the same, and this is what matters the most for the benefit incidence. The data from the CWIQ is principally used to allocate spending according to quintile levels, and the quintile assignment in the CWIQ is based on data from the GLSS5 valid for 2005/06. Thus the underestimation of enrolled students is not a major issue (what could change benefit incidence results is a change in demographics for example).

A number of adjustments had to be made to the data for the estimations. First, the 2007 district budget data covered 138 districts, while the 2003 CWIQ survey covers only 110 districts (this is due to the increase in the number of districts between the two years). To reconcile the data sets, the analysis was carried on 110 districts by aggregating the budget data for the new districts. As mentioned earlier, the detailed budget data enable us to compute unit costs for many different levels: Pre-school, primary, JSS, SSS, vocational and technical training, teacher training, and tertiary. More recently JSS has been renamed JHS for Junior High School and similarly SSS been renamed SHS for Senior High School. For each level of schooling, we have data on expenditures for personnel per district, but most of the data on spending for general administration is at the regional or national level. All nondistrict budget data (i.e., regional and national administrative budgets) were attributed to the different district on a pro-rated (number of students) basis, but with two exceptions. Vocational education and teacher training data were used at the regional levels only, and data on spending for tertiary education were used only at the national level. In the CWIQ survey, the number of students estimated to compute the unit costs was based on the students enrolled in state-funded schools, taking into account the survey sample weights. The data on student enrollment were disaggregated into the seven education levels described above. To compute national and regional level unit costs, the corresponding data on student enrollment were aggregated at those levels.

The resulting unit costs are provided in table 11.2. The first panel in the table provides key statistics on our budget data, which differ a bit from the estimates in table 11.1, especially at the tertiary level. Primary schools benefited from the largest overall budget (302 million GH¢), closely followed by the tertiary level (293 million GH¢). Secondary schools had a budget of 219 million GH¢ (159 million GH ¢ for JHS and 60 million GH¢ for SHS). It was possible to provide breakdown of those budgets by region in all cases except for tertiary education. The second panel in the table provides school enrollment data by level and region as obtained from the 2003 CWIQ. For all level prior to SHS, the Ashanti region is by far the region with the largest number of students. At higher levels Ashanti shares its position with the greater Accra region.

Table 11.2: Budget, enrollment and unit costs, per region and national

Region	Pre-school	Primary	JHS	SHS	Tertiary	Vocational	Teacher training
Total Annual Budget, in 1,000 GH¢, 2007							
Western	4,071	27,119	13,683	4,267	—	433	1,750
Central	2,197	31,811	19,126	7,962	—	402	2,199
Greater Accra	1,527	24,795	16,965	6,240	—	1,090	1,461
Volta	3,570	30,930	23,337	6,901	—	814	4,481
Eastern	5,187	43,528	23,531	8,573	—	—	5,055
Ashanti	5,747	58,519	31,020	13,328	—	749	5,586
Brong Ahafo	4,973	39,348	16,498	5,760	—	—	2,537
Northern	1,207	28,366	7,051	3,966	—	354	2,410
Upper East	1,028	10,720	4,210	1,914	—	618	1,028
Upper West	861	6,518	3,745	1,479	—	157	1,112
National	30,501	301,736	159,086	60,258	292,931	4,617	27,600
School enrollment, 2003							
Western	74,436	254,673	80,846	32,294	5,942	4,589	1,644
Central	63,643	227,494	82,855	22,333	6,796	3,814	1,377
Greater Accra	25,103	170,010	98,507	64,186	31,388	9,822	1,282
Volta	54,422	248,412	89,325	22,448	5,347	3,036	1,853
Eastern	79,151	316,595	110,853	31,770	4,509	4,873	2,420
Ashanti	131,553	431,374	157,381	72,387	18,987	7,215	4,438
Brong Ahafo	76,785	251,289	73,268	25,086	5,702	1,968	775
Northern	36,271	226,576	44,272	19,992	4,864	2,541	1,807
Upper East	20,195	131,440	25,261	11,109	1,969	1,583	1,508
Upper West	7,076	51,719	10,722	3,828	1,305	771	314
National	568,636	2,309,582	773,289	305,434	86,809	40,211	17,418
Unit cost in GH¢							
Western	55	107	169	132	—	94	1,065
Central	35	140	231	357	—	105	1,597
Greater Accra	61	146	172	97	—	111	1,140
Volta	66	125	261	307	—	268	2,418
Eastern	66	138	212	270	—	—	2,089
Ashanti	44	136	197	184	—	104	1,259
Brong Ahafo	65	157	225	230	—	—	3,275
Northern	33	125	159	198	—	139	1,333
Upper East	51	82	167	172	—	391	682
Upper West	122	126	349	386	—	203	3,541
National	54	131	206	197	3,374	115	1,586

Source: Authors.
Note: — = not available.

The last panel in table 11.2 shows our unit costs defined as the total budget for any given level divided by our estimates of school enrollment (for the pre-school, primary, and secondary levels, we also estimated unit costs at the district level, as mentioned above). On average the unit cost at the primary level is estimated at 131 GH¢ per pupil per year, while it is estimated at around 200 GH¢ at the secondary level. Unit costs are significantly higher at the tertiary level, at 3,374 GH¢. For most levels, the Upper West region has higher unit costs that other regions, and only its primary level unit cost is in line with the national average. It is likely that those much higher unit costs results from smaller class sizes and higher per student administrative cost, with lower school enrollment in the Upper West region stemming not only from lower population density, but probably also in part from a demand side issue (some households in extreme poverty may not be able to send their children to school). In the more densely populated Upper East region, unit costs are more in line with national averages. Similar data are available by district but not shown here due to space limitation.

Results from the Benefit Incidence Analysis

Table 11.3 provides the results from the benefit incidence analysis, with each of the quintiles representing 20 percent of children in age of schooling rather than 20 percent of the population. The data are thus based on all children aged 5 to 25 plus any student enrolled who is aged above 25. The benefit incidence analysis estimates are computed using nationwide unit costs as well as district- and region-specific unit costs. The use of district-level estimates tends to reduce the estimates of the benefits obtained by children in the poorest quintiles, and increase the share received by the children in the richest quintiles.

As expected the distribution of public spending in education as a whole (all levels) is rather unequal since the bottom quintile received around 12 percent of total spending while the top quintile obtains more than a third of total spending. It should be recalled that the results are obtained for children attending publicly funded institutions. The distribution is monotonically increasing. The results by level are also as expected. At the primary level, public spending is about neutral, if one uses the district-level unit costs. For all other levels, the very poor tend to have a much smaller share of benefits than their share of the population in age of schooling. The higher levels of schooling (SHS, vocational, teacher training and tertiary) have public spending pattern greatly benefitting the top quintile, especially at the tertiary level.

Conclusion

The benefit incidence analysis of public spending for education provided in this chapter suggests that despite an increase in funding for primary education in 2007, the poorest quintiles of children in age of schooling still benefit only from a relatively small share of total education spending (12 percent). This is essentially because at higher levels of schooling, children from the better of quintiles in the population are much more likely to go to school. Some of the conditions on the ground may however have changed since the implementation of the GLSS5 survey, given that there has been a sharp increase in schooling thanks in part to capitation grants, and that this increase in schooling is likely to have benefitted the poor in priority, with likely ripple effects from primary education to higher levels of schooling. The analysis should thus be replicated when new household survey data become available.

Table 11.3: Benefit incidence analysis of public spending for education (%)

Quintile	Pre-school			Primary			JHS			SHS		
	District	Region	National	District	Region	National	District	Region	National	District	Region	National
Lowest	15.0	16.4	15.8	18.9	20.9	22.6	13.2	13.5	13.4	9.3	9.8	9.1
Second	25.0	27.8	28.0	24.9	26.0	25.6	20.5	20.6	20.2	11.8	12.6	12.2
Third	29.2	30.1	30.1	23.7	23.4	22.9	23.3	23.4	22.9	15.9	16.2	15.6
Fourth	20.8	17.9	18.1	19.5	18.3	17.9	22.8	23.2	23.4	24.9	24.6	24.0
Highest	10.1	7.9	8.0	13.0	11.4	11.1	20.2	19.3	20.1	38.0	36.9	39.1
Total	100.0	100.0	100.0	100.0	100.0	100.0	100.0	100.0	100.0	100.0	100.0	100.0

Quintile	Vocational			Teacher training			Tertiary			All levels		
	District	Region	National	District	Region	National	District	Region	National	District	Region	National
Lowest	14.9	14.9	8.0	10.7	10.7	11.7	4.0	4.0	4.0	11.8	12.6	13.1
Second	10.0	10.0	10.2	10.8	10.8	10.2	4.1	4.1	4.1	15.8	16.3	16.0
Third	11.4	11.4	10.1	17.6	17.6	15.5	7.8	7.8	7.8	17.7	17.7	17.3
Fourth	24.4	24.4	27.4	14.5	14.5	15.9	19.2	19.2	19.2	20.3	19.8	19.7
Highest	39.2	39.2	44.3	46.3	46.3	46.6	64.8	64.8	64.8	34.4	33.6	33.8
Total	100.0	100.0	100.0	100.0	100.0	100.0	100.0	100.0	100.0	100.0	100.0	100.0

Source: Coulombe and Wodon (2009).

Notes: District columns were computed using district-level unit costs. Similarly "region" and "national" columns used respectively region-specific and national unit costs. Those unit costs are found in Table 11.1.

CHAPTER 12

Targeting Performance of School Lunches in Ghana

George Joseph and Quentin Wodon[1]

The Government of Ghana is currently implementing a large school lunch program with the aim to reach up to one million children. As was the case with school uniforms, this program aims to lower the private cost of schooling for households, but it also has some other objectives such as contributing to better nutrition and learning outcomes. This chapter first provides some lessons from international experience with school lunches from Bundy et al. (2009). The chapter then provides an analysis of the targeting performance of school lunches using district and school level administrative data, as well as data from the CWIQ survey. It turns out that school lunches are poorly targeted today, and less well targeted than what would be feasible under simple geographic targeting. Thus adopting one of the targeting systems proposed for example for school uniforms might greatly enhance the benefits for the poor of the school lunch program.

School Lunches: Outlays in Ghana and Lessons from International Experience

Ghana's school lunch program started in 2005 with a pilot in 10 schools, one per region. In 2008, the program reached 560,000 students in all 170 districts, which accounts for about 20 percent of total primary school enrollment. Plans are to expand the program to reach 1,040,000 students by the end of 2010. The 2008 budget of the program was 43.6 million GH¢ but actual expenditures reached only 33.0 million GH¢. The budget for 2009 at 51.1 million GH¢ was more than 20 percent higher than the budget for 2008.

The program provides children in public primary schools and kindergartens with a hot and nutritious meal on every school day. It has multiple objectives, which complicates the choice of the indicator to be used for assessing targeting performance. Key objectives include increasing school enrollment rates, improving attendance and retention (i.e., avoiding students dropping out), and improving the nutrition and food intake of children so that they are better prepared to concentrate and learn in the classroom. The meals that are distributed are prepared using locally grown food, so that the program contributes to the local economy by generating income for farmers, although the impact of this dimension of the program is not easy to consider here.

Ghana is not an outlier in implementing a school lunch program. As noted by Bundy et al. (2009), most countries today provide food in one way or another to their children in school both for nutritional purposes and to transfer benefits to the poor so as to encourage schooling. Because high- and middle-income countries can afford to fund such programs more generously, coverage rates tend to be highest in those countries. In poorer countries, despite external support principally from the World Food Programme (WFP), coverage is lower. Given how widespread school lunches are, and given that for political economy reasons these programs are difficult to abolish even if they are poorly performing, the policy issue in most countries is less whether countries should implement them but how. When coverage is far from universal, the issue of targeting becomes important to ensure that the poorest are the segment of society most likely to receive the lunches.

The review of the international experience with school lunches by Bundy et al. (2009) emphasizes that school feeding programs provide an explicit or implicit transfer to households of the value of the food distributed. The programs are relatively easy to scale up in a crisis and can provide a benefit per household of more than 10 percent of household expenditures, even more in the case of take-home rations. In many contexts, well-designed school feeding programs can be targeted moderately accurately, though rarely so effectively as the most progressive of cash transfers. In the poorest countries, where school enrollment is low, school feeding may not reach the poorest people, but in these settings alternative safety net options are often quite limited, and geographically targeted expansion of school feeding may still provide the best option for a rapid scale-up of safety nets. Targeted take-home rations may provide somewhat more progressive outcomes.

Further research is required to assess the longer-term relative merits of school feeding versus other social safety net instruments. There is evidence that school feeding programs increase school attendance, cognition, and educational achievement, particularly if supported by complementary actions such as deworming and micronutrient fortification or supplementation. In many cases the programs have a strong gender dimension, especially where they target girls' education, and may also be used to benefit specifically the poorest and most vulnerable children. What is less clear is the relative scale of the benefit with the different school feeding modalities, and there is a lack of engagement of educators on research around these issues. The education benefits of the programs are a justification for the education sector to own and implement the programs, while these same education outcomes contribute to the incentive compatibility of the programs for social protection. Policy analysis also shows that the effectiveness and sustainability of school feeding programs is dependent upon embedding the programs within education sector policy. Hence, the value of school feeding as a safety net and the motivation of the education sector to implement the programs are both enhanced by the extent to which there are education benefits. It must be pointed out that well-designed school feeding programs, which include micronutrient fortification and deworming, can provide nutritional benefits and should complement and not compete with nutrition programs for younger children, which remain a clear priority for targeting malnutrition overall.

The concept of a school feeding "exit strategy" has tended to confound thinking about the longer-term future of school feeding programs. Countries do not seek to exit from providing food to their schoolchildren, but rather to transition from externally supported projects to national programs. For 28 countries previously assisted by WFP, this has already happened, and there are case studies of how externally assisted programs have transitioned into sustainable national programs, which in some cases have themselves gone on to provide technical support to others (for example, Brazil, Chile, and India).

In terms of financial sustainability the review by Bundy et al. (2009) suggests first that school feeding programs in low-income countries exhibit large variation in cost, with concomitant opportunities for cost containment. Second, as countries get richer, school feeding costs become a much smaller proportion of the investment in education. For example, in Zambia the cost of school feeding is about 50 percent of annual per capita costs for primary education; in Ireland it is only 10 percent. Further analysis is required to define these relationships, but supporting countries to maintain an investment in school feeding through this transition may emerge as a key role for development partners. Third, the main preconditions for the transition to sustainable national programs are mainstreaming school feeding in national policies and plans, especially education sector plans; identifying national sources of financing; and expanding national implementation capacity. Mainstreaming a development policy for school feeding into national education sector plans offers the added advantage of aligning support for school feeding with the processes already established to harmonize development partner support for the Education for All-Fast Track Initiative. A key message is the importance of both designing long-term sustainability into programs from their inception and of revisiting programs as they evolve. Countries benefit from having a clear understanding of the duration of donor assistance, a systematic strategy to strengthen institutional capacity, and a concrete plan for the transition to national ownership with time frames and milestones for the process.

There are trade-offs in the design of school feeding programs. The effectiveness of school feeding programs is dependent upon several factors, including the selection of modality (in-school meals, fortified biscuits, take-home rations, or some combination of these); the effectiveness of targeting; and the associated costs. Take-home rations (average per capita cost US$50 per year) can be more finely targeted and can give high-value transfers, but have significant administrative costs. They have strong safety net potential and appear to result in increases in attendance, and perhaps educational achievement, on a similar scale to in-school meal programs. Thus, from a social protection point of view they may be preferred to in-school meal programs. In-school meals (average per capita cost US$40 per year) tend to be less finely targeted and capped in the value of their transfer, have potentially large opportunity costs for education, and incur higher administrative costs, but have the potential not only to increase attendance but to act more directly on learning, especially if fortified and combined with deworming. In-school snacks and biscuits (average per capita cost US$13 per year) have lower administrative costs but also lower transfer and incentive value, though the scale of benefit relative to meals needs to be better quantified.

Designing effective programs that meet their objectives requires an evidence base that allows careful trade-offs among targeting approaches, feeding modalities, and costs. There is a need for better data on the cost-effectiveness of the available approaches and modalities. Few studies compare in-school feeding with take-home rations in similar settings, and the few that have gone further with this suggest that both programs lead to similar improvements over having no program at all. The issue is that in selecting any modality, there are important trade-offs dependent upon context, benefit, and cost. In some contexts, school feeding programs combine on-site meals with an extra incentive from take-home rations targeting a specific group of vulnerable children, such as those affected by HIV or girls in higher grades.

District-Level Targeting Performance

The review by Bundy et al. (2009) does not focus on the targeting performance of school lunches. Data quoted by Grosh et al (2009) provide additional insights. Their estimates for various programs suggest that in many countries the incidence of school lunches is progressive, but that nevertheless the share of school lunches accruing to the poor is not necessarily high (performance was lower for example in India than in Latin American countries such as Chile, Costa Rica, and Jamaica, but there are exceptions; in Guatemala for example, most of the benefits accrued to the middle class). Thus targeting performance depends on design, and a detailed analysis of such performance within any specific country is needed.

In principle, school lunches should be targeted to schools in deprived education districts, and especially to deprived schools, but it is unclear whether this is the case and whether the program reaches the poor in priority. The Ghana household surveys do not have modules to assess household participation in various programs and do not ask whether households benefit from school lunches. However, adding such questions on the questionnaire would help in tracking targeting performance in the future. But in Ghana since the program was expanded only after the completion of the GLSS5, we would not have been able to assess targeting performance with that survey anyway. Targeting performance must be evaluated using administrative data. This can be done at the district and school levels, and we focus here on the district level data (school level data provide similar estimates of targeting performance).

To carry the analysis of targeting performance at the district level, administrative data on the benefits provided to 170 districts were transformed to obtain data for 138 districts (these districts are those for which we have poverty data, by expanding the poverty map presented in chapter 4 that is valid for 110 districts into estimates for 138 districts; this means that some districts that resulted from the scission of a previous district in two have the same poverty estimate from the poverty map). The total outlays to the districts indicated in the administrative data available to us amount to 26.3 million GH¢. This is below the level of spending for 2008, at 33.0 million GH¢, but part of the difference may be due to administrative costs.

To assess targeting performance at the district level, we assumed first that within a district the distribution of the benefits from school lunches by quintile of well-being follows the distribution of the population according to those national quintiles of well-being. The same is done for assessing the share of benefits going to the poor. If a district has a poverty headcount of 35 percent, we assume that 35 percent of the benefits from the school lunches provided to that district accrue to the poor, and the same rules are used when looking at benefits by quintile. The results are presented in table 12.1. The poor, who represent 28.5 percent of the population, benefit from only slightly more than a fifth (21.3 percent) of the school lunches. In table 12.1, the profile of benefits by quintile suggests clearly that outlays for the top quintiles are significantly (twice) higher than those for the bottom quintiles. Other approaches were used to assess whether those

Table 12.1: Targeting performance of school lunches using district level allocations

Program	Share of population benefiting	Q1	Q2	Q3	Q4	Q5	Poor	Total expenditure
School lunches	2.77%	3,449.6	4,618.7	5,235.1	6,182.0	6,789.4	5,597.1	26,274.9
Share of benefits		13.1%	17.6%	19.9%	23.5%	25.8%	21.3%	

Source: Authors.

results were robust (for example to considering targeting according to deprived education districts as opposed to poverty), and the same message on targeting performance was obtained.

Conclusion

Ghana's large school lunch program reaches up to one million children and aims to lower the private cost of schooling for households, while also contributing to better nutrition and learning outcomes. This chapter has provided some lessons from international experience with school lunches. Next, it has provided an analysis of the targeting performance of school lunches using district level administrative data, as well as data from the CWIQ survey. Unfortunately school lunches are poorly targeted today, and less well targeted than what would be feasible under simple geographic targeting. Adopting a better geographic targeting formula might greatly enhance the benefits for the poor of the school lunch program.

Note

1. The first section of this paper is reproduced with minor edits from the executive summary in Bundy et al. (2009).

CHAPTER 13

National Health Insurance Scheme in Ghana

Clarence Tsimpo and Quentin Wodon

The National Health Insurance Scheme (NHIS) was created in 2003 in an effort to increase the access to and affordability of health care. The scheme relies on premiums from participants, but it is also heavily subsidized through indirect taxation (special levy on the VAT and import duties). Today the scheme has managed to enroll about 60 percent of the population according to NHIS data. Indigent persons benefit from exemptions, but there are strict controls on the registration of indigents at the district level. This chapter provides a brief description of the scheme, and then uses a range of different data sources (GLSS5, other surveys, LEAP single registry, and administrative district level data) to assess its benefit incidence. The results suggest that while the scheme does reach some among the poor, it benefits much more the better-off segments of the population; the premiums to be paid are often too high for the very poor. A number of options for increasing NHIS enrollment among the poor are considered.

Description of the National Health Insurance Scheme

The National Health Insurance Scheme (NHIS) was established by the National Health Insurance Act in 2003. It is managed by the National Health Insurance Authority. The objective of the NHIS is to provide in a sustainable way affordable and quality care for all Ghanaians. Data from the NHIS website suggests that as of June 2009 some 13,779,806 individuals were registered in the scheme, representing close to 60 percent of the population. Exempt groups, which do not have to pay to be part of the scheme, accounted for close to 70 percent of all registered members. The program is managed at the district level by District Mutual Health Schemes. In addition to members participating through district schemes all (mostly formal sector) workers contributing to the SSNIT (Social Security and National Insurance Trust) are enrolled. On the provider side, public facilities are automatically accredited to participate in the scheme. In addition NHIS has provisionally accredited 1,551 private health care facilities, including 400 hospitals and clinics, 237 maternity homes, 451 pharmacies, 329 licensed chemical shops and 128 diagnostic facilities (laboratories and diagnostic imaging facilities). Finally, facilities from the Christian Health Association of Ghana have been granted provisional accreditation.

The program is funded through a 2.5 percent addition to the Value Added Tax (VAT) and import duties known as the National Health Insurance Levy (import duties are administered by the Customs, Excise and Preventive Service, or CEPS in table 13.1). The program also benefits from contributions from employees enrolled in the SSNIT and, as needed, from resources from the MOH and donors. Insurance premiums paid by households who are not exempt from contributions also contribute to funding the scheme, but they account only for a small portion of the scheme's budget. As noted in ODI (2009), and as shown in table 13.1, contributions to the National Health Insurance Fund (which excludes the revenue of the district mutual schemes) were estimated at GH¢ 318 million for 2008 and GH¢ 375 million for 2009.

Table 13.1: Contributions to the national health insurance fund

	2008 Original budget	2008 Provisional outturn	2009 Budget estimates
SSNIT	35,424,000	104,419,539	117,377,746
VAT collection	74,405,513	72,029,861	98,831,416
CEPS collection	125,600,000	141,866,300	159,000,000
Total NHI Fund	235,429,513	318,315,700	375,209,162

Source: ODI (2009), based on NHIS 2009 Budget Statement, Appendix 3A MTEF 2007–2009 Total receipts.

Several categories of individuals are exempted from paying premiums to participate in the scheme. First, formal sector workers who already contribute to SSNIT do not need to make any additional payments to the NHIF. Second, dependent children under 18 years of age are exempt from premiums if both of their parents are already members of the scheme. Third, all individuals aged above 70 are exempt, as are all pensioners from SSNIT. The last category of exempted individuals consists of the "indigent", who are a subset of the poor. Specifically, according to regulation 58, *"A person shall not be classified as an indigent under a district scheme unless that person (a) is unemployed and has no visible source of income; (b) does not have a fixed place of residence according to standards determined by the scheme; (c) does not live with a person who is employed and who has a fixed place of residence; and (d) does not have any identifiable consistent support from another person."*

The above definition of the indigent can be interpreted in a rather strict way, since a working poor would not in principle qualify even if his or her income were very low. The lack or residence is also a rather stringent criteria and the combination of both criteria may explain why only very few individuals have been accepted into the scheme as indigent. In addition, district schemes are in charge of verifying individual eligibility under the "indigent" category; they must keep and publish the list of indigents in their area of operation and submit the list to the National Health Insurance Council for validation. If the number of indigents on a district's list exceeds half a percent of the total membership of the district scheme, the Council must verify the list (the method to do so is left at the discretion of the Council). In addition, individuals who are members of a district's scheme and who are in disagreement with the inclusion of a specific individual as an indigent in the scheme may complain to the scheme first and if needed next to the District Health Complaint Committee which must investigate whether the complaint is appropriate. All these measures may also contribute to social exclusion and stigma, and to the extent that the list of beneficiaries is made public in a district or at the local level, this may discourage participation by households or individuals who might need an exemption badly due to very limited resources.

Benefit Incidence of NHIS Subsidies in 2005–06

The NHIS is heavily subsidized through contributions from the VAT and import duties. It is thus legitimate to ask whether these subsidies reach the poor. GLSS5 data can be used to assess the benefit incidence of NHIS subsidies at an early stage of the program, namely in 2005–06. The survey included a special one-page module on the type of access to health insurance enjoyed by households and the obstacles to access. Table 13.2 provides the main results from the analysis. First, in 2005–06, only a small minority (17 percent) of the population was registered and/or covered (as noted earlier, about 60 percent of the population is now covered). Registration and coverage were much higher in the upper quintiles of consumption per equivalent adult than in the lower quintiles. For example, registration and coverage rates were 2.5 times higher in the top quintile as compared to the bottom quintile. The main reason for non-registration was the cost of the premium which was perceived to be too high for what households could afford. Lack of knowledge about the NHIS was also a reason for non-registration, as well as other reasons which are not detailed in the survey but may relate to some households not feeling the need to register, perhaps because they were relatively healthier than the average population. Among those who registered, only a very small minority had left the scheme, with the main reason being the cost of the premiums, apart from the "other" category for which we do not have details on what it entails.

Most households had registered through the district mutual schemes, and most expected that both OPD and out-patient services would be covered in case of need. About 41 percent of households had paid premiums, with 22 percent exempted, and another 33 percent belonging to neither category (again it is not fully clear what this category represents). Some 16 percent of households had made use of the insurance scheme, with a slightly higher proportion of users among registered/covered households from the poorest quintile. Thus overall, one could argue that the scheme benefited in 2005–06 mostly better off households, although it should be recalled that some among the better households were paying premiums through the SSNIT (this would for example be the case for households with formal sector workers).

The fact that the NHIS benefited more the better off than the poor in 2005–06 is also illustrated in figure 13.1 that provides CD curves for the use of health services and the registration into the NHIS. The top curve represents the share (on the vertical axis) of total episodes of illness declared by the population with a consumption level below a certain threshold (on the horizontal axis, with a value of one denoting the poverty line). The curves entitled "Public", "Private", and "Religious" represent the share of health services provided by public, private, or religious providers used by the corresponding shares of the population. The last two curves represent the shares of registered individuals in the NHIS, as well as the share of those who used the NHIS coverage for health care. The fact that the two NHIS curves are well below other curves confirms visually the better coverage and use of the NHIS among richer households.

Technically, what figure 13.1 implies is that from a pure benefit incidence analysis, a balanced budget subsidy reform to reduce subsidies for the NHIS and increase subsidies for health care facilities to reduce the cost of health care at those health facilities should be poverty reducing. This does not mean that such a policy should be implemented however, given that it would reduce the reach of the NHIS which has proven a useful scheme to expand access to care overall. A better way to proceed would be to improve

Table 13.2: Data on participation in health insurance scheme from GLSS5, 2005–06

	Residence area			Welfare quintile					Total
	Accra	Other urban	Rural	Q1	Q2	Q3	Q4	Q5	
Have you ever been registered or covered with a health insurance scheme? (%)									
Yes, registered	8.7	13.6	6.4	2.4	5.6	7.8	10.5	16.2	8.5
Yes, covered	6.7	12.6	6.5	3.2	7.0	9.0	10.4	11.0	8.1
No	84.6	73.8	87.1	94.3	87.4	83.2	79.1	72.8	83.4
Total	100.0	100.0	100.0	100.0	100.0	100.0	100.0	100.0	100.0
If you have never been registered why? (%)									
Premium is too high	17.2	40.5	32.9	33.4	31.8	35.3	32.2	30.7	32.8
Don't have confidence in operators	13.9	6.4	4.4	3.4	4.1	6.0	7.3	10.2	6.0
Covered by other avenues	7.8	1.3	0.5	0.4	1.0	1.2	1.6	4.1	1.6
No knowledge of any scheme	15.5	10.9	16.1	12.8	15.5	18.2	14.5	13.2	14.8
Other	45.7	40.9	46.2	50.0	47.6	39.4	44.4	41.8	44.9
Total	100.0	100.0	100.0	100.0	100.0	100.0	100.0	100.0	100.0
Are you still registered, or covered? (%)									
Yes, registered	56.6	51.7	47.4	42.0	43.9	44.1	49.0	59.4	50.2
Yes, covered	43.1	47.2	48.7	56.4	53.4	53.1	47.6	39.3	47.5
No	0.3	1.1	3.8	1.5	2.7	2.8	3.4	1.3	2.4
Total	100.0	100.0	100.0	100.0	100.0	100.0	100.0	100.0	100.0
Reason for not being registered anymore (%)									
Premium is too high	0.0	19.0	14.5	22.5	6.5	17.1	10.1	28.9	15.2
Don't have confidence in operators	0.0	6.0	4.3	15.2	5.2	3.9	2.6	6.4	4.6
Covered by other alternatives	32.7	0.0	0.0	0.0	0.0	0.0	0.0	2.6	0.5
Was not getting benefits	67.3	31.2	13.7	32.5	3.8	25.4	22.6	8.6	17.9
Other	0.0	43.8	67.5	29.8	84.5	53.7	64.7	53.5	61.8
Total	100.0	100.0	100.0	100.0	100.0	100.0	100.0	100.0	100.0
Type of coverage if registered (%)									
District mutual	86.9	95.6	97.1	96.3	97.5	95.5	94.7	94.5	95.3
Private mutual	2.0	1.3	0.9	0.6	2.0	0.2	1.7	1.1	1.2
Private company	10.6	1.4	0.4	1.6	0.0	1.1	2.1	3.3	2.0
Other	0.5	1.7	1.6	1.5	0.5	3.1	1.5	1.1	1.5
Total	100.0	100.0	100.0	100.0	100.0	100.0	100.0	100.0	100.0

(Table continues on next page)

Table 13.2:   (continued)

	Residence area			Welfare quintile					Total
	Accra	Other urban	Rural	Q1	Q2	Q3	Q4	Q5	
	Expected benefits/type of coverage (%)								
Only OPD services	16.1	14.3	7.8	8.2	9.3	6.5	13.4	14.5	11.4
Only in-patient services	3.8	1.0	1.8	1.7	2.3	3.1	0.9	1.1	1.7
Both	80.1	84.7	90.5	90.1	88.4	90.4	85.7	84.5	86.9
Total	100.0	100.0	100.0	100.0	100.0	100.0	100.0	100.0	100.0
	Payment of premium (%)								
All	47.9	44.6	36.7	35.0	32.7	37.0	40.7	49.4	41.2
Part	6.8	2.4	4.4	3.0	4.9	4.9	3.2	3.3	3.8
Exempted	20.6	23.0	21.6	19.2	23.3	26.9	21.6	19.5	22.1
N/A	24.6	30.0	37.3	42.7	39.1	31.3	34.5	27.8	32.9
Total	100.0	100.0	100.0	100.0	100.0	100.0	100.0	100.0	100.0
	Benefits from the scheme among population registered (%)								
Yes	9.0	15.6	18.1	18.3	15.4	17.4	16.5	14.9	16.1
No	91.0	84.4	81.9	81.7	84.6	82.7	83.5	85.1	83.9
Total	100.0	100.0	100.0	100.0	100.0	100.0	100.0	100.0	100.0

Source: Authors' estimations using GLSS5 data.

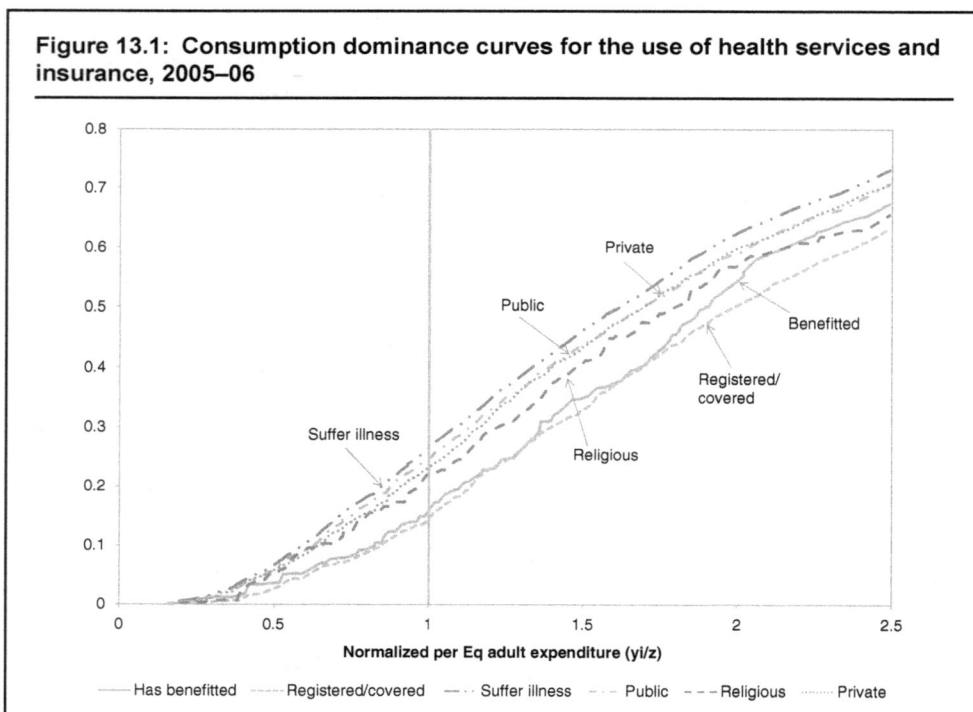

Figure 13.1: Consumption dominance curves for the use of health services and insurance, 2005–06

Source: Authors' estimations using GLSS5 data.

the benefit incidence of the NHIS (i.e., to shift the curves for the NHIS up in figure 13.1) by enrolling more poor individuals. This could be done for example by relaxing some of the strict criteria used to identify the indigent or by encouraging districts to register a larger number of poor households into the scheme under the indigent category. Other possibilities would include ensuring that some very poor households who participate in other programs such as LEAP be enrolled automatically into the scheme (we will come back to this below, as well as to other options that are being considered).

Benefit Incidence of NHIS in 2007 and 2008

Since the implementation of the GLSS5 in 2005/06, registration and coverage under the NHIS have increased considerably. Several sources of data can be used to assess the benefit incidence of the scheme in 2007 and 2008 and the obstacles preventing registration. On the basis of a special purpose household survey implemented in 2007, Asante and Aikins (2007) provide evidence that the enrollment rate into the NHIS by the poor in 2007 remained much lower among lower quintiles of wealth than among the richest households (see figure 13.2). On the positive side, the authors find that most households were aware of the scheme (this was not as much the case in 2005/06 as noted above) and satisfaction with the scheme was high, as revealed among others by high rates of re-enrollment into the scheme. Appiah-Denkyira and Preker (2007), also quoted by ODI (2009), found that in some regions a substantial majority of the NHIS registered members belonged to exempt categories. In addition a participatory monitoring and evaluation report implemented in 2008 confirmed that barriers to enrollment by the poor remain significant (NDPC, 2008). Approximately three-quarters (77 percent) of the individuals not registered into the scheme declared that affordability was the reason for not enrolling. Among households not renewing their premiums (this was the case for 5 percent of respondents), cost was again the main reason to not to re-enroll, especially among the poor. The fact that affordability remains an issue is not surprising given that as noted by ODI (2009), the GHS 11 (USD 9.5) fee required to register represents more than

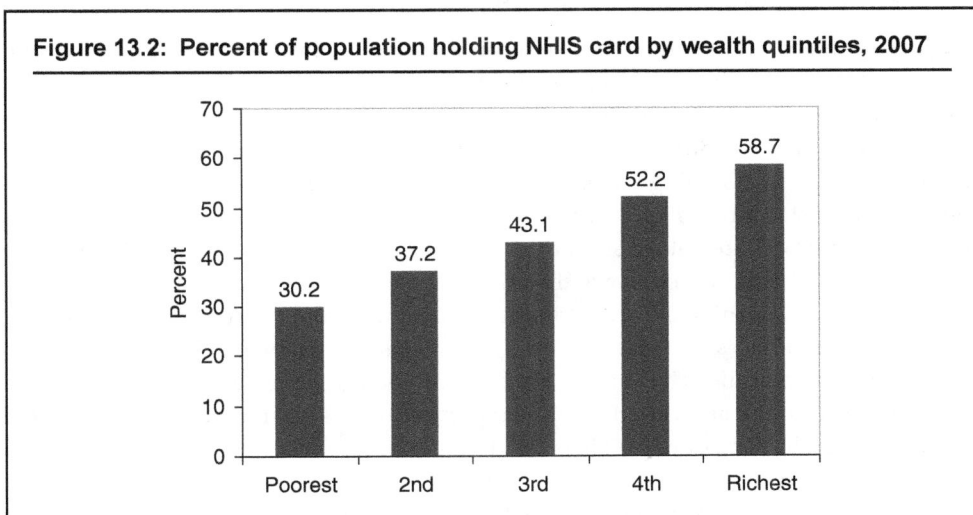

Figure 13.2: Percent of population holding NHIS card by wealth quintiles, 2007

Source: Asante and Aikins (2007).

45 percent of the monthly consumption of a household living with resources equivalent to the extreme poverty line.

Another source of information on the incidence of NHIS registration, or more specifically on the lack of registration among the very poor, comes from the LEAP single registry. As discussed in chapter 14 LEAP was launched in March 2008 to supplement through cash transfers the income of "dangerously poor households." The program is administered by the Ministry of Employment and Social Welfare and it targets five categories of beneficiaries: orphans, and vulnerable children (OVCs); pregnant and lactating women; elderly individuals in poverty; individuals with severe disabilities[10]; and finally subsistence food crop farmers and fishermen in poverty. The program currently serves 32,000 households. LEAP maintains a single registry with detailed information on program beneficiaries that can be used to classify these households by level of predicted consumption. Data are currently available for all households that were enrolled in 2008 (there are 16,000 of them). As shown in table 13.3, only 18.3 percent of all LEAP households were registered with the NHIS, and the share was even lower among the poorest of LEAP beneficiaries (15.7 percent in the bottom national quintile).

Table 13.3: Share of LEAP household members registered with NHIS, 2008 (%)

| | Predicted quintile of consumption by national quintile | | | | | |
	Q1	Q2	Q3	Q4	Q5	Total
Share of LEAP households in quintile	46.3	30.2	16.0	4.6	2.9	100.0
Registration with NHIS						
Yes	15.7	16.8	23.9	31.5	23.3	18.3
No	84.3	83.2	76.1	68.6	76.7	81.7
Total	**100.0**	**100.0**	**100.0**	**100.0**	**100.0**	**100.0**

Source: Authors' estimation using LEAP single registry data.

Assessment of the Indigent Provision in the NHIS

Data are available from administrative records regarding the number of registered indigents in the NHIS. These data are available at the district level, but we do not have information on the individual characteristics of the indigents. District level data can be used to assess in a very imperfect way how well targeted the indigent exemption is. The method consists in assuming that indigent participants are representative of the population of a district. Thus if 40 percent of the population of a given district belongs to the poorest quintile of national consumption, we assume that 40 percent of the indigent registered in that district also belong to the poorest national quintile, and this is repeated for other quintiles. Summing up across all districts, the distribution of indigents by district gives us an assumed share of all the indigents registered in NHIS that belong to each of the national quintile. That information is provided in table 13.4, which shows that under this method of analysis, the indigent provision does reach much more the bottom quintiles than the richer ones. This is good news, and it simply means that poorer districts tend to have a larger share of their population registered as indigents in the NHIS. It should be clear however that the benefit incidence reported in table 13.4 is likely to underestimate the share of the indigents who actually belong to the poorest quintiles

Table 13.4: District-level data on the benefit incidence of the NHIS indigent provision, 2008

Program	Share of population benefiting (%)	Q1	Q2	Q3	Q4	Q5	Poor	Total expenditure
2008	0.13	566,405	316,811	274,885	254,715	247,457	611,982	1,660,274
2009	0.13	754,728	402,894	338,684	298,431	284,865	800,486	2,079,602

Source: Authors' estimation using NHIS administrative data.
Note: District level data will underestimate the targeting performance of a program like the indigent provision.

because the program is likely to be well targeted within districts (given the relatively strict controls mentioned above imposed by the Council).

While the indigent provision under the NHIS is likely to be well targeted to the poor, it is clearly too strict currently. In 2009, only about 2 percent of total enrollment in the NHIS, and only about one percent of the overall population consisted of individuals classified as indigent. By contrast, the share of Ghana's population living in poverty was 28.5 in 2005–06, and the share of the population living in extreme poverty was 18 percent (Coulombe and Wodon, 2007).

What could be done to increase enrollment among the poor? Several measures have been already taken or are under consideration (ODI, 2009). First, following in part on advocacy efforts by UNICEF, it has been proposed in 2008 to extend fee exemptions to all children under 18 (so that children registration in the NHIS is now delinked from their parents' registration). Second, as of July 2008, free NHIS enrollment is to be provided to all pregnant women, with a full package of benefits provided for one year, including maternal health services but not restricted to those (pre-natal care was already provided for free). Newborn children are also covered for up to three months. It has also been proposed to extend exemptions to all LEAP beneficiary households, which are shown to be in most cases in (extreme) poverty. Proposals have also been made to exempt children in large families from registration fees when their parents are enrolled, and to make sure that all children are indeed enrolled in beneficiary families (the NHIS participatory monitoring and evaluation report suggested that this was not always the case). Another avenue for promoting enrollment among the poor would consists of reducing further premiums for those who are poor, and the eligibility for such a reduction could be dependent on a proxy means-testing mechanisms such as the mechanism implemented by LEAP to avoid abuses.

Conclusion

The National Health Insurance Scheme (NHIS) was created in 2003 in an effort to increase the access to and affordability of health care. Today the scheme has managed to enroll about 60 percent of the population according to NHIS data. Indigent persons benefit from exemptions, but there are strict controls on the registration of indigents at the district level. This chapter suggests that while the scheme does reach some among the poor, it continues to benefit much more the better off segments of the population. On the other hand, the indigent exception seems to be fairly well targeted based on the available data, and it could thus be expanded in various ways to achieve a higher coverage among the extreme poor without risking high leakage rates to the nonpoor.

CHAPTER 14

Ghana's Livelihood Empowerment Against Poverty

Clarence Tsimpo and Quentin Wodon

The Government of Ghana launched the LEAP (Livelihood Empowerment Against Poverty) Program in March 2008 to supplement through cash transfers the income of "dangerously poor households." The program is administered by the Department of Social Welfare (DSW) in the Ministry of Employment and Social Welfare (MESW). It targets five categories of beneficiaries: OVCs; pregnant and lactating women; elderly individuals in poverty; individuals with severe disabilities, and finally subsistence food crop farmers and fishermen in poverty. Currently approximately 32,000 household benefited from LEAP in 74 districts. The aim is to scale up the program to reach 165,000 households within five years. Using data from LEAP's single registry of program participants, this chapter shows that LEAP appears to be a well targeted program reaching the extreme poor.

Design and Targeting Mechanism of LEAP

As noted in a recent ODI (2009) report, LEAP has a complex targeting mechanism. First, districts are selected on the basis of their poverty incidence, rate of HIV/AIDS prevalence, rates of child labor, and lack of access to social services (DSW 2008). Next, within selected districts Community LEAP Implementation Committees (CLICs), which include representation from traditional leaders, District Assembly members, teachers and nurses, religious leaders and other community leaders, identify the most vulnerable households in their communities. Third, social welfare officers from DSW administer a survey questionnaire to the households proposed by local communities to select those who are likely to be the poorest (proxy means-testing). The survey questionnaire implemented by LEAP has two parts. The first part includes about 40 questions on the housing conditions of the household, selected household characteristics including a series of assets, and the household roster. The second part includes about 30 questions on the characteristics of individual members of the household, including their demographic characteristics, their education and their employment status. The data on LEAP beneficiaries (as well as on households not selected into the program) are kept electronically in a single registry. The list of the proposed beneficiaries after taking into account results from proxy means-testing is sent back to each community's CLIC for approval.

The LEAP targeting mechanisms is not very far away from what has been implemented in some other countries such as Mexico, where proxy means-testing has been combined with geographic targeting to improve targeting performance. A key feature of the Mexico Oportunidades program (previously known as PROGRESA) is its three-stage targeting mechanism based on community and household characteristics (see among others Wodon, de la Briere, and Yitzhaki 2002). The first stage selects poor, rural localities to participate in the program. The second stage selects eligible families within participating localities. The third stage involves local meetings to incorporate eligible families and to check on the selection process, allowing for disputes of eligibility decisions. In selecting localities, census data are used to create a "marginality index" for localities. The index comprises seven variables for each locality: share of illiterate adults, share of dwellings without water, share of dwellings without draining systems, share of dwellings without electricity, average number of occupants per room, share of dwellings with dirt floor, and share of population working in the primary sector. The localities ultimately selected as eligible had to have a primary school, a secondary school, and a clinic, and could not have an extremely small population or be so isolated that access was limited. In the second stage of targeting, census data was used in a two-step process to classify households as poor or nonpoor. The first step involved constructing a per capita income indicator by summing all individual incomes in a given household and subtracting the income earned by children. This income was compared to a Standard Food Basket to create a binary variable for poor and nonpoor status. In the second step, a statistical analysis identified the non-income variables that best distinguish poor and nonpoor households. In the third stage, community meetings were held in each locality, for all eligible beneficiaries and local authorities. Each community was given the list of program participants, and it was still feasible at this stage to change the selection if it was believed that some poor families should be reclassified as nonpoor or vice versa. However, the proportion of households whose selection was disputed was very small. Mexico's program targeting mechanism has proven to be very effective. One key difference with LEAP is that the Oportunidades Program relies on a census of all households living in the poor areas selected for the programs, while LEAP at the time being collects data only on those households that are proposed for participation by the communities.

Coming back to LEAP, the program's payments to the final list of beneficiaries are processed through the Ghana Post. The transfers paid to households depend on the number of eligible dependents within the household, starting with GH¢ 8 (US$ 6.90) per month for households with one dependent to a maximum of GHS 15 (USD 12.90) for four dependents (DSW, 2008). Beneficiaries are expected to "graduate" from the program within three years, although the details of this graduation process have not been worked out and graduation may be difficult for some very poor households (such as the elderly or individuals with disability not able to work). The transfers for the elderly and households with individuals with disabilities are not conditional. The transfers to households with OVCs require in principle that the children be enrolled in school. Transfers targeted to pregnant and lactating women require the parents to obtain a birth certificate for their children, and to visit post-natal clinics regularly with the newborn babies. Full (EPI) vaccination is also required for children aged up to five in participating households. Finally, parents cannot allow their children to participate in any child trafficking scheme and the children cannot be involved in forms of child labor detrimental to their safety, health or development. MESW is also negotiating with the National Health Insurance Scheme how LEAP beneficiaries could be included in the scheme (given that premiums to be paid are often too high for the households to be able to afford them).

Is LEAP likely to be well targeted? There is some discretion on the part of community leaders in proposing households for benefits and one could fear that such discretion could lead to poor targeting if program benefits are used as a form of patronage by local elites. On the other hand, the fact that a verification of eligibility is done centrally by LEAP social workers should help in avoiding such patronage at the community level. That is, if the targeting mechanism is well implemented, the combination of community targeting and proxy means-testing could lead to fairly low errors of inclusion (few non-poor households included in the list of beneficiaries). Errors of exclusion (share of the poor not benefitting from the program) are likely to be large given the small coverage of the program as of today, but this is less of an issue because what matters from a poverty reduction point of view and for any given budget allocated to a program is that as large a share as possible of the program benefits reach the poor. This depends on the errors of inclusion and not the errors of exclusion. In fact the small size of the LEAP program is probably right now an advantage for targeting performance since it is typically easier within a community to identify a few very poor households while it may become more difficult to identify the near poor once a program is extended so that its benefit are to be spread on a larger share of the community.

It is important to note that under the initial implementation of the LEAP pilot, not all of the above design features were implemented strictly due to logistical as well as political reasons (as reviewed in ODI, 2009). The program provided initially transfers of GH¢ 16 to GH¢ 30 every two months to households, and procedures to decide on graduation out of the program have also not been fully fleshed out. The conditionalities of the program also have not been strictly enforced. However, the data available from the LEAP office are still good enough to provide an assessment of the programs' targeting performance.

Targeting Performance of LEAP

Since the LEAP program targets a large number of districts, some of which do not have high levels of poverty, it is the selection of the communities and individuals within selected communities that is key for good targeting. This also means that a benefit incidence analysis of beneficiaries at the district level would probably generate estimates of targeting performance that are well below actual performance, assuming that the combination of community identification of the very poor and the proxy means-testing procedure is working well to ensure that most program participants indeed belong to the very poor.

Our assessment of the targeting performance of LEAP is based on the individual and household level data collected by LEAP through its two part questionnaire mentioned above. The LEAP data sets provided to us comprised of about 16,000 households, so that it may not cover all of the program beneficiaries today (the number of LEAP beneficiaries in the database received is close to the number of beneficiaries of the program in 2008). A first (but imperfect) procedure for assessing the targeting performance of the program consists in simply predicting the likely consumption level of households, and reporting the results of this prediction together with a comparison to the same prediction for the GLSS5 sample, or for a sub-sample, of the GLSS5. A number of variables available in both the LEAP questionnaire and the GLSS5 are identified. A regression of the correlates (i.e., predictors) of the consumption per equivalent adult in the GLSS5 is estimated using the variables also available in the LEAP questionnaire. The parameter estimates from this regression are then used to predict the level of consumption of LEAP beneficiary households. We used several regression models as well as techniques (including step-wise regression) in the GLSS5 to test for the robustness of our assessment of LEAP's targeting performance, and changes in the regressions do not make much of a difference. We also used the full sample in the GLSS5 for the regression estimates, but the procedure could be repeated with a sub-sample of households with LEAP-like characteristics as in the case of the poverty mapping methodology which also takes into account the issue of standard errors (this is discussed in more details below).

The key results are presented in table 14.1. The first column shows that 20 percent of the population belongs to each of the quintiles of consumption in the GLSS5. This is obtained simply by construction of the quintiles (ties in consumption levels may increase or reduce slightly the share of the population in each quintile versus the norm of 20 percent). The next two columns in the table provide the proportion of the population in the GLSS5 survey and in the LEAP survey that have levels of consumption that fall within the bounds defined by the quintiles in the first column. The share of the population predicted to belong to the various quintiles is different in the GLSS5 than the share of the population actually belonging to the quintiles. This is due to the regression technique that tends to result in predicted values of consumption that reduce extreme values, since the error terms are not taken into account. Thus for example, only 15.3 percent of the population in the GLSS5 has a predicted value of consumption that falls within the interval of consumption defined by the actual consumption levels of the bottom 20 percent of the population. And similarly, the share of the population that has a predicted value of consumption that falls in the intervals of consumption defined by the top quintile is below 20 percent. To assess LEAP's targeting performance we need to compare the allocation of LEAP beneficiary households to the allocation of GLSS5 households using the predicted value of consumption in the GLSS5. LEAP appears to be very well targeted. Some 46.3 percent of the LEAP beneficiary population has a predicted level of consumption per equivalent adult that falls within the bounds of the first quintile, as compared to only 15.3 percent for the GLSS5 survey. Only 2.9 percent of beneficiary households in LEAP fall into the top quintile.

Table 14.1: Distribution of population quintiles (actual, predicted, and matched with propensity score) (%)

	Observed population share	Log consumption predicted shares		LEAP propensity score matching	
	GLSS-5	GLSS-5	LEAP	One-to-One	k-Nearest
Poorest quintile (Q1)	20.1	15.3	46.3	48.0	42.2
Q2	19.9	24.3	30.2	14.6	32.4
Q3	20.0	23.2	16.0	17.9	18.8
Q4	20.0	21.9	4.6	10.5	6.0
Richest quintile (Q5)	20.0	15.3	2.9	9.0	0.5
Population	100.0	100.0	100.0	100.0	100.0

Source: Authors' estimates using GLSS5 and LEAP single registry data.

An alternative to simply predicting consumption levels consists in using propensity score matching techniques to assess targeting performance. Usually propensity score matching is used to assess a program's impact. Consider as a treatment group households that benefitted from a program. We would like to compare this group to a control group constituted of households that did not benefit from the program but have characteristics similar to those of the households in the treatment group. If the control group constructed in the data is truly comparable to the treatment group, and if there are no issues of bias of selection in the treatment group, then differences in outcomes between the two groups can be associated with the program. The same technique can also be used to measure targeting performance. We simply consider LEAP households as the treatment groups, and we match these households to households in the GLSS5 that have similar characteristics. Then, we compare the consumption levels of the matched to the overall distribution of consumption in the GLSS5, and this gives us the data needed to assess targeting performance since we have an estimate of the likely consumption level of LEAP households. Note that there is no assessment of program impact here; we are looking at targeting only. There is also no possibility of bias in the estimate of the likely consumption level of LEAP households due to program impact, since the data on the characteristics of LEAP households were collected before they benefitted from the program. Technically, there are many alternative ways to implement this type of matching procedure, and we rely here on two of the most used alternatives: one-to-one matching (for each LEAP households, we find one match in the GLSS5), and k-nearest neighbors matching (we find the k households in the GLSS5 that are closest in characteristics to the LEAP households, with k equal to 5). The results obtained with k-nearest neighbors matching are often considered as more robust than those with the nearest neighbor, but both methods clearly confirm that LEAP is very well targeted.

To provide even more confidence in those results, table 14.2 gives a series of summary statistics for LEAP households as compared to the GLSS5 sample that suggest large differences between both samples (these are many of the variables common to both data sets and used for the predictive model). Some 80.2 percent of LEAP beneficiaries live in dwellings whose walls are made of mud or mud bricks, versus 53.2 percent in the GLSS5 sample. Earth, mud, or mud bricks are the main material for the dwelling's floor for 56.1 percent of LEAP beneficiaries, versus 14.7 percent in the GLSS5. Some 36.6 percent of LEAP beneficiaries have a roof made of palm, versus 17.0 percent in the GLSS5 sample. LEAP beneficiaries are much more likely to get their drinking water from a borehole than GLSS5 households, and they are also much more likely to use kerosene for lighting. Only 16.8 percent of LEAP beneficiaries own land versus 42.7 percent of GLSS5 households. The majority of LEAP beneficiaries in the data have a female household head (61.9 percent), while the proportion is much lower in the GLSS5 (27.9 percent). About half of LEAP beneficiaries are widowed (50.1 percent) versus only 10.6 percent in the GLSS5. Some 84.5 percent of household heads in the LEAP sample have no education, versus 34.6 percent in the GLSS5. Lack of employment affects more than half of the LEAP household heads (54.5 percent) versus only 5.8 percent in the GLSS5. Almost no LEAP households have any appliance, and most to not have access to electricity, while a third of GLSS5 households have a TV and more than two-thirds have a radio. Clearly, the LEAP beneficiary group appears to be overwhelmingly in poverty or even extreme poverty.

Table 14.2: Comparison of selected household characteristics in GKSS5 and LEAP samples (%)

	GLSS-5	LEAP
Main construction material used for the outer walls of dwelling: Mud/mud bricks	53.2	80.2
Main construction material used for the floor of dwelling: Earth/mud/mud bricks	14.7	56.1
Main construction material used for the roof of dwelling: Palm leaves/raffia/thatch	17.0	36.6
Main source of drinking water for household: Borehole	33.5	45.1
Type of toilet mainly used by household: No toilet (use of bush/beach)	25.0	53.9
Main source of lighting for the dwelling: Electricity	45.9	10.1
Main source of lighting for the dwelling: Kerosene	52.3	71.4
Main source of lighting for the dwelling: No light	0.4	11.1
Does household own land Yes	42.7	16.8
Gender of household head: Female	27.9	61.9
Marital status of household head: Widowed	10.6	51.0
Education level of household head: No education	34.6	84.5
Employment of household head: No employment	5.8	54.5
Household size	4.2	3.7
Household owns a TV	31.1	0.3
Household owns a radio	69.4	4.4
Household owns a electric fan	29.2	0.1
Household owns a fridge/freezer	21.2	0.1
Household owns a tape recorder	3.6	0.3
Household owns a mobile phone	18.3	0.7

Source: Authors' estimates using GLSS5 and LEAP single registry data.

It is important to point out that the good targeting performance is not related mainly to the fact that the program targets individuals with disability, pregnant and lactating women, and elderly individuals who are not working. Indeed, it can be shown that most of these groups are not that much poorer in the population as a whole than the average Ghanaian. This is shown in figure 14.1, which provides the cumulative share of the population in the various demographic target groups that have a level of consumption below a certain threshold, as well as the cumulative density for the population as a whole. Individuals with disability tend to live in poorer households (their cumulative density is higher than that for other groups and the population as a whole) than the population as a whole, and this is also the case at the margin for households with children below three years of age (simply because the poor tend to have more children). However, for most other target demographic groups, the curves are not very different from the cumulative density of the population as a whole, or are below the overall density, which suggests a lack of clear relationship between belonging to one of those demographic groups and living in poverty. Actually, orphans on average tend to live in slightly less poor households than the population as a whole (because they are welcomes by slightly better off households who can provide for them). Thus what enables a good targeting performance for LEAP is the combination of selecting potentially demographic vulnerable groups and the procedures used to indeed identify who in those groups are most likely to be very poor.

Figure 14.1: Cumulative density of groups targeted by LEAP in overall population

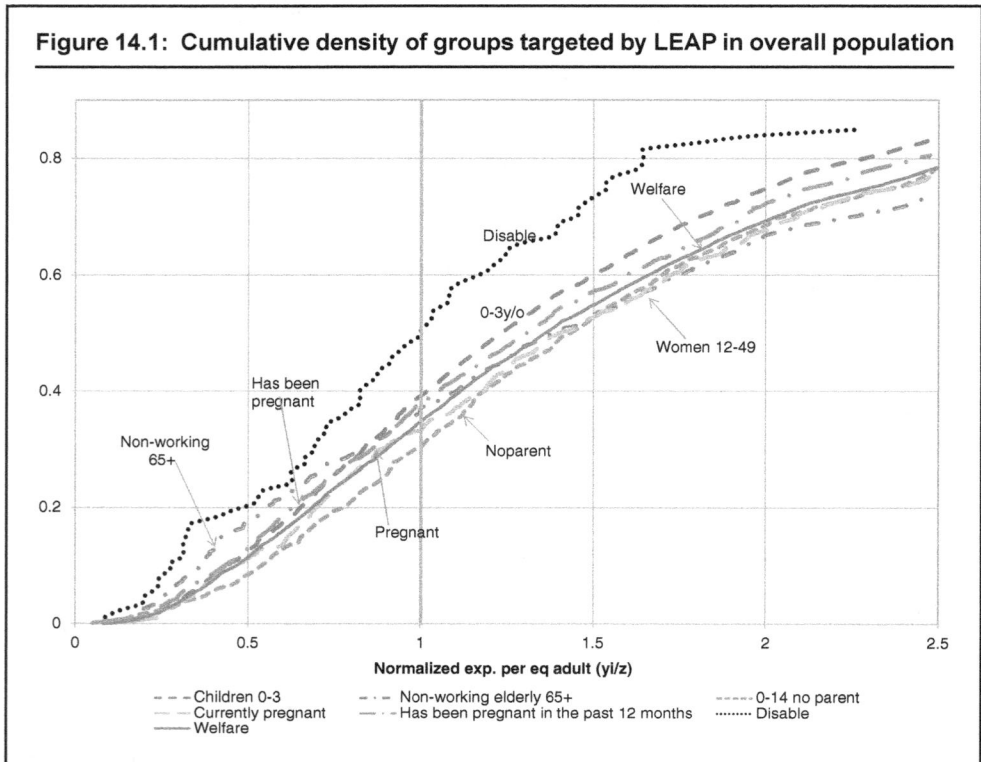

Source: Authors using GLSS5 data.

Scope for an Expansion of LEAP

How much demand could there be for LEAP in Ghana? This depends on whom one considers as eligible. Table 14.2 provides data from the GLSS5 as to the number of individuals falling in different demographic categories targeted by LEAP. Both the total number of individuals and the number of individuals in poverty are provided, using the official definition of poverty in the country. Data on the extreme poor are also provided with the extreme poverty line equal to the food poverty component of the overall poverty line (thus the extreme poor are those whose consumption is below what is needed to meet basic food needs).

The categories listed in the table are the demographic groups targeted by LEAP. We have listed children aged 0–3 because LEAP aims to provide support to selected households, including those with newborn children, for up to three years according to the program's guidelines. The elderly, especially those not working, are also a target group. Orphans are another target group, as are women currently pregnant or lactating (which can be assumed to correspond to women who were pregnant in the last 12 months). Finally, LEAP targets individuals with disabilities. For the elderly for example, some 252,000 of them live in poverty, and about half of those are not working (132,000). Paternal "orphans" living in poverty are estimated in the GLSS5 at 727,000, but this includes children whose father may have simply migrated outside of the household given that the information in the GLSS5 as to whether the father is alive or not is not available. There are also 388,494 maternal orphans in poverty and the number of double orphans in poverty is estimated at 293,296 (with the same caveat as to the limits of the data in the GLSS5 that tends to lead to an overestimation of the number of true orphans). The number of poor and pregnant women is estimated at 84,257, while the number of women in poverty who had a pregnancy in the last 12 months is estimated at 179,069. Finally, the number of individuals with disabilities in poverty is estimated at 17,983 (this is probably an underestimation of the issue of disability given that standard household survey questionnaires capture typically only the most severe forms of disability).

These statistics are also provided for the extreme poor. Note that all statistics in the first part of table 14.2 refer to the number of individuals in the demographic groups. The last two lines of table 14.2 provides the total number of households who have at least one individual in the following groups: Children aged 0–3; the elderly; the non-working elderly; double orphans (as proxied by the absence of both parents); pregnant women; women who were pregnant in the last 12 months; and individuals with disabilities. In one case we also include households with children aged 0–3, and in the other case we do not. If we take the more restrictive definition of the target groups for LEAP, we find an estimated total of 286,405 potential beneficiaries in the GLSS5. Thus, even if LEAP were to target only some of the subgroups identified in table 14.3 while also continuing to aim to reach only the poorest households, there is clearly room for expansion to reach households in need (in terms of potential population reach, it is useful to note that on average, a LEAP household consist of 3.7 individuals, versus 4.2 individuals for an average household, as recorded in LEAP's single registry).

LEAP's proposed expansion plan is reproduced in table 14.3. The objective is to reach in 2012 a total of 164,370 households. This would represent a population of more than 600,000 persons if the current household size of LEAP beneficiaries is

Table 14.3: Potential size of target demographic groups for LEAP benefits

	Total	Poor	Poor/ Total (%)	Extreme poor	Extreme poor/ Total (%)
Number of individuals					
Children aged 0–3	2,326,901	745,643	32.0	462,789	19.9
Elderly 65+	1,049020	252,068	24.0	165982	15.8
Non working elderly 65+	492,509	131,913	26.8	90595	18.4
Children 0–14 leaving without their father	2,940,394	727,470	24.7	420,984	14.3
Children 0–14 leaving without their mother	1,522,980	388,494	25.5	237,053	15.6
Children 0–14 leaving without any of the 2 parents	1,166,267	293,296	25.1	171,189	14.7
Women currently pregnant	329,616	84,257	25.6	56,602	17.2
Women pregnant in the last 12 months	598,795	179,069	29.9	115,313	19.3
Individuals with disabilities	460,66	17,983	39.0	11,225	24.4
Number of households					
Total number of households involved	2,821,646	729,015	25.8	446,224	15.8
Total number of households less children aged 0–3	1,874,937	462,268	24.7	286,405	15.3

Source: Authors using GLSS5 data.

maintained. Given the good targeting performance of the program, this expansion is positive and is likely to substantially reduce the share of program costs associated with administration and delivery of the benefits to households (this is discussed in more detail below). One could fear that the desire to cover a much larger number of districts by 2012 would increase costs versus concentrating interventions on a smaller number of districts that have the highest levels of poverty. However, if the LEAP targeting system were to be used to better target a range of other social programs currently implemented in Ghana, the fact that the LEAP program might cover a larger number of districts is a potential plus (this will also be discussed in more details below). The request put forward by LEAP to achieve its expansion is to increase its budget from the current level of 7.2 million GH¢ to 11.76 GH¢ in 2010, and ultimately 26.1 million GH¢ in 2012. While this level of funding would be substantial, it is not necessarily unwarranted given some other expenditures currently in place for poverty reduction that appear to be much less well targeted (and less strategic) than the LEAP program.

Table 14.4: Target expansion of LEAP program according to MESW

Year	2008	2009	2010	2011	2012
Number of households	15,000	35,000	65,000	115,000	164,370
Number of districts	50	50	70	100	138
Average number of households per district	300	700	929	1,150	1,188

Source: Ministry of Employment and Social Welfare, Annual Report 2008.

Cost Effectiveness of LEAP

LEAP is a well targeted program, but its targeting procedure implies administrative costs. The program is also very recent and it has not yet reached critical mass. This means that administrative costs as a share of the total LEAP budget are likely to be high. Data from LEAP suggest that for 2009, administrative costs may represent close to half of the program's budget (Subbarao 2009). This can lead to concerns regarding the cost effectiveness of the program, but three comments should be made regarding this cost effectiveness in terms of comparison with other social programs and likely changes in the future.

First, even if only half of LEAP's benefits were to reach the poor due to high administrative costs (which should not be the case when the program expands, as discussed below), this would not necessarily imply that the program is at a disadvantage versus some of the other social protection and poverty reduction programs currently implemented in Ghana. For example, it is often argued that less than half of the costs involved in public works programs end up representing additional net immediate income for program participants. This is partly because some benefits provided through wages to public works participants may substitute for earnings that those participants would have obtained if they had not participated in the program. It also has to do with the fact that public works also entail administrative costs as well as costs for the material used for construction which do not generate direct immediate benefits for program participants (although there should be some medium term benefits from local infrastructure built through public works). More generally, what matters for poverty reduction is the share of benefits from a program's costs that reach the poor. If we consider table 14.1, we see that about three fourths of program benefits reach the bottom 40 percent of the population. Even with very high administrative costs, three fourths of half of a program outlays reaching the poor represent a benefit to cost ratio of 37.5 cents to the dollar, which is still two to three times better than the benefit to cost ratio of food rice and electricity subsidies for the poor discussed in Part I of this report.

Second, once LEAP reaches a larger number of beneficiary households, the share of total costs of the program absorbed by administrative costs (including targeting costs) is likely to be reduced substantially. There are costs that will remain given the fact that the program is national in scope and that the proxy means-testing procedure must be maintained. But other costs related to central administration as well as delivery should be reduced in the future as a share of total costs thanks to economies of scale. Some of the current costs related to sensitization, workshops and training should also be reduced once the program is well established. And if some current costs appear to be too heavy in terms of expenditures for vehicles, fuel, staff trips and per diems, a detailed analysis of those costs could help in avoiding excesses and again an expansion of the program should result in a reduction in these expenses as a share of total outlays. Thus the current high administrative and delivery costs of LEAP are not likely to be a good indication of future benefit to costs ratios. For example, even if LEAP's total administration and delivery costs were to double between 2008 and 2012, the share of total costs allocated to administration and delivery would still be reduced by more than threefold if the targets in terms of beneficiaries are reached, since the expansion of the program aims to provide benefits to ten times more beneficiaries by 2012.

Third, and perhaps most importantly, LEAP is one of the only social programs that appear to be well targeted to the very poor in Ghana today. The targeting mechanism initiated by LEAP could potentially be used for many other programs, ranging from electricity subsidies to conditional cash transfers and fertilizer subsidies and possibly even public works. If LEAP's expertise in targeting were to be used to expand the use of the single registry to a larger set of programs, the administrative costs of the targeting mechanism could be shared by various programs so that as a proportion of the total outlays targeted through the mechanism, the administrative and delivery costs would be further reduced. This is what has been done in middle income countries, especially in Latin America, where a common targeting mechanism has been used to targeted many different social programs at relatively low cost.

Using a Common Targeting Mechanism for Multiple Programs: Chile's Experience[1]

For many years, the government of Chile has been using a proxy means-testing system for the targeting of many of its income transfers and other social programs. The system is based on the *ficha CAS*, a two-page form that households must complete if they wish to apply for benefits. The form includes information on housing conditions of the dwelling unit (e.g., material used for the construction of the housing unit, number and type of rooms, access to water, latrine and sanitary services, access to electricity, etc.) and on members of the dwelling unit (their occupation, educational level, date of birth, and income). Additional information is provided on material assets held by the household (such as housing status, television, heating equipment, and refrigerator). Points are allocated to households on the basis of the information provided, with the number of points fluctuating between 380 and 770 points. Households with a total of less than 500 points are considered as extremely poor and those with a total of between 500 and 540 points are considered as poor. The Ministry of Planning is responsible for the design of the *ficha CAS*. The recruitment of the employees administrating the form is done at the discretion of the municipality, but training must be provided by the Ministry. Municipalities usually separate the activities of data collection and data entry from those of needs assessment. Data collection and entry tend to be done by a department of social information within the municipality, while the control of the needs assessment is usually done by social workers and *técnico-sociales* (welfare assistants).

The national income transfer programs which are targeted using the CAS scoring system apply the formula in a strict manner to determine eligibility. The score obtained by a household automatically and exclusively prevails, so that eligibility depends only on the number of points obtained. The *ficha* is also used for targeting locally financed safety nets, but in this case social workers and other professionals can often give some weight to other eligibility criteria such as the presence of a chronic illness, the civil status of household members, and their actual financial resources at the time of request (the *ficha* is completed every three years, and there may be differences between the status of households when they apply for benefits, as compared to their status when they filled the form). For housing programs as well, differences can be observed in the use of the *ficha* at various levels of government. Professionals dealing with central government programs (*viviendas básicas* and *vivienda progresiva*) must follow the method of calculation defined by the Ministry of Housing, while professionals involved in municipal initiatives have some discretionary power.

The key advantage of using the ficha CAS for many different programs is that it reduces the cost of proxy means-testing. The cost of a CAS interview was about US$8.65 per household in the late 1990s. The Ministry of Planning estimates that 30 percent of Chilean households undergo interviews, which seems reasonable given that the target group for the subsidy programs is the poorest 20 percent. The CAS system is used as a targeting instrument for utility subsidies, income transfers, social housing subsidy, and pension subsidies among other programs. Because the fixed administrative costs of targeting are spread across several programs, the CAS is very cost-effective with administrative costs estimated at a mere 1.2 percent of the benefits distributed using the CAS system. For example, if the administrative costs of the CAS system were to be borne by the water subsidies alone they would represent 18 percent of the value of the subsidies. In addition, many national and local Government programs rely on the CAS system for their targeting. Locally, *Comunas* generate from their own budgets other safety net programs which vary in their amount and eligibility criteria. Overall, quantitative evaluations have suggested that the programs targeted using the *ficha CAS* have a good redistributive impact through good targeting. Chile's experience could be very beneficial for thinking about a potential expansion of the LEAP targeting system to cover other social programs that should benefit from an improvement in targeting.

Conclusion

The Government of Ghana launched the LEAP (Livelihood Empowerment Against Poverty) Program in March 2008 to supplement the income of "dangerously poor households" through cash transfers. This chapter shows that LEAP appears to be one of the best targeted programs in Ghana using data from LEAP's single registry of program participants. An expansion of the program would thus generate substantial benefits for the poor and would also help in reducing the share of program costs currently devoted to administration and delivery. LEAP's targeting mechanisms should however be reviewed to assess if it could be improved in terms of both its proxy means-testing and community-based components. In addition, a LEAP-inspired household questionnaire could be used to assess eligibility for other programs (possibly on a pilot basis) and for assessing ex post the targeting performance of some programs such as public works. There is thus scope for building on LEAP's experience to progressively design targeting mechanisms that could be used for multiple programs, or at least for those programs that are not geographically targeted. However, for programs serving the north, geographic targeting is often enough.

Note

1. This section is reproduced with minor changes from Clert and Wodon (2001).

CHAPTER 15

Ghana's National Youth Employment Program

Harold Coulombe, Moukim Temourov, and Quentin Wodon

To deal with youth unemployment, Ghana introduced in October 2006 the NYEP which initially aimed to employ 500,000 youth between 2006 and 2009. Wages paid by the NYEP appear to be high in comparison to market wages which makes the program costly. Administration costs are also substantial. In addition, the program essentially targets youth with a junior secondary education completed, which excludes many among the poor. To assess the potential impact of the NYEP on poverty we use the GLSS5 data and simulation techniques. We identify individuals who might be interested in participating in the NYEP and consider two parameters that affect the impact of the program on poverty: the program's targeting performance and substitution effects whereby only part of the wages paid to potential beneficiaries generate additional income since some beneficiaries would have done other work if they had not participated in the program. The results suggest that while the substitution effect may not be too large, overall targeting performance is likely to be very poor. While the simulations presented in this chapter rely on the distribution of NYEP beneficiaries for 2006–07, it is unlikely that the program's performance has changed substantially since then.

Youth Unemployment and Underemployment

Youth unemployment and underemployment is a major issue in sub-Saharan Africa as in many other areas of the developing world (World Bank 2007a). In many countries, children and youth represent up to 40 percent of the population. Thanks to programs such as the Education for All initiative, school enrollment rates are rapidly increasing, but many youth remain out of school, and are often without work or with work that do not build their skills. In Ghana, according to the GLSS5, the unemployment rate among youth ages 15–24 is about twice as high as the national unemployment rate (6 percent compared to 3 percent for the working population as a whole). In addition, many youths appear to be underemployed. Many declare working (hence are not considered unemployed) although they do not get any pay because they are trapped in subsistence activities. There is also a perception that although national poverty measures have been steadily decreasing in the country as a whole for the last 15 years, poverty in urban areas is increasing, especially in the capital area of Greater Accra, so that initiatives to help youth find jobs could contribute to increasing urban standards of living. This is however more a perception than a fact, as careful analysis of the available data suggests that over time, poverty in urban areas has decreased, even though there may have been a limited increase in Accra (Coulombe and Wodon 2007).

To deal with youth unemployment, various strategies can be used. One strategy consists in providing the right skills set to youth, so that they are better prepared to join the labor force. For this, traditional apprenticeships can prove to be a cost-effective alternative for especially lower skilled youth. Throughout West Africa, and especially in Ghana, traditional apprenticeships between a master craftsman and apprentice are a popular source of skills. The strengths of traditional apprenticeship are its practical orientation, self-regulation, and self-financing. Apprenticeships also cater to individuals who lack the educational requirements for formal training, but at the same time, evidence from Ghana from Adams et al. (2008) suggest that the impact from apprenticeships on occupational choice and wages may be limited.

Another approach consists in providing combined employment and training opportunities. Ghana introduced in October 2006, NYEP, a large program which aims to employ some 500,000 young people between 2006 and 2009. Ghana has a number of other employment-related programs, such as the Special Presidential Initiatives, the Rural Enterprise Development Program, the National Board of Small Scale Enterprises, and other small programs run by a number of sectoral ministries and agencies. But the new NYEP is by far the largest. Apart from providing temporary employment, the NYEP aims to train youths in various trades and occupations (Ministry of Manpower, Youth and Employment, 2006).

The launch of the NYEP may appear to be a sound idea to help youth find employment and improve their skills. According to lessons from a Youth Employment Inventory of 289 programs and interventions from 84 countries recently carried out by the World Bank (2007), public works and training program are more suitable than formal sector wage subsidy programs for youth in developing countries, since wage subsidies do not go far in developing countries due to the small size of the formal wage sector and hence do not reach the poor. Public works and training programs are also more likely to succeed than targeted youth entrepreneurship schemes because while these schemes may improve opportunities for young entrepreneurs in low-income countries where job growth in the formal economy is slow, but not all youth will be well suited for self-employment and failures rates for young entrepreneurs may be high.

However, careful targeting and screening for these programs is important to success and cost-effectiveness, and it may well be that training programs are substantially more expensive than public works program, especially if the training programs target relatively better educated workers and pay a high wage for the period of training. Training programs are also more successful when they involve the private sector in providing practical work experience and in identifying the kind of skills required. Engagement of the private sector in training is an effective tool to mitigate the risk of high-cost training disconnected from market demand and to increase on-the-job training. This is something that is also attempted in the NYEP, but it is unclear whether it is actually working.

While on paper the NYEP has a number of attractive characteristics, its actual implementation is not an example of best practice. In a country such as Ghana where public resources remain scarce, difficult trade-offs must be arbitrated to ensure that public spending is allocated to improve the well-being of the population. The NYEP appears to be an expensive program, because wages paid and administration costs are high. The program also targets to some extent urban areas, probably because that's in part where the issue of youth unemployment is most visible, and that's also where it is easier to provide meaningful training to youths participating in the program thanks to the network of firms and non-profit organizations that can employ youths there. But to the extent that poverty is much more severe in rural areas, one may wonder whether the high budgetary cost of the program is justified from the point of view of the objectives set forth in Ghana's growth and poverty reduction strategy.

Assessing the impact of the NYEP on poverty is a complicated matter, because the program is supposed not only to provide temporary employment, but also to build skills which may lead to a stream of higher future incomes for participants. Furthermore, the NYEP started to be implemented right after the last nationally representative survey with data on income and consumption was carried out in 2005–06, so that it is not possible to assess the impact of the program on poverty by looking using impact evaluation techniques such as matching procedures using survey data. At the same time, given that Ghana implements national consumption and income surveys only once every seven years on average, we cannot wait for the next survey to begin to try to assess what the potential impact of the program might be.

To provide a preliminary assessment of the potential impact of the NYEP on poverty, we rely in this chapter on simulation techniques rather than on impact evaluation techniques. The approach is very simple. We assess who may be potentially interested in participating in the NYEP by identifying working individuals without pay, as well as for every level of proposed wage in the NYEP, those individuals who work but now earn less than the NYEP wage, since all these individuals may indeed be interested in participating in the program to increase their earnings. We also consider as potential beneficiaries the unemployed whose reservation wage is below the proposed NYEP wage. Next, we randomly select among the pool of potential beneficiaries of the program a number of participants so as to match the distribution of NYEP beneficiaries by region that is available from administrative records of the program. Finally, we estimate for the assumed participants to the program two key parameters which affect the potential impact of the program on the poor: the targeting performance of the program, and the substitution effect of the program, whereby only part of the wages paid to beneficiaries generate additional income, because at least some of the beneficiaries would have done other work if they had not participated in the program. But first we provide some background on the program in the next section.

Brief Description of NYEP

NYEP aims to promote job creation for youths, defined as young people between the ages of 18 to 35. Launched in October 2006, the program aims to "empower the youth to be able to contribute more productively towards the socio-economic and sustainable development of the nation" according to the Youth Employment Implementation Guidelines (Government of Ghana, 2006). The NYEP program is built on the experience of the Skills Training and Employment Placement Program (STEP), which focused mainly on vocational training, including apprenticeship for graduates of junior and senior secondary schools, agricultural training for rural areas, and the teaching of entrepreneurship skills to college graduates. According to information from the Ministry of Manpower, Youth and Employment, between 2002 and 2004, 18,000 beneficiaries (9,384 men and 8,928 women) were trained by STEP.

The NYEP target of 500,000 jobs to be created over several years comes from a national youth employment survey/registry carried out prior to the program. This survey identified and registered approximately 175,000 young people willing to work, with only about 50 percent of them employed at the time of the survey (table 15.1). The survey revealed large regional disparities in youth unemployment, with the highest unemployment rates in large urban areas, particularly Ashanti and Greater Accra regions. At the same time, while youth unemployment may be higher in these areas, these are also the richest areas in the country, which suggests that the impact on poverty of the program may not be large.

Table 15.1: NYEP youth employment registry data

Region	No. of youth registered	Actual no. of youth employed	Share of youth employed (%)
Ashanti	24,322	7,537	31.0
Brong Ahafo	19,868	7,932	39.9
Central	13,016	7,697	59.1
Eastern	19,100	8,600	45.0
Greater Accra	22,363	7,922	35.4
Northern	21,959	16,528	75.3
Upper East	13,271	9,530	71.8
Upper West	12,590	9,688	76.9
Volta	18,094	8,674	47.9
Western	10,087	7,967	79.0
Total	174,670	92,075	52.7

Source: Ministry of Manpower, Youth and Employment 2005.

NYEP is a broad-based program, involving a number of national ministries and agencies, district assemblies, community-level groups, as well as NGOs and the private sector. The youth employment program targets a wide range of activities in different sectors, such as education, health, water and sanitation, agriculture, and others, and given its national coverage, the program operates in all 10 regions of the country. To reach its objectives, the program interacts on regular basis with a number of governmental structures at the national and regional levels and it also contracts out some of its activities to NGOs and the private sector. Many of the beneficiaries are employed to provide basic social services in the public sector. In 2007, NYEP provided employment to 92,075 young people (table 15.2), with about 42,000 of them working as teaching assistants and health and sanitation workers. Agrobusiness (16,383) was another important module that promotes farm and nonfarm income-generating activities in rural areas. The internships module (5,041) targeted mainly the educated youth in urban areas seeking employment with the private and public sectors. The employment modules for trades and vocation and ICT were still being developed. Administrative data from 2008 suggests a somewhat similar profile for the employment created, with an increase in the employment generated by some of the modules like water and sanitation. For that year, there were 132,976 beneficiaries, of which 28,778 were involved in community education, 4,602 were health workers, 29,263 were in agro-business, 21,005 were in water and sanitation, and 13,795 had paid internships (the other categories of employment were smaller). Thus overall the largest share of NYEP employment is still in the public sector, with teaching and nurse assistants financed by NYEP filling in for needed teachers and medical staff, especially in remote areas of the country. While the program is providing important social services, the youth hired by the program often lack proper training and may not have all necessary qualifications to carry out their tasks.

Table 15.2: NYEP beneficiary data

Employment modules	Beneficiaries 2006–07	Beneficiaries 2008
Community education teaching assistants	23,021	28,778
Agro-business	16,383	26,263
Health extension workers	14,000	14,602
Internship	5,200	13,795
Waste and sanitation	5,041	21,005
Community protection	1,300	3293
Others	26,760	22,180
Program staff	370	0.0
Afforestation	0.0	2,263
Self employed	0.0	797
Total	92,075	132,976

Source: Ministry of Manpower, Youth and Employment for 2006–07 and Subbarao (2009) for 2008.

The program is financed from four main sources: (a) specialized funds and national programs, such as Poverty Alleviation Fund, HIPC, Road Fund, Ghana Education Trust (GET) Fund, National Health Insurance System (NHIS), Women Development Fund, Food and Agriculture Budget Support Funds; (b) cost-sharing schemes and collaborative funding by district assemblies common funds (DACF), government agencies, civil society organizations, etc.; (3) funds recovered from the program participants; and (iv) other state sources. An earmarked amount from each specialized fund is used annually to financing various NYEP employment modules.

A key concern with the NYEP is its cost. Originally the Government of Ghana has planned an earmarked annual allocation of about 1,300,000 million GHC in old currency units (US$120 million) to finance NYEP activities. Based on the available data, the NYEP budget allocations for 2007 were estimated at a lower 677,000 million GHc, but this was still five times the total budget of the Ministry of Manpower, Youth, and Employment (estimated at 103,000 million GHc for 2007). By the end of 2007, since the program's launch in October 2006, the government had spent about 445,000 millions GH¢ (US$42 million) to benefit 92,075 young people, or about US$450 per beneficiary (some jobs were paid at much higher rates). NYEP's total budget for 2009 is higher at 273,840,039 GHc (new currency). This includes allowances to trainees, but also staff costs, workshops, monitoring and evaluation, vehicles and software, etc. Yet the program was expected to transfer to trainees only 76.8 million GH¢, so that less than a third of total costs are paid in allowances. In the past only part of the funds allocated were actually executed, so that total spending could be lower than the budget allocation, but the program does remain expensive.

Another concern is the long-term sustainability of the NYEP interventions and their impact. The program focuses mainly on short-term goals and tasks that project beneficiaries would not be able to carry out independently of program subsidies. Since most of the NYEP interventions are creating temporary jobs in the public sector, this approach may also create unrealistic expectations about future employment and earning prospects among the youth and could affect long-term employability of the beneficiaries.

Assessment of the Likely Targeting Performance of the NYEP

To assess the NYEP's targeting performance, we rely on simulations using the GLSS5. This is because administrative data on the share of total employment created by district combined with district level data on poverty would tend to overestimate the share of the benefits accruing to the poor. Indeed within districts beneficiaries tend to have relatively high levels of education (at least in comparison to the poor) so that the program will benefit better off individuals and households than the district data would suggest.

We start by providing estimates from the GLSS5 of the number of youths aged 18 to 35 who could be interested by a national youth employment program such as the NYEP or a public works program. We distinguish the NYEP from a public works program in two ways (the analysis for public works is provided in the next chapter using an approach similar to the simulations for the NYEP). First, we assume that the NYEP targets youth who have at least a junior secondary education completed, while the public works program is open to all without any education requirement. Second, we assume the NYEP pays much higher wages than a public works program would, which is indeed the case.

While we have no detailed data on the distribution of wages paid under the NYEP, anecdotal evidence suggests that these wages are high. In 2007, those with a Master degree may have received up to 2 million GHc (in old currency units) on a monthly basis, while wages may have been of the order of 1.5 million GHc for a Bachelor degree, one million for the Higher National Diploma offered at the polytechnic level, 800,000 GHc for Senior Secondary School graduates and 500,000 GHc for Junior Secondary School graduates. The majority of program participants are likely to be Higher National Diploma and Senior Secondary School graduates. These wages are well above the level of the minimum wage which was at the time of the GLSS5 survey at 13,500 GHc per day. By contrast, it is likely that a public works program would pay substantially lower wages, probably even well below the minimum wage, given that the minimum wage itself is high in comparison to the earnings of youth (Coulombe and Wodon, 2008).

For the simulations for the NYEP, to test the robustness of our results to our assumptions, we consider wages ranging from 500,000 GHc to 2 million GHc per month. These values for the wages to be paid are indicative only and somewhat arbitrary. Yet we are using enough different values to be able to assess the NYEP's likely targeting performance and potential impact on poverty. Table 15.3 provides data on the distribution of earnings of target individuals who are already working, as well as the distribution of the reservation wage declared by individuals who are unemployed and looking for work. The groups of individuals are presented in the first column of the table in terms of their monthly wages in thousand GH¢. Only youth who have completed their junior secondary education are included. Thus table 15.3 enables us assess the potential population that could be interested in a job in the NYEP. Note that in the actual NYEP program

Table 15.3: Potential beneficiaries of NYEP, individuals aged 18–35 with JSS completed, 2005–06

	Wage of workers					Unemployed reservation wage				
	% group	#people group	Monthly wage	Weekly hours	% poor	% group	#people group	Monthly wage	Weekly hours	% poor
Total										
0	23.8	399,946	0.0	34.0	22.3					
1–50	5.5	92,056	31.4	35.4	15.4	0.2	622	50.0	—	0.0
51–100	5.7	95,166	79.0	39.1	10.8	1.1	3,110	78.1	—	23.6
101–200	10.2	171,672	157.4	42.1	13.1	6.2	17,416	192.7	—	16.0
201–300	9.5	159,854	260.3	42.3	11.4	7.1	19,904	281.8	—	27.9
301–400	6.6	110,094	363.3	42.8	10.2	9.3	26,124	386.8	—	26.7
401–500	7.4	124,400	459.1	43.4	3.3	22.3	62,822	494.5	—	19.3
501–600	4.8	81,482	557.7	44.1	3.7	9.3	26,124	598.3	—	14.2
601–700	4.0	67,798	662.0	44.4	7.0	4.0	11,196	693.9	—	18.1
701–1,000	8.5	143,060	862.8	46.8	5.0	25.4	71,530	923.9	—	6.6
1,001–2,000	9.7	162,342	1,420.3	50.3	1.9	12.4	34,832	1,526.3	—	8.7
2,001+	4.3	72,774	3,749.0	50.9	0.8	2.7	7,464	4,081.5	—	8.6
Urban										
0	14.9	138,706	0.0	39.6	7.1	—	—	—	—	—
1–50	3.9	36,076	32.5	41.6	9.8	—	—	—	—	—
51–100	4.3	39,808	79.2	44.8	5.1	1.4	3,110	78.1	—	23.6
101–200	9.4	87,702	159.1	46.8	4.9	4.7	10,574	188.7	—	9.8
201–300	9.8	91,434	264.1	47.7	2.5	5.0	11,196	280.5	—	28.7
301–400	7.6	70,908	366.4	44.7	6.9	8.1	18,038	387.3	—	9.2
401–500	8.5	78,994	464.3	45.7	1.3	22.9	51,004	495.8	—	21.6
501–600	6.2	57,846	561.7	46.8	3.1	10.3	23,014	598.1	—	16.0
601–700	4.7	44,162	663.5	47.1	3.9	4.2	9,330	697.6	—	8.8
701–1,000	11.3	105,118	866.6	49.3	2.5	26.5	59,090	916.7	—	6.4
1,001–2,000	13.3	123,778	1,419.7	53.1	1.0	14.0	31,100	1,518.2	—	6.7
2001+	6.3	58,468	3,880.1	51.8	0.0	2.8	6,220	4,189.6	—	0.0
Rural										
0	34.9	261,240	0.0	30.9	30.8	—	—	—	—	—
1–50	7.5	55,980	30.6	31.3	19.1	1.1	622	50.0	—	0.0
51–100	7.4	55,358	78.9	34.7	15.2	—	—	—	—	—
101–200	11.2	83,970	155.6	37.1	21.8	11.7	6,842	200.0	—	27.6
201–300	9.2	68,420	255.9	35.9	21.7	14.9	8,708	283.6	—	26.8
301–400	5.2	39,186	358.4	39.6	15.3	13.8	8,086	386.0	—	56.7
401–500	6.1	45,406	450.1	39.5	6.7	20.2	11,818	489.7	—	10.1
501–600	3.2	23,636	549.6	38.4	5.0	5.3	3,110	600.0	—	0.0
601–700	3.2	23,636	659.1	39.4	13.0	3.2	1,866	678.2	—	57.5
701–1,000	5.1	37,942	853.3	40.9	11.1	21.3	12,440	952.6	— /	7.7
1,001–2,000	5.2	38,564	1,422.3	41.7	4.7	6.4	3,732	1,615.5	—	30.4
2001+	1.9	14,306	3,277.6	47.7	3.6	2.1	1,244	3,640.4	—	43.6

Source: Authors' estimation using GLSS5 data.

Note: — = not available.

documentation, it is not entirely clear whether a strict education eligibility condition is imposed, but due to the training component of the program and the types of jobs proposed to participants, it seems that the program indeed targets youth with at least junior secondary education completed as opposed to youth with lower levels of education.

Table 15.3 suggests that there are a large group of eligible youths who are working without pay. These individuals are likely to be interested the NYEP. Clearly, some may not apply for such a program due to various constraints (they may not be paid, but still doing important work that has to be done for their household, and hence they may not be able to participate in the program). Also, depending on the wage paid by the NYEP, more individuals could be interested in participating in the program if their current wage is below that proposed by the program. We cannot identify those who would actually be interested and those who would not. But for the purpose of the simulations, all the individuals unpaid for their work, as well as all individuals who earn less than the proposed wage are potential beneficiaries of the program, and we can randomly chose some of these individuals as participants in public works for each proposed wage level to simulate the impact of the program on poverty. Finally, among the unemployed, those who have a reservation wage below the NYEP wage are also potential beneficiaries.

The estimates in table 15.3 therefore give us an upper estimate for the potential number of youths that might be interested in the NYEP depending on the wage provided in the program, and without any eligibility condition apart from the age and education of the individual. Figure 15.1 summarizes the data on the potential number of participants by quintiles of consumption per equivalent adult of the households to which the individuals who are potential beneficiaries belong. This is done for the four potential wage levels. Two findings stand out. First, the number of individuals potentially interested in the program appears to be large (albeit less large than what is observed for the public works in the next chapter due to the education requirement assumed for the NYEP), in part because many youth are working without pay and might thereby be interested in getting cash income through the NYEP. Second, the targeting performance or likely benefit incidence of the program depends fundamentally on whether the program is implemented mostly in urban or rural areas. Clearly, in urban areas, the program would probably be regressive, since most of the potential beneficiaries belong to the better off quintiles of the population (this is because urban households tend to have much higher levels of consumption than rural households). By contrast, the programs could potentially be better targeted to individuals belonging to households who tend to be poor if the focus were placed on providing employment in rural areas, but even there, the benefits accruing to the poorest would probably be smaller than those accruing to the better off.

The number of potential beneficiaries as estimated from the survey is much larger than the number of persons actually employed by the NYEP or the number of youths registered in the program. To assess the potential impact of the NYEP on the basis of the numbers of jobs actually created, we randomly select among all potential beneficiaries of the program (the number of which depends on the wage provided) a number of participants so as to match the distribution of the actual program participants provided in table 15.1 by region. This is done using 25 random replications, and average values obtained with the 25 replication are reported. This is also done for each of the wages assumed to be provided. In these simulations, we make sure that we select a number of simulated beneficiaries from the NYEP equal to the number of participants in the program in each of the geographic areas for which we have data on participants. This

Figure 15.1: Distribution of potential beneficiaries of NYEP National

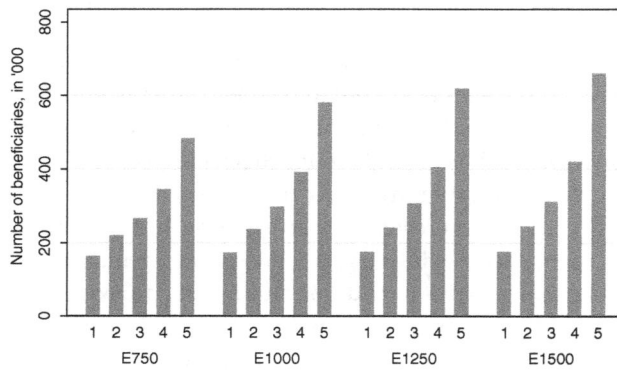

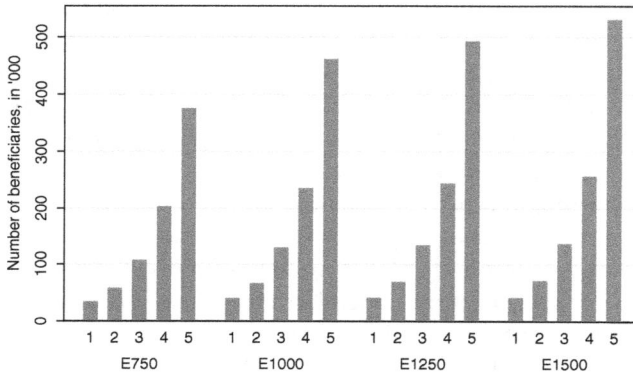

Urban

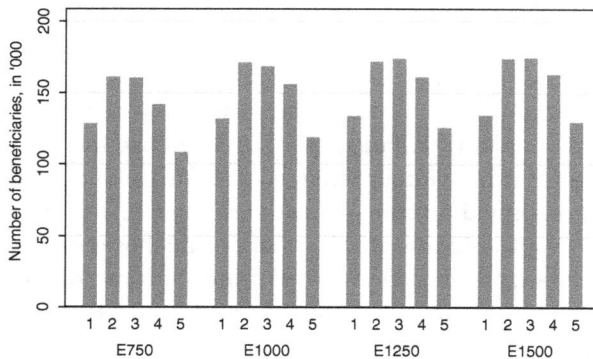

Rural

Source: Authors' estimation using GLSS5 data.

was done using data on participants at the end of 2007, but the limited changes in the number of jobs created since then, for example in 2008, as well as the limited changes in the geographic location of the jobs created would not affect the results much.

Table 15.4 provides estimates of the leakage to the nonpoor of the program, as well as potential wage substitution effects. The first column provides the estimate of the total

Table 15.4: Potential leakage effects of the NYEP for poverty reduction by region, 2005–06

	Region	#of people	Poverty headcount (%)	Additional wage In '000 monthly	Leakage rate (%)	#registered/ #people (%)	#job/ #people (%)
E750	Western	139,950	10.9	557.0	91.9	7.2	5.7
	Central	105,118	14.6	578.3	88.7	12.4	7.3
	Greater Accra	263,728	8.9	488.7	94.2	8.5	3.0
	Volta	118,802	19.9	573.9	84.8	15.2	7.3
	Eastern	187,222	12.1	583.4	90.6	10.2	4.6
	Ashanti	357,650	11.1	580.7	91.4	6.8	2.1
	Brong Ahafo	135,596	18.8	581.3	85.4	14.7	5.8
	Northern	62,822	22.5	542.9	83.7	35.0	26.3
	Upper East	51,004	46.6	603.3	62.5	26.0	18.7
	Upper West	57,846	62.7	672.5	43.8	21.8	16.7
	Total	1,479,738	14.2	560.5	89.4	11.8	6.2
E1000	Western	156,122	9.6	765.1	92.7	6.5	5.1
	Central	121,912	14.5	795.3	88.5	10.7	6.3
	Greater Accra	338,990	7.8	679.1	94.7	6.6	2.3
	Volta	125,022	19.3	803.6	84.5	14.5	6.9
	Eastern	209,614	11.0	768.6	91.5	9.1	4.1
	Ashanti	396,214	10.4	788.7	91.8	6.1	1.9
	Brong Ahafo	144,926	18.4	797.4	85.3	13.7	5.5
	Northern	69,664	21.4	725.3	84.5	31.5	23.7
	Upper East	57,846	46.0	857.6	60.6	22.9	16.5
	Upper West	60,956	61.8	896.9	44.6	20.7	15.9
	Total	1,681,266	13.1	761.3	90.0	10.4	5.5
E1250	Western	162,964	9.3	984.0	92.7	6.2	4.9
	Central	126,266	13.9	1010.5	88.8	10.3	6.1
	Greater Accra	362,626	7.4	891.9	94.7	6.2	2.2
	Volta	129,376	18.9	1034.5	84.4	14.0	6.7
	Eastern	213,968	11.1	1003.1	91.1	8.9	4.0
	Ashanti	414,874	10.1	1009.1	91.8	5.9	1.8
	Brong Ahafo	148,658	17.8	1022.0	85.4	13.4	5.3
	Northern	70,286	21.2	969.4	83.6	31.2	23.5
	Upper East	58,468	46.6	1098.1	59.1	22.7	16.3
	Upper West	62,822	62.3	1130.6	43.7	20.0	15.4
	Total	1,750,308	12.7	983.4	90.0	10.0	5.3

(Table continues on next page)

Table 15.4:   (continued)

	Region	#of people	Poverty headcount	Additional wage	Leakage rate	#registered/ #people	#job/ #people
			(%)	In '000 monthly	(%)	(%)	(%)
E1500	Western	166,074	9.6	1215.1	92.2	6.1	4.8
	Central	129,376	13.6	1235.3	88.8	10.1	5.9
	Greater Accra	392,482	6.8	1093.8	95.0	5.7	2.0
	Volta	133,108	18.4	1252.6	84.6	13.6	6.5
	Eastern	218,322	10.8	1225.1	91.2	8.7	3.9
	Ashanti	427,936	9.7	1225.5	92.1	5.7	1.8
	Brong Ahafo	153,012	17.3	1240.3	85.7	13.0	5.2
	Northern	71,530	20.7	1196.6	83.5	30.7	23.1
	Upper East	61,578	45.2	1313.8	60.4	21.6	15.5
	Upper West	62,822	62.3	1380.6	42.7	20.0	15.4
	Total	1,816,240	12.3	1199.3	90.2	9.6	5.1

Source: Authors' estimation using GLSS5 data.

number of potential beneficiaries of the program depending on the wage level, as estimated from table 15.3 at the national level. For example, at a wage level of one million GHc per month, 156,122 individuals in the Western region might be potential beneficiaries of the NYEP according to our method for identifying such potential beneficiaries. The second column provides the share of individuals living in households who are poor among potential beneficiaries of the program. For example, at a wage of one million GH¢, 9.6 percent of the potential beneficiaries in the Western region live in a household in poverty according to the official definition of poverty (see Coulombe and Wodon, 2007). The third column provides the additional wage to be obtained by each individual, on average, depending on the wage proposed for the program. At a wage of one million GH¢, out of that amount, on average 765,100 GH¢ represents additional income for potential participants to the program, and this provides an estimate of potential wage substitution effects.

The next column provides the leakage rate, which is computed as one minus the product of the poverty rate times the additional wage divided by the reference wage of the program. The overall leakage rate is very high. The main driver is not the substitution effects (even though about one quarter of the wage is "lost" due to the fact that some of the participants would have to give up other earnings to participate in the program), but rather poor targeting to the poor. The last two columns provide data on the ratios of the number of individuals registered in the NYEP or participating in the program as compared to the number of potential beneficiaries of the NYEP as we estimate them by region. With a wage rate of one million GHc per month, the registration rate among potential participants is 10.4 percent and jobs are provided to only 5.5 percent of potential participants. We are overestimating the potential number of participants since we do not know about specific constraints that some individuals may have in participating in the program, but this helps to show that at the high wages provided under the NYEP, there could be a large demand for jobs that would be difficult to supply at an affordable cost.

The results in table 15.4 suggest that while the substitution effects are not negligible, most of the wages obtained by NYEP participants are likely to be additional wages for them and their household. This is in part because some of the individuals concerned are now working without pay and are considered as potential beneficiaries of the program. By contrast, losses for poverty reduction due to the fact that many potential participants are not poor are much larger. This results in a high overall leakage rate from the point of view of poverty reduction of 90 percent at the national level for all the wage levels. The poor performance in terms of reaching the poor with the NYEP is observed despite efforts to target the program, at least to some extent, to poorer areas. Because in poorer areas there are few individuals with junior secondary education completed, the number of program participants as a share of the number of potential beneficiaries is higher in poorer areas. Remember that we simulate the NYEP impact using data on how the program is geographically targeted. For example, the ratio of participants to potential beneficiaries is lowest in Ashanti and Greater Accra. In terms of registered youth as compared to potential beneficiaries, the ratio is 6.6 percent in Greater Accra (for a wage of one million GH¢), as compared to a rate of 31.5 percent in the Northern area. Clearly, the simulated NYEP has pro-poor regional bias when we take into account the eligibility criteria, but this does not help much for its potential impact on poverty due to the education requirement. The main benefit of the program for the poor then must come from the fact that some program participants are involved in the provision of education and health services in poor areas, so that there may be positive impacts from their work later on through higher human capital accumulation, especially among children.

Assessment of the Likely Poverty Impact of the NYEP

The estimated potential impact of the NYEP is given in table 15.5. The estimates are obtained in a very simple way. For program participants (as simulated by us on the basis of the distribution of workers in the NYEP by region) who belong to households living in poverty, we add to the consumption aggregate of the household the gains in earnings obtained by the participants, and we recomputed poverty using the same poverty lines. In other words, we assume that the full amount of the earnings gains for program participants translate into additional consumption for their households. For higher wages, the impact is higher, since the additional earnings obtained by participants are higher, but note that the number of participants is kept unchanged since it is based on the data provided in table 15.2 for the NYEP.

At the wage level of the NYEP which prevailed in 2007, which was probably on average of the order of one million GHc per month or higher, one can conjecture that

Table 15.5: Potential impact on poverty of the NYEP, National, 2005–2006

	Within target group of potential beneficiaries		Whole population	
	Headcount	Poverty gap	Headcount	Poverty gap
E750	0.845	0.276	0.057	0.019
E1000	0.778	0.245	0.059	0.019
E1250	0.784	0.241	0.062	0.019
E1500	0.757	0.232	0.062	0.019

Source: Authors' estimation using GLSS5 data.

the program is reducing the headcount index of poverty at the national level by only 0.059 percentage point, which is very small. As will be discussed in the next chapter, the impact of public works on poverty may not be much larger, but the cost of public works would be significantly lower than the cost of the NYEP. A similar story emerges with the poverty gap, which takes into account the distance separating the poor from the poverty line (with a zero distance given to the nonpoor). The NYEP clearly does not have a large impact despite its cost.

Conclusion

As in many other countries, youth unemployment is a major issue in Ghana. In October 2006, the National Youth Employment Program (NYEP) was created by Ghana's government to provide temporary employment as well as training to up to 500,000 people between the ages of 18 and 35 over the period from 2006 to 2009. Even though efforts are made to serve the rural areas of the northern regions, the program still appears to have a bias in favor of urban and relatively wealthier areas (at least in terms of the number of registered youths in the program). This may be due in part to the fact that these are the areas where the issue of youth unemployment is most visible, and that's also where it is easier to provide meaningful training to youths participating in the program thanks to the network of firms and non-profit organizations that can employ youths there. More importantly, the program targets youth with a junior secondary education completed or higher, and this is likely to mean that the impact of the program on poverty is likely to be limited. Wages also appear to be very high, so that the program is costly, and perhaps leading to unrealistic expectations in terms of future wages for the youth enrolled in the program.

Using the GLSS5 and simple simulation techniques, we have estimated in this chapter the likely targeting performance and impact on poverty of the program. Our estimates suggest that at assumed prevailing wages for the NYEP of about one million GHc per month on average (in old currency units), the program is reducing the headcount of poverty at the national level by only a very small amount. This is in part because the leakage rate (with considers both wage substitution effects and leakage of the program to the nonpoor) is high, at about 90 percent. The main reason for this high leakage rate is less the fact that there is a substitution effect of the program whereby only part of the wages paid to beneficiaries generates additional income since some beneficiaries would have done other work if they had not participated in the program. Rather, the limited impact and poor targeting performance of the program is due mainly to the education criteria implicitly used to screen participants and the fact that the program does not focus explicitly on poor areas. When compared to a public works program (as discussed in the next chapter), the NYEP appears to be four to five times more expensive for reducing poverty than public works.

CHAPTER 16

Simulating Labor Intensive Public Works in Ghana

Harold Coulombe and Quentin Wodon

Labor intensive public works are a popular program to implement in time of crisis. They provide earnings to program participants while at the same time building local infrastructure. Ghana has had previous experience in such programs, albeit at a small scale. A scale-up of such programs is being envisioned as part of a World Bank project on productive safety nets. This chapter provides first a brief review of some of the international experience with public works. Next the chapter relies on simulation techniques to provide an assessment of the potential targeting performance and impact of labor intensive public works on poverty following the same method as that used for the assessment of the NYEP in the previous chapter. We use the GLSS5 to identify individuals who might be interested in participating in public works and consider two parameters that affect the impact of the program on the poor: targeting performance and substitution effects. The results suggest that public works might not target the poor very well if they were implemented nationally, but targeting performance could be good if the program were targeted to rural areas and especially to the rural north. In this case, labor intensive public works could be four to five times more efficient to reduce poverty than the NYEP.

Labor Intensive Public Works: A Brief Review[1]

Labor intensive public works (sometimes also referred to as workfare although the workfare concept is more general) provide employment through public works projects. One classic example is Trabajar in Argentina. In this program, projects are identified by local governments, NGOs and community groups, and can provide employment for no more than 100 days per participant. Project proposals are reviewed by a regional committee, and projects with higher poverty and employment impacts are favored. Workers hired by the project are paid by the Ministry of Labor. The other costs are financed by local authorities. Examples of eligible projects include the construction or repair of schools, health facilities, basic sanitation facilities, small roads and bridges, community kitchens and centers, and small dams and canals.

While public works are often assumed to benefit the poor who are unemployed or underemployed, this is not necessary the case and steps often have to be taken to ensure good targeting, for example by ensuring that wages are below the minimum wage if that minimum wage is higher than the market wage, and by targeting programs geographically.

In addition, a key benefit of the program resides in the local infrastructure that is being built, but it is therefore needed to make sure that the projects do correspond to local priority needs. In a reform of Trabajar implemented in the late 1990s, several steps were taken to improve the performance of the program in these areas. The focus of the reform was placed on increasing community participation and funding in the choice of the projects to be financed. Trabajar now works in collaboration with local community groups, NGOs, and municipalities who present projects for selection. Projects must first be approved for technical feasibility. Next, they are selected on a points basis. More points are awarded to projects located in poorer areas, yielding larger public benefits, benefiting from well-regarded sponsoring community groups or NGOs, and reducing labor costs below the minimum wage. These new features have improved targeting both at the geographic and individual levels. The involvement of local groups has also improved the quality of monitoring and feedback for the projects.

Local projects funded by labor intensive public works can (but need not) be fairly similar to those financed by social funds. One important difference between a social fund project and a workfare project is that the workfare project is likely to be supervised by local authorities, rather than by independent agencies, and construction is typically not contracted to the private sector, but is carried out by the sponsoring agency, which can include local and provincial governments, private groups, and national organizations. Another difference is that workfare programs have the generation of employment and income as their priority, while social funds focus more on the quality of the infrastructure generated.

Projects financed by Trabajar are limited to poor areas as identified by a poverty map. Moreover, wages are set to be no higher than 90 percent of the prevailing market wage, so that the workers have an incentive to return to private sector jobs when these are available. Thus, the program involves self targeting apart from geographic targeting. Overall, targeting of the poor under Trabajar II (the second round of the project) has been reported to be good, with 75 percent of the funds reaching the bottom 20 percent of the income distribution, and 40 percent reaching the bottom 5 percent. However, the supply of jobs in the program depends on budgetary allocations as well as the ability of local communities to identify viable projects. Trabajar has provided employment to no more than 1 or 2 percent of the labor force, at a time when unemployment has ranged from 13 to 18 percent of the labor force.

Many other countries have implemented public works in virtually all regions of the world. The advantages of workfare programs include their ability to expand quickly during a crisis, once the basic mechanisms have been established, and to reach the poor through area targeting and, within poor areas, through self targeting thanks to the low wages. However, a problem is that the cost of generating one dollar in additional income for the poor through public works is typically large, in the range of three dollars or more. To understand why, a measure of cost effectiveness and a simple decomposition are useful.

Consider as a measure of cost effectiveness the share of total program costs which reaches the poor through net increases in earnings. In the spirit of Ravallion (1999), assume that without public works, an individual has a probability F^* to find employment at market wage W^*. Expected earnings are F^*W^*. With public works, the individual earns the public works wage W. If the individual can continue to search for private or self-employment while participating in public works, with probability F of finding such employment, the expected wage with public works is $FW^*+(1-F)W$. The net wage benefit from the program for the worker is NWB = (1-F)W - (F* - F)W*. If the worker gets unemployment benefits or a subsistence allowance S, the wage benefit is reduced to NWB = (1-F)W - (F* - F)W* - (1-F*)S. If the program costs G to the Government per worker employed, a measure of cost effectiveness is the share of public expenditures transferred to workers as wage gain NWB/G. This measure can be decomposed as:

$$\frac{NWB}{G} = \frac{C}{G}\frac{(W+L)}{C}\frac{W}{(W+L)}\frac{NWB}{W}$$

$$\begin{array}{cccc} / & | & \backslash & \backslash \end{array}$$

budget wage targeting proportionate
leverage share performance wage gain

The determinants of cost-effectiveness are then (a) the leverage ratio C/G, where C is the total cost per worker including community funding; (b) the wage share (W+L)/C, where W stands for wages paid to the poor and L stands for leakage due to wages paid for the nonpoor; (c) the targeting performance W/(W+L) which is the percentage of wages reaching the poor; and (d) the proportionate wage gain NWB/W. In a country like Ghana a reasonable value for the proportionate wage gain may be as high as 0.8 because even though the workfare wages are low and the poor typically find some other way to generate resources, for example through part-time informal employment when they do not have access to the programs, many participants in the program are likely to work without pay or for a very low pay. While the self-selection involved and the priorities given to poor areas may help in targeting public works in middle income countries such as Argentina, this is more difficult in a country like Ghana, especially if geographic targeting is weak for example due to political economy pressures to provide jobs in urban areas as well as in rural areas. Thus the targeting performance may be low, at about 0.5.

The wage share can often be obtained from administrative records by multiplying the number of work days created by the program by the wage rate, and dividing this amount by the total cost of the program. In many cases, the wage share will not exceed 0.7. Finally, when the program is almost entirely financed by the federal state (even though project selection may be done at the local level), the budget leverage is equal to one (in the case of Trabajar, there is budget leverage, but while this saves money for the central government, it still has to be paid by local governments). The measure of cost effectiveness is obtained by multiplying the various parameters. In our illustrative examples, this measure would be equal to 0.8*0.5*0.7=0.28, in which case the total cost of generating one dollar in net additional wage earnings for program participants is 1/0.28=3.6 dollars. It thus typically costs three or more dollars to the national or federal government to transfer one dollar to the poor in additional wages.

The notion that it costs three or more dollars to transfer one dollar of income to the poor through workfare could be challenged, in that the benefits could be higher for two reasons (for a fuller discussion of these points, see Wodon 2000). First, the decomposition method presented above does not take into account the benefits of the public works themselves, which can be substantial if the workers are put to good use. The problem, however, is that these benefits will be enjoyed during the whole life of the infrastructure built, while what the poor need in times of crises is immediate income support. If the poor have high discount rates (which they do in general, but especially in times of crisis when their resources do not provide for basic subsistence), the discounted value of the benefits generated by the public works may be quite low. Moreover, since the emphasis is on job creation rather than investments, there may be a bias toward "make work" or prestige projects that may not be highly valuable. This may be particularly true in a crisis, when a rapid expansion of the program exhausts the backlog of viable projects. Second, the decomposition presented assumes that only the net proportionate wage gain must be taken into account for measuring the program's impact. However, in periods of high unemployment, it could be argued that at least part of the difference between the public works wage and what the program participant would have earned by himself without the program will be available as earnings for another worker who does not participate in the program and who is also under-employed. At the extreme, the whole wage rate could be taken into account in the cost-benefit analysis, which would enhance cost-effectiveness. In the Africa context however, as will be shown below, substitution effects tend to be small, and much of the loss for poverty reduction that takes place in public works is likely to come from mis-targeting the poor.

On the other hand, arguments could also be put forward to argue that the net transfers to the poor may be lower than predicted by the decomposition. For example, since workers are paid by local authorities, the opportunities for corruption and political bias in the choice of projects may be more pronounced. With Trabajar, there remained some evidence when evaluations were carried out of political influences in the choice of participants and gender discrimination (few women are selected in some areas). Second, when contributions are required from communities, the poorest communities may not always be well positioned to submit proposals for projects and/or to contribute to non-wage costs. In this case, the targeting performance of the program may suffer, because the contribution of geographic targeting to overall targeting performance will be reduced. These weaknesses are less likely to arise in Ghana given that public works typically do not require there substantial co-funding at the local level.

In what follows, we focus on the wage component of the public works program and ignore other costs such as materials and administration. We use the GLSS5 to identify individuals who might be interested in participating in labor intensive public works and consider as was done for the NYEP in the previous chapter two parameters affecting the likely impact of the program: targeting performance and substitution effects, which correspond respectively to the ratios NWB/W and W/(W+L) in the above framework.

Assessment of the Likely Targeting Performance and Poverty Impact of Public Works

To assess the potential targeting performance of labor intensive public works, we use the GLSS5 in a way similar to what was done in the previous chapter for the NYEP. We start by providing in this section. The methodology is repeated for readers who may not have consulted the previous chapter. We start by estimating the number of youths aged 18 to 35 who could be interested by the public works program. While for the NYEP a minimum education was required in the simulations, for public works no education requirement is required since the jobs involved tend to require very low skills. It is likely that a public works program would pay low wage to achieve self-targeting, probably even well below the minimum wage, given that the minimum wage itself in Ghana is rather high in comparison to the earnings of youth (Coulombe and Wodon 2008). We will consider wages ranging from 50,000 to 200,000 GHc per month (old currency in 2005–06 value given that we use the GLSS5 for the estimations). These values for the wages to be paid are indicative only and somewhat arbitrary. Yet we are using enough different values to be able to assess the targeting performance and potential impact on poverty of the program.

Table 16.1 provides data on the distribution of earnings of individuals who are already working, as well as on the distribution of the reservation wage declared by individuals who are unemployed and looking for work. The groups of individuals are presented in the first column of the table in terms of their monthly wages in thousand GHc. All youths are included without restrictions since public works do not require specific skills. The choice of the age group is made to compare the results to the NYEP, but for public works that would be implemented in practice, older individuals would be eligible. Table 16.1 shows that there is a very large group of youth who are working but are not paid (37 percent of the youths who are working at the national level). These individuals are likely to be interested in public works. Some may not apply for such a program due to various constraints (they may not be paid, but still doing important work that has to be done for their household, and hence they may not be able to participate in the program). Also, depending on the wage paid by public works, additional individuals could be interested in participating in the program if their current wage is below that proposed by the program. We cannot identify those who would actually be interested and those who would not. But for the purpose of the simulations, individuals unpaid for their work, as well as those who earn less than the proposed wage are potential beneficiaries, and we can randomly chose some of these individuals as participants in public works for each proposed wage level to simulate targeting performance. Among the unemployed, those with a reservation wage below the public works proposed are also potential beneficiaries.

The estimates in table 16.1 therefore give us an upper bound for the potential number of youths that might be interested in a public works program, depending on the wage provided in the program, and without any eligibility condition apart from age. Figures 16.1a to 16.1c summarize the data on the potential number of participants by quintiles of per capita consumption of the households to whom the individuals who are potential beneficiaries belong. This is done for four potential wage levels, from 150,000 GHc per month to 300,000 GHc per month, which is about the level of the minimum wage at the time of the survey. Two findings stand out. First, the number of individuals potentially interested in the program appears to be very large, especially because many youth are working without pay and might thereby be interested in getting cash income through public works. Second, the targeting performance or likely benefit incidence of the program depends fundamentally on whether the program is implemented mostly in urban or rural areas. In urban areas, the program would be regressive, since most of the potential beneficiaries belong to the better off quintiles of the population (this is because urban households tend to have much higher levels of consumption than rural households). By contrast, the programs could potentially be better targeted to the poor if the focus is placed on providing employment solely in rural areas.

To assess the potential targeting performance of public works, we randomly selected, among all potential beneficiaries of the program (the number of which depends on the wage provided), a number of participants so as to match the number of jobs created under the NYEP simulations in the previous chapter. This is done using 25 random

Table 16.1: Potential beneficiaries of public works among individuals aged 18–35, National 2005–06

	Wage of workers					Unemployed reservation wage				
	Percent group	# of people group	Monthly wage	Weekly hours	Percent poor (%)	Percent group	# of people group	Monthly wage	Weekly hours	Percent poor (%)
Total										
0	37.0	1,503,374	0.0	33.5	42.8	—	—	—	—	—
1–50	7.2	290,474	30.1	33.1	30.2	0.7	3,732	39.0	—	77.0
51–100	6.9	278,656	78.7	36.5	23.9	1.7	8,708	82.9	—	52.1
101–200	9.3	379,420	156.3	38.8	18.6	7.5	39,186	184.5	—	26.3
201–300	8.6	348,320	254.6	40.0	19.5	11.9	62,200	272.1	—	38.8
301–400	5.4	220,188	357.8	40.1	17.3	13.0	68,420	384.8	—	36.1
401–500	6.0	243,202	455.9	41.9	12.7	22.8	119,424	489.0	—	32.3
501–600	3.2	130,620	556.8	42.3	7.4	7.5	39,186	596.5	—	24.8
601–700	2.7	110,716	659.7	41.7	10.6	4.3	22,392	685.1	—	34.7
701–1000	5.5	223,298	852.9	44.8	8.5	19.2	100,764	920.2	—	9.1
1,001–2,000	5.5	223,920	1403.9	48.2	3.6	9.7	51,004	1,539.1	—	14.5
2,001+	2.7	109,472	3855.1	46.8	5.1	1.8	9,330	3,859.2	—	7.1
Urban										
0	16.9	236,982	0.0	37.1	15.7	—	—	—	—	—
1–50	5.0	70,908	30.7	38.1	18.6	—	—	—	—	—
51–100	5.5	77,750	78.5	42.7	13.0	1.4	4,354	80.4	—	12.4
101–200	9.9	139,328	158.4	44.2	6.4	5.9	18,660	179.6	—	13.6
201–300	10.6	148,658	260.0	46.8	6.0	9.0	28,612	272.6	—	21.9
301–400	7.9	111,338	363.9	44.7	8.8	11.1	35,454	384.2	—	14.1
401–500	8.3	116,936	463.7	44.7	4.3	21.1	67,176	493.7	—	23.4
501–600	5.8	80,860	559.6	45.7	5.4	9.2	29,234	598.6	—	17.6
601–700	4.5	62,822	662.1	44.6	7.4	3.7	11,818	697.0	—	9.7
701–1,000	9.9	138,706	861.4	48.5	3.5	24.4	77,750	912.7	—	6.6
1,001–2,000	10.6	149,280	1,417.8	52.3	1.2	12.1	38,564	1,516.9	—	12.0
2001+	5.1	71,530	3,976.9	50.4	1.6	2.1	6,842	4,198.5	—	0.0
Rural										
0	47.7	1,266,392	0.0	32.7	49.3	—	—	—	—	—
1–50	8.3	219,566	29.9	31.3	34.2	1.8	3,732	39.0	—	77.0
51–100	7.6	200,906	78.7	33.9	28.5	2.1	4,354	85.8	—	100.0
101–200	9.0	240,092	155.0	35.5	26.0	10.0	20,526	190.8	—	42.5
201–300	7.5	199,662	250.8	35.3	29.0	16.3	33,588	271.5	—	61.2
301–400	4.1	108,850	352.2	35.9	25.0	16.0	32,966	385.5	—	61.9
401–500	4.8	126,266	448.9	39.3	20.2	25.4	52,248	480.7	—	48.2
501–600	1.9	49,760	552.9	37.6	10.0	4.8	9,952	588.7	—	51.1
601–700	1.8	47,894	656.6	38.0	14.7	5.1	10,574	668.9	—	68.9
701–1,000	3.2	84,592	839.0	39.0	16.5	11.2	23,014	947.2	—	18.2
1,001–2,000	2.8	74,640	1,376.2	40.0	8.2	6.0	12,440	1,635.1	—	25.4
2,001+	1.4	37,942	3,623.4	40.0	11.7	1.2	2,488	3,091.9	—	23.1

Source: Authors' estimation using GLSS5 data.
Note: — = not available.

Figure 16.1: Distribution of potential beneficiaries of public works

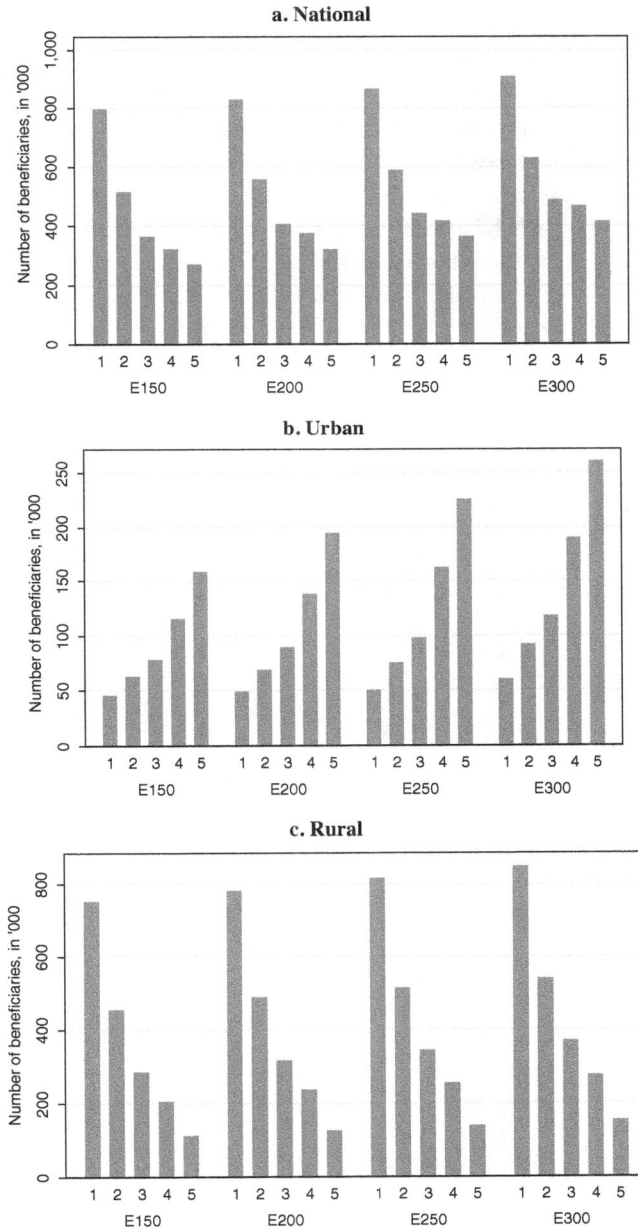

a. National

b. Urban

c. Rural

Source: Authors' estimation using GLSS5 data.

replications, and average values obtained with the 25 replication. This is also done for each of the wages assumed to be provided. The results of this procedure and the related statistics on targeting performance are provided in table 16.2. The first column provides the estimate of the total number of potential beneficiaries of the program depending on the wage level. For example, at a wage level of 250,000 GHc per month, some 348,320 youths might be interested in the program solely in the Upper West region. The second column provides the share of those individuals living in households who are poor. For example, at a wage of 250,000 GHc, 83.7 percent of the potential beneficiaries in the Upper West region live in a household in poverty according to the official definition of poverty. The third column provides the additional wage to be obtained by each individual, on average, depending on the wage proposed for the program. For the case considered, on average 244,500 GHc represents additional income for potential participants to the program, so there are almost no substitution effects in that geographic area. Overall, at a wage of 250,000 GHc, only 17.9 percent of that amount would be lost in the Upper West region for poverty reduction due to targeting errors and substitution effects. Thus, if the public works were targeted to that area, it would be very well targeted to the poor. Nationally by contrast, performance is much weaker with a leakage rate of 73.2 percent at that wage rate.

Table 16.2: Potential leakage effects of public works for poverty reduction, by region

	Region	# of people	Poverty headcount	Additional wage	Leakage rate
			(%)	in '000 monthly	(%)
E150	Western	161,098	21.4	125.9	82.0
	Central	111,338	19.0	114.6	85.5
	Greater Accra	120,046	7.7	100.7	94.8
	Volta	163,586	37.8	119.1	70.0
	Eastern	190,954	20.7	119.0	83.6
	Ashanti	326,550	24.7	124.1	79.6
	Brong Ahafo	238,848	34.4	129.0	70.4
	Northern	368,224	57.4	127.1	51.4
	Upper East	246,312	69.6	126.4	41.4
	Upper West	335,258	83.8	146.4	18.2
	Total	2,262,214	36.4	123.5	70.0
E200	Western	178,514	20.2	162.5	83.6
	Central	125,022	18.4	152.7	86.0
	Greater Accra	142,438	7.6	134.5	94.9
	Volta	188,466	36.2	151.6	72.6
	Eastern	219,566	19.5	152.3	85.2
	Ashanti	375,688	23.0	157.5	81.9
	Brong Ahafo	255,020	33.7	170.5	71.3
	Northern	391,860	55.2	168.3	53.5

(Table continues on next page)

Table 16.2: (continued)

	Region	# of people	Poverty headcount	Additional wage	Leakage rate
			(%)	in '000 monthly	(%)
	Upper East	264,350	69.7	168.9	41.1
	Upper West	340,856	83.7	195.6	18.1
	Total	2,481,780	34.6	160.8	72.2
E250	Western	193,442	20.0	199.1	84.1
	Central	137,462	17.2	190.8	86.9
	Greater Accra	155,500	7.0	172.7	95.2
	Volta	200,906	35.8	190.2	72.8
	Eastern	241,958	18.5	187.8	86.1
	Ashanti	409,276	22.0	195.9	82.8
	Brong Ahafo	271,192	33.6	210.9	71.7
	Northern	434,156	54.1	200.7	56.6
	Upper East	277,412	69.7	214.6	40.2
	Upper West	348,320	83.9	244.5	17.9
	Total	2,669,624	33.7	198.7	73.2
E300	Western	213,346	18.8	229.3	85.6
	Central	154,256	17.9	223.2	86.7
	Greater Accra	190,332	8.2	194.2	94.7
	Volta	222,676	34.7	223.8	74.1
	Eastern	266,216	17.9	220.4	86.8
	Ashanti	457,792	21.5	228.2	83.6
	Brong Ahafo	283,632	32.7	251.6	72.6
	Northern	460,280	52.3	236.3	58.8
	Upper East	297,316	70.5	257.6	39.5
	Upper West	355,162	84.1	293.0	17.9
	Total	2,901,008	32.6	232.4	74.7

Source: Authors' estimation using GLSS5 data.

The estimated potential impact of the program on poverty is given in table 16.3. As in the case of the NYEP, the estimates are obtained in a very simple way. For the participants in the program who belong to households living in poverty, we add to the consumption aggregate of the household the gains in earnings obtained by the participants, and we recomputed poverty using the same poverty lines. In other words, we assume that the full amount of the earnings gains (taking into account substitution effects) for program participants translate into additional consumption for their households. For higher wages, the impact is higher, since the additional earnings obtained by participants are higher, but the number of participants is kept unchanged (based on the number of NYEP recipients in 2007 at slightly less than 100,000). With public works wages of 250,000 GHc per month, the reduction in the national headcount index is

0.047 percentage point. This impact is small because the simulated program is itself small in comparison to the needs of the population for poverty eradication. But in terms of cost efficiency, public works are much better than the NYEP discussed in the previous chapter since the cost is about four times lower for public works than for the NYEP, and the impact is about the same (actually, when using the poverty gap which is a better measure of poverty than the headcount, public works perform better than the NYEP). If the public works were geographically targeted to the poorest areas, the poverty impact would be even larger.

Table 16.3: Potential impact on poverty of public works, national, 2005–06

	Within Target Group of Potential Beneficiaries		Whole population	
	Headcount	Poverty Gap	Headcount	Poverty Gap
E150	0.307	0.169	0.032	0.017
E200	0.350	0.189	0.039	0.021
E250	0.384	0.207	0.047	0.025
E300	0.397	0.215	0.052	0.028

Source: Authors' estimation using GLSS5 data.

Comparison with Other Countries

As mentioned earlier, implementing or expanding labor intensive public works programs are one of the popular alternatives being considered by many governments confronted with the economic crisis. The implicit assumption is that such programs are relatively well self-targeted to the poor because they typically provide low wages so that only the poor are interested in participating in them, and that they provide direct cash or king benefits for program participants which may help in reducing the negative impact of higher food prices. In addition, public works may help in reducing youth unemployment and underemployment, which is high in many countries. However, in the African context where a large share of the population is employed at very low wages or without pay, it is not certain à priori that public works are well targeted. In addition, public works often suffer from substitution effects whereby program participants have to give up other employment to participate in public works, which may lead to only part of the wage outlays being effective in reducing poverty (although this is likely to be less serious in Africa). Finally, public works may entail substantial costs in terms of administration and materials.

In this section, we compare the results obtained above with Ghana with the results from similar simulations conducted for three other countries using nationally representative household surveys (see table 16.4): Liberia (using the 2007 CWIQ survey), Chad (using the 2004 ECOSIT II survey), and Rwanda (using the 2006 EICV 2 survey). The overall leakage rates vary from 50 percent to close to 75 percent in all four countries. While the leakage rate at the national level is higher in Ghana because the country has a lower share of its population in poverty, even in rather poor countries such as Chad, Liberia, and Rwanda, more than half of the funds appear to not directly contribute to

Table 16.4: Simulated targeting performance of labor intensive public works, African countries (%)

Country and survey year	Simulated public works wage	Share of individuals among potential beneficiaries who are poor (percent) (1)	Share of public works wage representing net additional income for participants (percent) (2)	Overall leakage rate (percent) 1-(1)*(2)
Chad (2002–03)	20,000 CFAF/month	63.0	74.4	53.1
Poverty at 55.0 percent	30,000 CFAF/month	57.2	73.5	58.0
	40,000 CFAF/month	55.6	73.8	59.0
	50,000 CFAF/month	53.8	74.7	59.8
Ghana (2005–06)	150,000 GHc/month	36.4	82.33	70.0
Poverty at 28.5 percent	200,000 GHc/month	34.6	80.40	72.2
	250,000 GHc/month	33.7	79.48	73.2
	300,000 GHc/month	32.6	77.47	74.7
Liberia (2007)	10,000 L$/year	68.9	72.6	50.0
Poverty at 63.8 percent	15,000 L$/year	66.9	71.2	52.4
	20,000 L$/year	65.3	74.6	51.3
	25,000 L$/year	64.7	78.2	49.4
Rwanda (2006)	30000 RwF/month	66.6	56.2	62.6
Poverty at 56.9 percent	40000 RwF/month	66.1	57.1	62.3
	50000 RwF/month	65.4	59.1	61.3
	60000 RwF/month	64.7	60.4	60.9

Source: Authors' estimation.

poverty reduction either because they are provided to nonpoor households (some of whom are however likely to be near the poverty line), or because of the wage substitution effects at work. Reducing the public works wage helps in reducing leakage rates, but not by a lot. Again, the key to good overall targeting performance seems to be the use of geographic targeting.

Conclusion

Using recent household survey data and simple simulation techniques, we have estimated the likely effectiveness of labor intensive public works program as a tool for helping the poor confronted with the economic crisis while at the same time building productive and/or social physical investments in communities. Our estimates suggest that at various wage levels, some of which are very low, unless the programs are geographically targeted public works programs are likely to suffer from substantial leakage mainly from imperfect targeting to the poor and to a lower extent from substitution effects whereby only part of the wages paid end up representing additional income for program participants. One key reason for the high leakage rates is the fact that without some form of geographic (or other) targeting, public works may not necessarily reach the poor because so many individuals work for no or little pay, even in slightly better off families. It could be that if there is a stigma associated with participating in public works program, or if the work involved is difficult, many among the better off segments of the population would not participate in such programs, so that we would then have over-estimated the extent of the leakage of funds in our simulations. But on the basis of what can be observed in the household surveys in terms of work patterns and pay levels, as well as declared reservation wages, the simulations clearly indicate that leakage could be high. However, if the program were targeted to the poorest areas of the country, leakage rates could be reduced dramatically so that case targeting performance would be good.

Note

1. This review is reproduced with minor changes from Hicks and Wodon (2002).

References

Adams, R., A. Cuecuecha, and J. Page. 2008. "Remittances, Consumption and Investment in Ghana," Policy Research Working Paper 4515, World Bank, Washington DC.

Adams, A. V., H. Coulombe, and Q. Wodon. 2009. "Education, Employment and Earnings in Ghana," in World Bank, *Ghana: Job Creation and Skills Development*, Report No. 40328–GH, Volume 2, Washington, DC, 1–18.

Ahmad, Yusuf and Chor-ching Goh. 2007a. "Poverty Maps of Yunnan Province: Uses and Lessons for Scaling-Up in China," in Tara Bedi, Aline Coudouel and Kenneth Simler (eds.), *More Than A Pretty Picture: Using Poverty Maps to Design Better Policies and Interventions*, Washington D.C.: The World Bank.

Ahmad, Yusuf and Chor-ching Goh. 2007b. "Indonesia's Poverty Maps: Impacts and Lessons, In Tara Bedi," Aline Coudouel and Kenneth Simler (eds.), *More Than A Pretty Picture: Using Poverty Maps to Design Better Policies and Interventions*, Washington D.C.: The World Bank.

Alderman, H., et al., 2002, "How Low Can You Go? Combining Census and Survey Data for Mapping Poverty in South Africa," *Journal of African Economies* 11(2): 169–200.

Angel-Urdinola, D., and Q. Wodon. 2007a. "Do Utility Subsidies Reach the Poor? Framework and Evidence for Cape Verde, Sao Tome, and Rwanda," *Economics Bulletin*, 9(4): 1–7.

Araujo, Maria Caridad 2007, "The 1990 and 2001 Ecuador Poverty Maps," in Tara Bedi, Aline Coudouel and Kenneth Simler (eds.), *More Than A Pretty Picture: Using Poverty Maps to Design Better Policies and Interventions*, Washington D.C.: The World Bank.

Arias, Omar and Marcos Robles. 2007. "The Geography of Monetary Poverty in Bolivia: The Lessons of Poverty Maps," in Tara Bedi, Aline Coudouel and Kenneth Simler (eds.), *More Than A Pretty Picture: Using Poverty Maps to Design Better Policies and Interventions*, Washington D.C.: The World Bank.

Ahmad, E., and N. H. Stern. 1984. "The Theory of Reform and Indian Indirect Taxes," *Journal of Public Economics* 25: 259–98.

Akuffo-Amoabeng, B. 2009. "Targeting Mechanisms Used for Various Social Protection Intervention by Ministries, department and Agencies," mimeo, Accra.

Appiah-Denkyira, E., and A. Preker. 2007. "Reaching the poor in Ghana with National Health Insurance—an Experience from the Districts of the Eastern Region of Ghana," in J. Holst and A. Brandrup-Lukanow (ed.) *Extending Social Protection in Health: Developing Countries' Experiences, Lessons Learnt and Recommendations*. Germany: GTZ.

Asante, F. A. and Aikins, M. 2007. "Does the NHIS cover the poor?," Danida Health Sector Support Office, Accra.

Bedi, T., A. Coudouel, and K. Simler. 2007. *More than a Pretty Picture: Using Poverty Maps to Design Better Policies and Interventions*, Washington, DC: The World Bank.

Bundy, D., C. Burbano, M. Grosh, A. Gelli, M. Jukes, and L. Drake. 2009. *Rethinking School Feeding: Social Safety Nets, Child Development, and the Education Sector,* Washington, DC: The World Bank.

Carletto, Calogero, Andrew Dabalen and Alia Moubayed. 2007. "Constructing and Using Poverty Maps for Policy Making: The Experience in Albania," in Tara Bedi, Aline Coudouel and Kenneth Simler (eds.), *More Than A Pretty Picture: Using Poverty Maps to Design Better Policies and Interventions,* Washington D.C.: The World Bank.

Clert, C., and Q. Wodon. 2001. "The Targeting of Government Programs in Chile: A Quantitative and Qualitative Assessment," in E. Gacitua-Mario and Q. Wodon, editors, *Measurement and Meaning: Combining Quantitative and Qualitative Methods for the Analysis of Poverty and Social Exclusion in Latin America,* Technical Paper No. 518, World Bank, Washington, DC.

Coady, D., and E. Skoufias. 2001. "On the Targeting and Redistributive Efficiencies of Alternative Transfer Programs," Food Consumption and Nutrition Division Discussion Paper 100, International Food Policy Research Institute, Washington, DC.

Coady, D., Grosh, M. and Hoddinott, J. 2004. "Targeting Outcomes Redux," *World Bank Research Observer* 19 (1): 61–85.

Coady, D., Grosh, M. and Hoddinott, J., 2002, "The Targeting of Transfers in Developing Countries: Review of Experience and Lessons," Social Protection Discussion Paper. World Bank, Washington DC.

Cox, D., and E. Jimenez. 1995. "Private Transfers and the Effectiveness of Public Income Redistribution in the Philippines," in van de Walle and K. Nead, eds., *Public Spending and the Poor,* Baltimore: Johns Hopkins University Press.

Coulombe, H. 2008. Ghana Census-based Poverty Map: District and Sub-District-Level Results, in Ernest Aryeetey and Ravi Kanbur (eds.), *The Economy of Ghana: Analytical Perspectives on Stability, Growth and Poverty,* Oxford: James Currey.

Coulombe, H., and Q. Wodon. 2007. "Poverty, Livelihoods and Access to Basic Services in Ghana, in World Bank," *Ghana: Meeting the Challenge of Accelerated and Shared Growth* (Country Economic Memorandum), Report No. 40934-GH, Volume III: Background Papers, World Bank. Washington DC.

Coulombe, H., and Q. Wodon, 2008. "Assessing the Geographic Impact of Higher Food Prices in Guinea," Policy Research Working Paper 4743, World Bank, Washington DC.

Coulombe, H., M. Temourov, and Q. Wodon. 2009. "Ghana's National Youth Employment Program and Poverty Reduction," in *Ghana: Job Creation and Skills Development,* Report No. 40328–GH, Volume 2, World Bank, Washington, DC, 97–118.

Datt, G., and M. Ravallion. 1992. "Growth and Redistribution Components of Changes in Poverty Measures: A Decomposition with Applications to Brazil and India in the 1980s," *Journal of Development Economics* 38:275–95.

Demery, L. 2003. "Analyzing the Incidence of Public Spending," in F. Bourguignon and L. Pereira da Silva, editors, *The Impact of Economic Policies on Poverty and Income Distribution: Evaluation Techniques and Tools,* Washington D.C.: The World Bank.

DSW. 2008. "Livelihood Empowerment Against Poverty (LEAP): Highlights of 2008 Annual Report," Department for Social Welfare: Accra.

Duclos, J. 1995. "Modeling the Take-up of State Support," *Journal of Public Economics* 58: 391–415.

Duclos, J. Y., P. Makdissi, and Q. Wodon. 2005. "Poverty-Efficient Program Reforms: The Role of Targeting and Allocation Rules," *Journal of Development Economics*, 77(1): 53–73.

Duclos, J. Y., P. Makdissi, and Q. Wodon. 2008. "Socially Efficient Tax Reforms," *International Economic Review*, 49(4): 1505–1537.

Demombynes, G., Elbers, C., Lanjouw, J. O., Lanjouw, P., Mistiaen, J., Özler, B. 2002. "Producing an improved geographic profile of poverty: methodology and evidence from three developing countries." in van der Hoeven, R., Shorrocks, A. (Eds.), *Growth, Inequality and Poverty: Prospects for Pro-Poor Economic Development*. Oxford University Press, Oxford.

Elbers, Chris, Jean Olson Lanjouw, and Peter Lanjouw. 2002. "Welfare in Villages and Towns: Micro level Estimation of Poverty and Inequality," Policy Research Working Paper No. 2911, DECRG-World Bank, Washington DC.

Elbers, Chris, Jean Olson Lanjouw, and Peter Lanjouw. 2003 "Micro-Level Estimation of Poverty and Inequality," *Econometrica*, 71(1), 355–64.

Emwanu, T., J. G. Hoogeveen, and P. Okiira Okwi. 2006. Updating Poverty Maps with Panel Data, *World Development* 34(12): 2076–88.

Fiszbein, A., and N. Schady. 2009. *Conditional Cash Transfers: Reducing Present and Future Poverty*, Washington, DC: The World Bank.

Fujii, Tomoki. 2007. "To Use or Not to Use? Poverty Mapping in Cambodia," in Tara Bedi, Aline Coudouel and Kenneth Simler (eds.), *More Than A Pretty Picture: Using Poverty Maps to Design Better Policies and Interventions*, Washington D.C.: The World Bank.

Ghana Statistical Service. 2007. *Pattern and Trends of Poverty in Ghana, 1991–2006*, Accra.

Gotcheva, Boryana. 2007. "The Poverty Mapping Exercise in Bulgaria," in Tara Bedi, Aline Coudouel and Kenneth Simler (eds.), *More Than A Pretty Picture: Using Poverty Maps to Design Better Policies and Interventions*, Washington D.C.: The World Bank.

Grosh, M. E. 1992. "The Jamaican Food Stamps Programme: A Case Study in Targeting," *Food Policy* 17:23–40.

Grosh, M., C. del Ninno, E. Tesliuc, and A. Ouerghi. 2009. *For Protection and Promotion: The Design and Implementation of Effective Safety Nets*, World Bank, Washington, DC.

GSS. 2007. *Pattern and Trends of Poverty in Ghana 1991–2006*, Accra: Ghana Statistical Service.

Hoogeveen, J. G., and Y. Schipper. 2005. "Which inequality matters? Growth evidence based on small area welfare estimates in Uganda," Policy Research Working Paper No. 3592, World Bank, Washington, DC.

Jensen, R. 1998. "Public Transfers, Private Transfers, and the 'Crowding Out' Hypothesis: Evidence from South Africa," JFK School of Government Faculty Working paper, Cambridge, MA: Harvard University.

Jitsuchon, Somchai and Kaspar Richter. 2007, "Thailand's Poverty Maps: From Construction to Application," in Tara Bedi, Aline Coudouel and Kenneth Simler (eds.), *More Than A Pretty Picture: Using Poverty Maps to Design Better Policies and Interventions*, Washington DC: The World Bank.

Litvack, Jennie. 2007. "The Poverty Mapping Applications in Morocco," in Tara Bedi, Aline Coudouel and Kenneth Simler (eds.), *More Than A Pretty Picture: Using Poverty Maps to Design Better Policies and Interventions*, Washington D.C.: The World Bank.

Lopez-Calva, Luis F., L. Rodriguez-Chamussy and Miguel Székely. 2007. "Poverty Maps and Public Policy: Lessons from Mexico," in Tara Bedi, Aline Coudouel and Kenneth Simler (eds.), *More Than A Pretty Picture: Using Poverty Maps to Design Better Policies and Interventions*, Washington D.C.: The World Bank.

Makdissi, P., and Q. Wodon. 2002. "Consumption Dominance Curves: Testing for the Impact of Indirect Tax Reforms on Poverty," *Economics Letters* 75: 227–35.

Mistiaen, J., Özler, B., Razafimanantena, T., Razafindravonona, J. 2002. "Putting welfare on the map in Madagascar." Africa Region Working Paper Series 34, World Bank, Washington, DC.

Mistiaen, J. A. 2003. "Small Area Estimates of Welfare Impacts: The Case of Food Price Changes in Madagascar," mimeo, The World Bank. Washington, DC.

NDPC. 2007. *Implementation of the Growth and Poverty Reduction Strategy 2006–09: 2006 Annual Progress Report.* Accra: National Development Planning Commission, 31 March 2007.

Nouve, K. and Q. Wodon. 2008. "Impact of Rising Rice Prices and Policy Responses in Mali: Simulations with a Dynamic CGE Model," Policy Research Working Paper 4739, World Bank, Washington DC.

Parra, J. C., and Q. Wodon, 2008, Comparing the Impact of Food and Energy Price Shocks on Consumers: A Social Accounting Matrix Analysis for Ghana, Policy Research Working Paper 4741, Washington D.C.: The World Bank.

ODI. 2009. *Social Protection for Children: Opportunities and Challenges in Ghana*, London.

Ravallion, M. 1993. "Poverty Alleviation through Regional Targeting: A Case Study for Indonesia," in K. Hoff, A. Braverman, and J. E. Stiglitz, eds. *The Economics of Rural Organization*, Oxford: Oxford University Press.

Ravallion, M., and K. Chao. 1989. "Targeted Policies for Poverty Alleviation under Imperfect Information: Algorithms and Applications," *Journal of Policy Modeling* II(2): 213–24.

Ravallion, M. 1993. "Poverty Alleviation through Regional Targeting: A Case Study for Indonesia," in K. Hoff, A. Braverman, and J. E. Stiglitz, eds., *The Economics of Rural Organization: Theory Practice and Policy*, New York: Oxford University Press.

Ravallion, M. 1999. Appraising Workfare, *World Bank Research Observer* 14:31–48.

Sancho, A. 1992. "La Ficha Cas Como Instrumento de Focalización del Gasto Social en el Nivel Local," in Margaret Grosh, ed., *Platitudes to Practice: Targeting Social Programs in Latin America*, Vol. II, Case Studies III, Latin America and the Caribbean Technical Department, World Bank Regional Study Program, Report 21, Washington, D.C.

Sen, A. 1988. "The Concept of Development," in H. Chenery and T. N. Srinivasan, eds., *Handbook of Development Economics*, Vol. I, Amsterdam: North Holland.

Skoufias, E., B. Davis, and J. Behrman. 1999. "Evaluacion del Sistema de Seleccion de Familias Beneficiarias en Progresa," in *Progresa: Mas Oportunidades para las Familias Pobres*, Mexico City.

Swinkels and Turk. 2007. "Poverty Mapping: The Experience of Vietnam," in Tara Bedi, Aline Coudouel and Kenneth Simler (eds.), *More Than A Pretty Picture: Using Poverty Maps to Design Better Policies and Interventions*, Washington D.C.: The World Bank.

Tuck, L., and K. Lindert. 1996. "From Universal Food Subsidies to a Self-Targeted Program—a Case Study in Tunisian Reform," Discussion Paper 351, World Bank. Washington D.C.

USAID Mali. 2008. "Mali—Periodic Update on the domestic food security situation (Situation as of July 7, 2008)," mimeo, Bamako.

Vishwanath, Tara and Nobuo Yoshida. 2007. "Poverty Maps in Sri Lanka: Policy Impacts and Lessons," in Tara Bedi, Aline Coudouel and Kenneth Simler (eds.), *More Than A Pretty Picture: Using Poverty Maps to Design Better Policies and Interventions,* Washington D.C.: The World Bank.

Wodon, Q., with contributions from R. Ayres, M. Barenstein, N. Hicks, K. Lee, W. Maloney, P. Peeters, C. Siaens, and S. Yitzhaki. 2000. *Poverty and Policy in Latin America and The Caribbean,* Technical Paper No. 467, Washington D.C.: The World Bank.

Wodon, Q., B. de la Brière, C. Siaens and S. Yitzhaki. 2003. "The Impact of Public Transfers on Inequality and Social Welfare: Comparing Mexico's PROGRESA to Other Government Programs," in Y. Amiel and J. A Bishop, editors, *Fiscal Policy, Inequality and Welfare, Research on Economic Inequality,* Volume 10, Elsevier Science/JAI Press, Amsterdam.

Wodon, Q., C. Tsimpo, and H. Coulombe. 2008. "Assessing the Potential Impact on Poverty of Rising Cereals Prices: The Case of Ghana," Policy Research Working Paper 4740, World Bank. Washington DC.

Wodon, Q., C. Tsimpo, P. Backiny-Yetna, G. Joseph, F. Adoho, and H. Coulombe, 2008, "Potential Impact of Higher Food Prices on Poverty: Summary Estimates for a Dozen West and Central African Countries," Policy Research Working Paper 4745, World Bank, Washington, DC.

Wodon, Q., and X. Ye, 2009, "Benefit Incidence Analysis Adjusted for Needs and Costs: Assessing the Equity of Public Education Sending in Sierra Leone," mimeo, Washington D.C.: The World Bank.

Wodon, Q., and H. Zaman. 2010. "Higher Food Prices in Sub-Saharan Africa: Poverty Impact and Policy Responses," *World Bank Research Observer* 25: 157–76.

World Bank. 1999. *Improving Social Assistance in Armenia,* Human Development Unit, Country Department III, Europe and Central Asia Region, World Bank Report No. 19385-AM, Washington, D.C.

World Bank. 2009. *International Development Association Program Document for the Economic Governance and Poverty Reduction Credit in the Amount of SDR 193.8 million (US$300 million equivalent) to the Republic of Ghana,* Report No. 47723-GH, Washington D.C.: The World Bank.

World Bank. 2007a. *World Development Report 2007: Development and the Next Generation,* Washington D.C.: The World Bank.

World Bank. 2007b. *Global Inventory of Interventions to Support Young Workers,* Washington D.C.: The World Bank.

ECO-AUDIT
Environmental Benefits Statement

The World Bank is committed to preserving endangered forests and natural resources. The Office of the Publisher has chosen to print World Bank Studies and Working Papers on recycled paper with 30 percent postconsumer fiber in accordance with the recommended standards for paper usage set by the Green Press Initiative, a non-profit program supporting publishers in using fiber that is not sourced from endangered forests. For more information, visit www.greenpressinitiative.org.

In 2010, the printing of this book on recycled paper saved the following:
- 11 trees*
- 3 million Btu of total energy
- 1,045 lb. of net greenhouse gases
- 5,035 gal. of waste water
- 306 lb. of solid waste

---

* 40 feet in height and 6–8 inches in diameter

green press
INITIATIVE